Ulster Presbyterians in the Atlantic World

ULSTER AND SCOTLAND

General editors
Professor John Wilson and Dr William Kelly

A series published by Four Courts Press
in association with the
Institute of Ulster Scots Studies
University of Ulster

Ulster Presbyterians in the Atlantic World

Religion, Politics and Identity

David A. Wilson and Mark G. Spencer

EDITORS

FOUR COURTS PRESS

Set in 10.5 on 12.5 Ehrhardt for
FOUR COURTS PRESS LTD
7 Malpas Street, Dublin 8, Ireland
e-mail: info@four-courts-press.ie
http://www.four-courts-press.ie
and in North America
FOUR COURTS PRESS
c/o ISBS, 920 N.E. 58th Avenue, Suite 300, Portland, OR 97213.

ISBN (10-digit) 1–85182–949–0
ISBN (13-digit) 978–1–85182–949–1

Printed in England by
Antony Rowe Ltd, Chippenham, Wilts.

Contents

Acknowledgments

This book would never have been written without the financial support of the Ulster-Scots Agency, and the initiatives of John Wilson and William Kelly of the Institute of Ulster Scots Studies at the University of Ulster. Through developing close links between the Institute and the Celtic Studies Program at St Michael's College, the University of Toronto, John Wilson and William Kelly laid the groundwork for Mark G. Spencer's postdoctoral fellowship at St Michael's College, and for the conference on which this book is based. The Principal of St Michael's College, Mark G. McGowan, was a constant source of encouragement, as were Ann Dooley and Máirín Nic Dhiarmada. Jean Talman organized the conference with her usual blend of patience, good humour and efficiency. Kate Merriman skillfully copyedited the manuscripts, and imposed order on the stylistic anarchy of our first drafts. At Four Courts Press, Michael Adams and Martin Fanning were a pleasure to work with. Our deepest thanks go to all of the above, and to Zsuzsa Balogh and Kelly Spencer for keeping our feet on the ground and our hearts in the right place.

Introduction

Partition is not only an enduring reality in contemporary Ireland; it is also a striking characteristic of Irish-American historiography. Traditionally, the Irish-American experience has been divided into two discrete phases. In the first, beginning in the early eighteenth century and ending somewhere around the American Revolution, it has been presented primarily as the story of Ulster Presbyterianism, and located largely in the rural south and west. In the second phase, which gets under way in the early nineteenth century and peaks during the Famine, it becomes the story of Irish Catholics, and is located largely in the urban centres of the north and west. As with the partition of Ireland, however, the reality is much more complex, much more interesting, and much more surprising. The traditional view has major blindspots. It omits the experiences of Irish Catholics who arrived in North America during the eighteenth century, it leaves an enormous gap between the American War of Independence and the War of 1812, it ignores Irish Protestant immigration in the nineteenth and early twentieth centuries, and it privileges immigration over ethnicity. Sometimes the resulting distortions are quite remarkable. Everyone knows that 'Irish America' equals Irish Catholic America. But in fact, three separate surveys conducted in the 1980s reveal that over half the Americans who identified themselves as being of Irish origin were actually Protestants.[1]

This book, which grew out of a conference organized at the University of Toronto by the Celtic Studies Program and the Institute of Ulster Scots Studies, explores some of these forgotten fields, while emphasizing the interaction between Ulster Presbyterianism in America and in Ireland. David W. Miller's contribution, for example, presents a comparative analysis of Presbyterianism in Ulster and America, and examines the process of continuity and change in the transmission of Ulster Presbyterian evangelical traditions through several generations in the United States. He also points out that the great Ulster Revival of 1859 must be placed in a transatlantic context, since it drew much of its initial inspiration from events in America. At the same time, its character and course were shaped by local circumstances, as Kevin James demonstrates in his study of the subject.

The essays by Mark G. Spencer, Peter Gilmore, Katharine L. Brown and David A. Wilson focus on radical Ulster-American politics during the late eighteenth and early nineteenth centuries. Spencer's discussion of the Ulster students who attended Thomas Reid's moral philosophy class at Glasgow University reminds us that the Ulster Enlightenment was part of a Scottish–

---

1 Donald Harman Akenson, *The Irish diaspora: a primer* (Toronto, 1993), pp 219–20.

Irish–American matrix, raises important questions about the relationship between education and ideology, and points the way towards further research on the various careers of Reid's graduates. Gilmore, Brown and Wilson examine Ulster Presbyterian United Irishmen in the United States; in each case, the idea is to deepen our understanding of individual experiences within a field that has largely been approached in very broad terms, and only recently at that.

If the study of Ulster Presbyterianism in the United States after 1783 is a relatively new endeavour, this is – surprisingly – also true of Ulster Presbyterianism in Ireland after the Rising of 1798. As Kerby A. Miller argues, most studies of radical Ulster Presbyterianism stop in 1798, or at the very latest 1803. Once again, the transatlantic perspective offers an entry point into this relatively neglected world. Specifically, Miller draws on a letter from Belfast to America about 'Belfast's first bomb' to open up a discussion about class conflict, hegemony and identity in Ulster. And what he calls the 'taming' of Ulster's Protestant 'lower orders' – the ways in which political radicalism and trade unionism were eclipsed by conservative unionism – was also part of a wider transatlantic development, in which radical Presbyterians were reborn as the respectable Scotch-Irish in the United States.

For three centuries, the Ulster-American connection has operated like a push-pull oscillator. Ulster Presbyterians have helped to shape the religious and political culture of America, and American ideas have pulsed back across the Atlantic to influence the political and religious culture of Presbyterian Ulster. Historians are increasingly catching on; there remains, however, a great deal of catching up to do.

RELIGION

As David W. Miller argues, modern religious fundamentalism in the United States has hidden but deep roots in Scottish and Ulster Presbyterianism. In tracing these roots, he emphasizes the importance of the confessionalist Presbyterian tradition in which salvation hinges not only on moral rectitude, but also on a deep knowledge of doctrinal detail – on 'having the right answers' to questions about Calvinist orthodoxy. During the eighteenth century, the Scottish Seceders transmitted this tradition to Ulster, where it was particularly popular among congregations that were opposed to New Light theological liberalism. A central point about the 'old leaven', as Miller calls the confessionalist tradition, was that it enabled lay folk to insist that their ministers adhere to doctrinal orthodoxy. Just as conversionist evangelicalism inverted established patterns of authority, the 'old leaven' provided the poor and uneducated with the means to assert popular community values before their wealthy and university-trained religious leaders.

Along with haggling over doctrine, the 'old leaven' was characterized by outdoor gatherings of prayer and preaching. Socially integrative occasions that were intended to rejuvenate the faithful and impress the unregenerate, these 'holy fairs' were not the same as revival meetings, which emphasized mass conversion and the new birth. There was, in fact, no revivalist tradition in eighteenth-century Ulster Presbyterianism, and even the 'holy fairs' began to fade during the early nineteenth century, disappearing altogether by the 1830s. The confessionalist component of the 'old leaven', however, proved to be more durable. Henry Cooke in the 1820s was able to force New Light clergy out of the General Synod for both their theological and political liberalism; the New Lights not only failed to subscribe to the Westminster Confession of Faith, but were also sympathetic to the campaign for Catholic Emancipation. By marginalizing the liberals, Cooke paved the way for union between the General Synod and the Seceders in 1840, and for a Calvinist consensus within mainstream Ulster Presbyterianism. Ironically, his success spelled the demise of the 'old leaven' haggling tradition, since all the Presbyterian ministers were now impeccably orthodox.

In Ulster, then, holy fairs had died out, and the haggling tradition had become superfluous. But at the very time that a Calvinist religious consensus was forming, social divisions within Presbyterianism were growing. The industrialization of Ulster produced a prosperous Presbyterian middle class, a relatively impoverished urban working class, and a 'deskilled underclass' in the domestic textile sector of the economy. Within the 'lower orders', there was a marked decline in religious observance. In the absence of effective 'old leaven' solutions, the gap was eventually filled by the religious revival of 1859 that broke out in mid-Antrim – an area characterized by 'a large underclass of nominal Presbyterians and a few pro-revival ministers'. Amid trances, apparitions and even the appearance of stigmata, the dispossessed became possessed with the Holy Spirit, and believed that supernatural forces were transforming their world. There was much here to alarm and embarrass middle-class Presbyterians; as a result, the clergy worked hard to make the revival respectable, and to ensure that it was compatible with confessionalism.

Ulster had never seen anything quite like it before; America, however, had plenty of experience in such matters. Faced with the Great Revival of 1800, mainstream Presbyterian ministers in the Ulster-Scots heartland of western Pennsylvania attempted to combine the conversionist and confessionalist strands of the evangelical tradition. It was not an easy task; they would later reassert their confessionalism when it became clear that many revivalists in the Presbyterian church were prepared to compromise with Calvinism. As long as revivalism could be contained within the framework of Calvinist orthodoxy, however, 'old leaven' ministers remained receptive to conversionism. In 1857, they welcomed the so-called 'businessmen's revival', which helped to stimulate the Ulster revival of 1859. Despite their different trajectories, Ulster-Scots Presbyterians on both sides of the Atlantic had reached a point of convergence; they accepted what Miller calls a 'tamed conversionist spirituality' within a predominantly confessionalist transatlantic tradition.

Just as conversionism had been rendered respectable, confessionalism was also adapted to the anxieties of middle-class lay folk over cultural change. As Miller wryly puts it, 'having the right answers' remained constant, but the questions kept changing. The 'essential points of doctrine' that the General Assembly adumbrated at the beginning of the twentieth century were very different from those put forward by the Confessing Church Movement at the beginning of the twenty-first century, when the key issues were the singularity of Christ, the infallibility of scripture and the exclusive sanctity of heterosexual marriage. In a sense, there was nothing new about this. Confessionalist ministers had consistently emphasized those points of doctrinal orthodoxy that spoke to the fears of their constituents – fears of increasing Catholic political power in nineteenth-century Ulster, for example, or fears of same-sex marriage in twenty-first century America. And they consistently appealed to the laity to ensure that pressure from below was exerted on religious liberals.

While David W. Miller has taken a broad interpretive sweep spanning three centuries of Presbyterianism in Scotland, Ulster and the United States, Kevin James has focused his attention on the Ulster revival of 1859. In particular, he challenges the assumptions, methodology and conclusions of Peter Gibbon's analysis of the revival in *The origins of Ulster Unionism*. According to Gibbon, the industrial revolution in Ulster undermined the independent farmers and weavers who worked in the linen economy. The revival, in Gibbon's view, was symptomatic of this deeper change, and became part of the process through which Presbyterian weaving districts shifted from democratic radicalism to conservative unionism.

In response to Gibbon's analysis, James does what all good historians are trained to do: he starts asking awkward questions. Do we actually know the occupational profile of those who participated in the revival? There are no hard data, and contemporary accounts are too formulaic to help us answer this question. It may well be, as David Miller suggests, that the revival particularly appealed to a Presbyterian underclass, but more research is needed before the point can be firmly established. Was there, in fact, significant social differentiation in the mid-Antrim heart of the revival? In some respects, there was; patterns of literacy and endogamy suggest that there was indeed a wide gap between male farmers and other male rural workers. But there is also evidence that the social boundaries were more easily crossed by women in rural mid-Antrim, for reasons that remain to be explored. What about Gibbon's contention that the revival was related to a growing sexual imbalance, with women marrying at a later age? While this might have been true for County Antrim as a whole, it did not apply at all to mid-Antrim, where the sexual balance remained constant; any attempt to relate the revival's 'hysteria' with women's sexual or marital insecurity is not only implicitly suspect, but also statistically insupportable.

Underlying all this is the larger socio-economic question: was Gibbon correct to argue that the linen trade become urbanized and proletarianized by the middle of the nineteenth century? Not in mid-Antrim, argues James; there is little evidence in this area of significant migration to urban centres, or that the power loom displaced hand-loom weaving. On the contrary, hand-loom weaving remained an important part of the mid-Antrim economy right up to the 1890s; this was because the area specialized in fine shirting linen, and hand looms were better suited for this kind of production. The most striking characteristic of mid-Antrim, argues James, was not social upheaval, but social stability – and this was at the very time that the revival was taking place. It may well be the case, he suggests, that the revival in mid-Antrim was actually an expression of 'the strength and power of the laity in a region of relative demographic, social and economic stability'.

If David W. Miller surveys the historical terrain from a great height, and points out important features that would be missed on the ground, James stresses the importance of local conditions, and demonstrates the importance of details that can become blurred from a distance. A central problem with Gibbon's interpretation, in James' view, lies in its tendency to over-generalize; this results, he argues, in a homogenized and highly misleading portrayal of a diverse and complex rural society. Unless general interpretations draw on a deep understanding of local circumstances, they will be fundamentally flawed; unless local studies are conducted with an eye on the broader issues, they will descend into particularist irrelevance. The key, of course, is to find the right balance.

POLITICS

Miller and James have focused on religion, while keeping politics in mind; our other contributors generally focus on politics, while keeping religion in mind. If one is looking for the intellectual roots of radical Ulster Presbyterian politics during the eighteenth century, the logical place to begin is Glasgow University – and in particular, the Moral Philosophy course that was at the heart of the Scottish Enlightenment, and that was taught by such brilliant figures as Francis Hutcheson (1730–45), Adam Smith (1752–63) and Thomas Reid (1764–79). Mark G. Spencer sets out to examine the Ulster Presbyterians who studied Moral Philosophy at Glasgow, and who were dismissed by Reid as 'stupid Irish teagues'.

Reid's remark, made only weeks after he took up his appointment in 1764, is as intriguing as it is insulting. There have always been a few professors who privately deride their students, generally after decades of teaching have numbed their senses or heightened their cynicism. But at least three things are surprising about Reid's particular remark: it was made after only a few weeks on the job; it was spectacularly unenlightened; and it uses a derogatory epithet about Irish Catholics to describe Ulster Presbyterians. They were all the same, it seems, once they left Ireland. And those Ulster Presbyterians who sensed this attitude would hardly have been endeared to their host society. It is entirely possible that such students would have left Glasgow with a sharpened consciousness of Irishness, which could under the right circumstances glissade into nationalism. Ultimately, of course, Reid's comments tell us much more about Reid himself than about his students, 'stupid', 'teagues', 'Irish' or otherwise.

Spencer's analysis reveals that the vast majority of students matriculating in the Moral Philosophy course came from Ulster; 77 per cent of Reid's students came from the province, with County Down supplying the greatest number. One such student was the little-known William Bingham, who matriculated from Glasgow in 1774, and later emigrated to North Carolina. Bingham may have been involved with the United Irishmen, and was on the radical wing of Jefferson's Republican Party; his militancy, it appears, cost him his job as Professor of Ancient Languages at the University of North Carolina. He founded his own school, and acquired a reputation as one of the best teachers in the state; it is highly likely that his own teaching was influenced by the education he had received in Reid's Moral Philosophy course. As Spencer suggests, Bingham was part of a much larger story that remains to be told, and that will shed considerable light on Ulster's contribution to the Enlightenment on both sides of the Atlantic. A collective biography of the Ulster Presbyterians who studied Moral Philosophy at Glasgow is crying out to be written.

Another of Reid's students was Thomas Ledlie Birch, the revolutionary and millenarian Presbyterian minister who was compelled to leave Ireland after the Rising of 1798, and who resettled in western Pennsylvania. In the most thoroughly researched and sophisticated analysis of Birch's career yet to be written, Peter Gilmore examines the contrasts and contradictions between Birch's experiences in Ireland and America. Here was a man who fought the forces of political and religious conservatism in Ireland – the government, the established church, and the Seceders – and who identified so closely with American republican principles that he convinced himself that the Second Coming would occur in the United States. Yet in western Pennsylvania, he was expelled from the Presbyterian church, denounced as 'a Minister of the Devil', and formed an alliance with the very Seceders whom he had fought back in Ireland. What, asks Gilmore, was going on, and what might this tell us about Ulster-American Presbyterianism?

The answer, he suggests, lies in the very different experiences of Presbyterianism in Ulster and in western Pennsylvania. In Ulster, where

Presbyterians had endured a significant degree of discrimination at the hands of church and state, it was not surprising that a significant minority of ministers would support the revolutionary democracy of the United Irishmen. But in western Pennsylvania, the greatest challenges facing Presbyterianism emanated not from the state, but rather from the disorder of the frontier and the challenges of rival denominations. While Birch focused on the threat from above and became a revolutionary, mainstream Presbyterians in western Pennsylvania focused on the threat from below and became conservatives. The political division was matched by equally intense theological differences. Birch remained rooted in the confessionalist Ulster Presbyterian tradition; his opponents were conversionists who believed that religious revivals could sustain the Presbyterian church and strengthen social stability on the frontier.

From Birch's perspective, the revivals that swept through the American west from 1799 were destroying true religious values; ostentatious displays of conversion, accompanied by shrieking and groaning, he believed, were all show and no substance. 'Man can only observe the outward appearance,' he wrote. 'God alone can see the heart.' In taking this position towards American revivalism, Birch found that he had much in common with the Seceders who had settled in western Pennsylvania. Back in Ireland, Birch had fought the Seceders for poaching his congregation, for their political conservatism and for their 'holy fairs', which he had denounced as noisy, drunken festivals of fornication. But in western Pennsylvania, Birch and the Seceders shared a common hostility to revivalism, as well as a common antipathy to the kind of psalms that were being sung in mainstream Presbyterian churches. And these issues brought them together in America, despite all the differences between them in Ireland.

Although there were some significant exceptions, most of Birch's supporters and many of the Seceders shared one crucial characteristic – they were recent arrivals from Ulster. Their opponents within the western Pennsylvania Presbyterian church, in contrast, were mainly American-born offspring from earlier Ulster Scots settlement. What we are seeing here, then, is a major conflict between immigration and ethnicity, which was expressed through political and theological terms. The gap was so wide that it could bring together old enemies, Birch and the Seceders, on the common ground of their Old Country faith. This in turn highlights a vitally important aspect of the experiences of Ulster's United Irishmen in the United States – despite, or possibly because of, their idealization of American republicanism, they often had a very difficult time in adjusting to a world that seemed familiar, but that in many respects appeared very strange.

While Peter Gilmore uses Birch's experiences to illuminate the contrasting forms of Presbyterian religion and politics in Ulster and western Pennsylvania, Katharine L. Brown traces the careers of the United Irishmen John Glendy, John Daly Burk and James Bones to examine the formation of radical Ulster

Presbyterian communities in the American South. Combining genealogical techniques with an impressive grasp of detail, she shows how patterns of chain migration drew United Irishmen from Ulster to Virginia, South Carolina and Georgia. Local connections were crucial. Radical Presbyterians from Maghera, County Londonderry, moved to Staunton, Virginia; United Irish sympathizers from communities in Counties Antrim, Down, Londonderry and Donegal wound up in Petersburg, Virginia; transatlantic radical Presbyterian family connections spanned Randalstown, County Antrim, and Augusta, Georgia. United Irish leaders such as Glendy, Burk and Bones moved through these networks, and helped to strengthen them; they were the visible figures in a cast of thousands.

Surprisingly, given his prominence in the Volunteers and the United Irishmen, Glendy has received relatively little attention from historians of Ulster-American radicalism. Like Birch, he was educated at Glasgow University, after which he became a Presbyterian minister at Maghera. Described by a government informer as being 'tainted with the blackest principles of revolution', he was forced to leave Ireland for the United States in 1798, and resurfaced as a strong supporter of the Republican Party. A brilliant preacher who rubbed shoulders with Thomas Jefferson and James Madison, he was appointed chaplain to the House of Representatives and later the Senate. Brown not only sheds new light on Glendy's career, but also shows how he gradually brought over family, friends and congregants from Maghera to Staunton. In the process, she enables us to catch glimpses of lesser-known United Irish sympathizers who have slipped through the historian's net – men like William Herron, who served as Glendy's singing clerk in Maghera, and rejoined his congregation in Staunton, and Robert Guy, who may also have left Ireland for political reasons.

John Daly Burk's career, in contrast, has featured prominently in studies of the United Irishmen in the United States. Although he was not an Ulster Presbyterian (he was actually a deist from Cork), Burk was at the centre of Petersburg's radical Irish community, which had a strong Ulster Presbyterian component. By placing Burk in the context of this close-knit community, Brown brings half-forgotten figures out of the shadows. Irish American historians have long been familiar with Burk's transatlantic career; the activities of Irish women in Petersburg such as Elizabeth Swail and Mary Cumming have not, however, received much attention. As Brown points out, Elizabeth Swail was an economically independent and politically radical midwife from Ballynahinch who played an important role in the town's United Irish circles. And Mary Cumming, the daughter of Lisburn's Presbyterian minister Andrew Craig, was an admirer of Burk's *History of Virginia* – a book that was infused with democratic republican principles, and that can be read as a subliminal history of the Irish Rising of 1798.[2]

2 On Mary Cumming, see also Kerby Miller, *Irish immigrants in the land of Canaan: letters and memoirs from colonial and revolutionary America, 1675–1815* (Oxford, 2003), pp 362–78.

James Bones, Brown's third figure, has also escaped the attention of historians of Irish American radicalism, possibly because he emigrated to the United States in 1810, a full twelve years after he and his brother Samuel led a contingent of United Irishmen against loyalist forces in Ballymena. Moving from Randalstown to join his sister in Winnsboro, South Carolina, Bones was followed by three of his brothers, including Samuel. The family network quickly extended to Augusta, Georgia, where members of the next generation established themselves as prominent businessmen who saw no contradiction between supporting civil and religious liberty in Ireland and owning slaves in America.

One of Brown's most significant findings is that the Ulster Presbyterian United Irishmen in the South retained a strong sense of ethnic identity, even as they integrated themselves into American economic life. This was reflected not only in a significant degree of endogamy, but also in continuing connections between the New World and the Old. As well as conducting transatlantic correspondence and making occasional return visits, Ulster Presbyterian Jeffersonians in the South read Irish-American newspapers, participated in St Patrick's Day parades, formed their own militia units, and supported Daniel O'Connell's campaign for Catholic emancipation. As Brown suggests, this provides a strikingly different picture from traditional accounts of the Ulster Scots in the South, which focus on their colonial and rural roots, and which emphasize individualism and acculturation rather than communal and familial networks and a continuing consciousness of Irishness.

Brown's conclusions fit well with David A. Wilson's case study of John Caldwell, the United Irishman from Ballymoney whose entire family left for the United States after the Rising of 1798. While Brown examines a wide range of sources to reconstruct transatlantic patterns of migration and settlement, Wilson focuses on a single document – the remarkable and revealing memoir that Caldwell wrote towards the end of his life in New York. By embedding ideas in the narrative, Wilson attempts to locate Caldwell's experiences in the broader context of Ulster-American ideological interchange, and to show how those experiences helped to influence that context. Like Brown's radicals, Caldwell was part of a transatlantic family network; his great-uncles were among the founders of Londonderry, New Hampshire, and two of his uncles were merchants in Philadelphia. The Caldwell family had a liberal, tolerant and politically radical ethos, although there were some elements of an underlying settler-radical tension. Within the family, the women played a powerful role; the memoir includes a striking series of letters from his aunts that shed light on the experiences and attitudes of middle-class Presbyterian women in late eighteenth-century Ulster.

In the best radical Ulster Presbyterian tradition, the Caldwell family were highly critical of the Irish system of government, which they associated with religious persecution, political corruption, economic exploitation and agrarian violence. This outlook prompted them to admire America as the political antithesis of Ireland, to support the War of Independence, and, in the case of John Caldwell and his younger brother Richard, to join the United Irishmen. John Caldwell was a principal fundraiser for the United Irishmen in north-east Ulster; Richard commanded a contingent of Ballymoney men during the Rising of 1798. John was arrested in Dublin shortly before the Rising; Richard was initially sentenced to death, but was later exiled to the United States. In retaliation for Richard's activities, and to demonstrate the price of disaffection, the military burned down the Caldwell family home in Ballymoney – an event that they would never forget. Not just Richard and John, but the entire Caldwell family crossed the Atlantic, and attempted to rebuild their lives in the United States.

At one level, Caldwell seemed to have landed on his feet in America, and wrote enthusiastically about the country's democratic republicanism, freedom of religion and meritocracy. Like Thomas Ledlie Birch, John Glendy, James Bones and other United Irishmen from Presbyterian Ulster, Caldwell tried to recreate in America the same political and social milieu that he had experienced in Ireland. He joined clubs such as the Hibernian Provident Society and the Friendly Sons of St Patrick, moved through transatlantic Masonic networks, and was part of the community that initiated the long tradition of Irish-American nationalism. Caldwell also became involved in American politics, aligning himself with De Witt Clinton's Republicans in New York, participating in the successful radical Irish attempt to defeat the Federalist Rufus King in the New York Assembly election of 1807, and supporting the War of 1812. His brother Richard, seeking to avenge the failure of 1798, marched with the American army towards Canada in 1812, only to die of dysentery en route. John, living in Salisbury, New York, concerned himself with strengthening the defences of West Point against a potential British attack. All in all, his political commitment to the American Republic was not in doubt.

Yet there remained a large gap between the ideal and the real in Caldwell's America. Although one purpose of his memoir was to praise America as the land of liberty, his writings reveal that he experienced loneliness, isolation, personal tragedy, economic difficulty and depression in the United States, and that he was always something of an outsider in his new environment. This is reflected not only in the content of his memoir, but also in the tone; his descriptions of life in Ireland are bursting with energy, while his account of life in the United States is relatively flat and occasionally melancholy. He missed the eccentric characters, the communalism and the customs of the Old Country. In Ireland, he was culturally at home and politically alienated; in America, he was politically at home and culturally alienated. His experiences were by no means exceptional; they were commonplace among Irish radicals in the United States from the United Irishmen to the Fenians and probably beyond. It is no wonder, under these circumstances, that so many of them retained a strong consciousness of exile in the United States.

IDENTITY

The historian who has done most to explore this sense of exile is, of course, Kerby A. Miller. In his contribution to this volume, however, Miller turns his attention to early nineteenth-century Ulster, and raises critically important questions about class and identity within Ulster Presbyterianism. Against the background of rapid population growth, economic dislocation and periods of severe distress, he argues, Protestant east Ulster experienced a species of class war during the first three decades of the nineteenth century. The most dramatic – and to the authorities terrifying – manifestation of this conflict came in 1816, when Protestant weavers bombed the home of Francis Johnson, a wealthy Belfast cotton manufacturer who had recently reduced his weavers' wages. Although the use of a bomb was exceptional, Protestant Ulster's lower orders – a group with a reputation for unruliness – had a long tradition of social resistance, reaching back to secret societies such as the Oakboys and Steelboys, and finding contemporary expression in combinations, or early trade unions. Yet by the 1830s, Miller argues, such intense social conflict had virtually disappeared in Protestant Ulster. The unions had been defeated, and there was no Ulster equivalent to British Chartism. Instead, a new set of values associated with 'the Protestant way of life' predominated; rather than social violence and class conflict, a pan-Protestant identity emerged, in which the central values were unionist, capitalist, pious and respectable. How and why, Miller asks, did this remarkable transformation come about?

Unconvinced that the change can be explained in terms of increased prosperity or sectarian conflict, Miller turns his attention to the hegemonic strategies of the Protestant upper and middle classes. He notes that upper- and middle-class Anglicans and Presbyterians formed a common front against trade unions, and argues that they relied heavily on the British state to suppress lower-class insubordination – thus cementing their loyalty to the union. Above and beyond this, however, they set out to impose their values on the Protestant population through a series of economic, social, religious and political initiatives. They encouraged loan societies through institutions such as the Belfast Savings Bank, they formed charitable and educational organizations, they promoted Sunday Schools, and they encouraged religious revivals that fostered a pan-Protestant identity.

On the role of religious revivals, it is instructive to compare Kerby Miller's analysis with that of David W. Miller. Two points are particularly relevant. First, David Miller notes that while Presbyterians moved slowly and reluctantly towards revivalism in the mid-nineteenth century, things were rather different within Anglicanism. After the Rising of 1798, David Miller argues, the Church of Ireland became more receptive to revivalism, 'at least partly in the interest of better securing the loyalty of the small Anglican lower class'. Second, David Miller also points out that revivalism only became acceptable to Presbyterians when it conformed to middle-class notions of respectability. It is no coincidence that David Miller examines the emergence of a 'tamed conversionist spirituality' while Kerby Miller focuses on the 'taming of Ulster's Protestant lower classes'.

Kerby Miller also argues that the Orange Order and the yeomanry helped to create a loyal and respectable climate by identifying and rewarding the 'right sort' of Protestants, and by strengthening the image of Catholics as the disloyal and unrespectable 'other'. The Anglican gentry and magistrates who led the Orange Order and the yeomanry ensured that the 'right sort' received preferential legal treatment, and helped to insulate loyal Protestants from the dangers of eviction, unemployment and emigration. Although relations between Anglicans and Presbyterians remained tense, lower-class Presbyterians were facing increased pressure to demonstrate their loyalty; after all, the 'right sort' could benefit from favourable leases, regular work, good wages, access to credit, and charity in time of need. Meanwhile, evangelical Protestantism encouraged wives and mothers to inculcate the values of hard work, thrift, sobriety, piety, chastity and loyalty in their husbands and children.

For those Presbyterians who found the new climate too uncongenial, there was always the option of emigration. As Miller argues, many different factors lie behind the decision to emigrate; nevertheless, it is striking that Presbyterians left Ulster in disproportionate numbers for most of the nineteenth century. While recognizing the importance of economic dislocation and increased competition for land and employment, Miller is convinced that the greater propensity of Presbyterians to emigrate was closely connected to Anglican discrimination and Orange intimidation. A subtle system of punishment and reward, usually operating at the local level, resulted in the acquiescence or departure of Presbyterians with more radical tendencies. By the middle of the nineteenth century, the 'Protestant way of life' was so closely associated with loyalty and respectability that it became difficult to imagine that things had once been very different indeed. A new Protestant identity had been forged – and the word is used advisedly.

* * *

Many questions remain, of course. More research is needed on the relationship between Ulster Presbyterianism and American evangelicalism, the precise nature of the Revival of 1859, the subsequent careers of students who studied moral philosophy at Glasgow University, the grassroots United Irishmen and

Defenders who crossed the Atlantic, and the changing character of early nineteenth-century Ulster Presbyterianism. It is also time to open up new perspectives about Ulster Presbyterians in the Atlantic world. Gilmore, Brown and Wilson have focused on the United Irishmen in the United States, but we need to know much more about the experiences of conservative Ulster Presbyterians who went to America. Similarly, Kerby Miller's analysis points towards a comparative analysis of Presbyterian and Anglican migration flows to the New World. Could it be that there was a kind of ideological, political and religious filter that took a greater proportion of Anglicans to Canada, and a greater proportion of Presbyterians to the United States? And what of those Irish Anglicans who did go to the United States during the nineteenth century? They have become a forgotten people, lost between Ulster Presbyterians on one side, and Irish Catholics on the other. To what extent did they – and, indeed, other Irish Protestants from a variety of denominations – fight old battles on new ground? There is a growing body of evidence, for example, that Irish Protestants played a significant role in American nativist movements during the mid nineteenth century. It is entirely possible that Orangeism did not so much disappear in the United States as mutate into other forms.

There are books here, waiting to be written. And if, as A.T.Q. Stewart has argued, 'the phrase "contrary to all expectations" rings through the story of the progress of human knowledge', there should be plenty of surprises in store.[3]

David A. Wilson

---

3 A.T.Q. Stewart, *The shape of Irish history* (Belfast, 2001), p. 33.

Religious commotions in the Scottish diaspora: a transatlantic perspective on 'evangelicalism' in a mainline denomination

DAVID W. MILLER

In the 1950s the Presbyterian Church, USA, seemed to be a comfortably liberal (or perhaps more accurately, neo-orthodox) denomination which could be described by a historian of its theology as 'the broadening church'.[1] A recent issue of the *Christian Century*, however, reported polling data showing members of that denomination divided almost equally between those favouring a church 'tolerant of social and theological diversity' and those preferring 'a stricter and more uniform body of believers'. This information had been presented to a meeting of a task force at denominational headquarters in Louisville simultaneously with a conference in nearby Indianapolis of the Association for Church Renewal, a coalition of 'evangelical/conservative' groups from seven different mainline denominations.

The tone of the Indianapolis conference, according to the *Century*, was set by a letter from eighteen theologians declaring 'The Holy Spirit has not abandoned our churches, neither will we.' A less irenic tone emerged on the day after the conference when five Presbyterian ministers turned up in Louisville to post on a wall of denominational headquarters a statement branding the church 'irretrievably apostate under current management' and, in seeming contradiction to the name of the body convoked in Indianapolis, declared any talk of 'renewal' to be 'ludicrous'. One of the five ministers was the pastor of the Butler, Pennsylvania, congregation (just north of Pittsburgh), whose resolution in early 2001 led to the formation of the Confessing Church Movement, a coalition of over 1,200 Presbyterian congregations committed to the infallibility of scripture, the singularity of Christ and the exclusive sanctity of heterosexual marriage.[2]

The late twentieth-century division of each mainstream American denomination into liberal and conservative parties, whose adherents seem to have more in common with the corresponding parties in other denominations than with the rival party within their own,[3] is of course well known. The widespread use of the

---

1 Lefferts Augustine Loetscher, *The broadening church: a study of theological issues in the Presbyterian Church since 1869* (Philadelphia, 1954). 2 'Mainline evangelicals vow to stay and witness,' *Christian Century* 119:23 (6–19 Nov. 2002), 14. See also http://www.confessing churches.org/acall.htm and http://www.confessingchurch.homestead.com. 3 Robert

term 'evangelical' to characterize the mainstream conservatives, along with their allies in non-mainstream churches, gives contemporary relevance to a substantial recent historical literature on the rise of 'evangelicalism' in America (and elsewhere) over the past three centuries.[4]

This essay is an effort by a historian of religion in modern Ireland to suggest to American historians some ways in which new understandings of the history of Presbyterianism in Ulster can shed light on its daughter denomination in America. I take as a warrant for my foolhardiness in venturing into a field of whose literature I am a mere consumer an observation by perhaps the most distinguished contributor to that literature, George Marsden. In an argument that fundamentalism was far more pervasive in American evangelical history than in that of England or indeed 'almost' any other country, Marsden remarks in a footnote that 'Ulster appears to be an exception'.[5] That very exception seems an implicit call for the analysis which I offer here.

Critics of the recent literature on American evangelicalism have pointed out its concentration on the Reformed (mainly Calvinist) roots of the subject at the expense of its holiness (mainly Methodist) roots.[6] The mirror image of this criticism might well be levelled at the corresponding literature for the British Isles,[7] which tends to construe the word 'evangelical' primarily in terms of the emphasis by John Wesley and his successors upon the importance of a palpable emotional conversion experience. In this respect it is faithful to the under-standing of many nineteenth-century English men and women who applied the term to themselves. In Scotland and Ulster, however, the term 'evangelical' was

Wuthnow, *The restructuring of American religion: society and faith since World War II* (Princeton, 1988); and *The struggle for America's soul: evangelicals, liberals, and secularism* (Grand Rapids, 1989), esp. pp 19–38. **4** Mark A. Noll, David W. Bebbington and George A. Rawlyk (eds), *Evangelicalism: comparative studies of popular Protestantism in North America, the British Isles, and beyond, 1700–1900* (New York, 1994). George Rawlyk and Mark A. Noll (eds), *Amazing grace: evangelicalism in Australia, Britain, Canada, and the United State*s (Montreal & Kingston, 1994). George M. Marsden, *Fundamentalism and American culture: the shaping of twentieth-century evangelicalism, 1870–1925* (Oxford, 1980). Mark Noll, *America's God from Jonathan Edwards to Abraham Lincoln* (New York, 2002). See also Paul K. Conkin, *Cane Ridge: America's Pentecost* (Madison,WI, 1990); John B. Boles, *The great revival, 1787–1805* (Lexington, KY, 1972); Christine Leigh Heyrman, *Southern Cross: the beginnings of the bible belt* (Chapel Hill, NC, 1997); Michael J. Crawford, *Seasons of grace: colonial New England's revival tradition in its British context* (New York, 1991); Paul E. Johnson, *A shopkeeper's millennium: society and revivals in Rochester, New York, 1815–1837* (New York, 1978); Curtis D. Johnson, *Islands of holiness: rural religion in upstate New York, 1790–1860* (Ithaca, 1989). **5** George Marsden, 'Fundamentalism as an American phenomenon, a comparison with English evangelicalism', *Church History* 46 (June 1977), 216. **6** Leonard I. Sweet, 'Wise as serpents, innocent as doves: the new evangelical historiography,' *Journal of the American Academy of Religion*, 56:3 (1988), 397–416. Douglas A. Sweeney, 'The essential evangelicalism dialectic: the historiography of the early neo-evangelical movement and the observer-participant dilemma,' *Church History*, 60 (March 1991), 70–84. **7** E.g., David Bebbington, *Evangelicalism in modern Britain: a history from the 1730s to the 1980s*

being applied retrospectively to the Popular Party which had opposed the dominant Moderates in the eighteenth-century Church of Scotland on grounds which had little to do with conversion. In a recent monograph which thoroughly surveys that party's theological writings, John R. McIntosh argues that although the Popular Party did eventually come to be dominated by 'broadly evangelical' thinkers, 'their perceptions of the nature of saving faith and such central doctrines as the Atonement were orientated towards an intellectual rather than an experiential conception of conversion and faith, and their preaching was not directed to the emotions of their hearers in the way that later nineteenth-century evangelical preaching often was'.[8]

Now as a social historian, I tend to find intellectual history – in particular, the history of theology – to be an unsatisfying way of accounting for religious behaviour of those who are not religious professionals. I am intrigued but not convinced by another approach: the recent efforts of sociologists to explain higher levels of religious practice in America than in Europe as the result of a 'free market' rather than a 'monopoly' in religious 'products'.[9] I find applications of this market *model* to be shallow and mechanical, but I think that a market *metaphor* can be quite useful. Yes, of course, religion is a commodity, but as a commodity it closely resembles whiskey: it is a commodity which can readily be manufactured by the consumer. The professionals of different religious systems compete not only with each other's products but also with the home-brewed output of their own customers, and the task of the historian of religion, in my view, is to understand those continual interactions between clergy and laity.[10]

ORIGINS OF POPULAR PRESBYTERIANISM

Some American historians have sought the popular side of this interaction, for example, in dreams, trances and other altered states of consciousness[11] which could and did support 'an experiential conception of conversion' which is central to the holiness/Methodist strain of evangelicalism. But the equally puzzling fascination of Scottish tenant farmers with 'the mysterious, abstruse and disputed points of systematic divinity'[12] reported by an early nineteenth-

(London, 1989); David Hempton and Myrtle Hill, *Evangelical Protestantism in Ulster society, 1740–1890* (London, 1992). 8 John R. McIntosh, *Church and theology in Enlightenment Scotland: the Popular Party, 1740–1800* (East Linton, 1998), p. 237. 9 Roger Finke and Rodney Stark, *The churching of America, 1776–1990: winners and losers in our religious economy* (New Brunswick, 1992). 10 See Raymond Gillespie, 'Popular and unpopular religion: a view from early modern Ireland', in James S. Donnelly, Jr and Kerby A. Miller (eds), *Irish popular culture, 1650–1850* (Dublin, 1998), pp 30–49. 11 Jon Butler, *Awash in a sea of faith: Christianizing the American people* (Cambridge, MA, 1990), pp 221–56. 12 David Daiches, *The paradox of Scottish culture: the eighteenth-century experience* (London, 1964), p. 7, quoting William Aiton, *General view of the agriculture of the county of Ayr* (Glasgow, 1811).

century observer is seldom if ever considered as an analogous popular foundation for the Reformed strain of evangelicalism. American students of the latter have very usefully traced the origins of the thinking of religious professionals in the common sense school of philosophy of Enlightenment Scotland.[13] However, Marsden dismissively characterizes the Scotch-Irish party in American Presbyterianism on the eve of the Great Awakening as 'notorious hagglers over doctrinal detail'.[14] This essay will argue that haggling – no less than ecstacies or apparitions – is a popular antecedent of Presbyterian evangelicalism which had two distinct, but intertwined, strands: conversionist and confessionalist. It offers a transatlantic analysis of development of the less-understood confessionalist strand of Scottish religiosity, especially in Ulster, the most direct contributor to American Presbyterianism, and in the United States, especially western Pennsylvania, arguably the most successful plantation of Scottish religious culture in the western hemisphere and, not coincidentally, the birthplace of the Confessing Church Movement which made such a stir in Louisville.

Popular confessionalism in Presbyterianism has its origins in what Margo Todd calls the 'logocentric' effort to impose Calvinism on a largely illiterate population between 1560 and 1640. Literally compelled to listen to the Word preached for at least two hours every week, the lay person might be excluded from communion not only for moral lapses but also for an inability to articulate points from the Calvinist orthodoxy in which he or she had been homiletically and catechetically indoctrinated.[15] One can scarcely wonder that simple folk – still accustomed to view access to the host as necessary to avoid physical disease as well as eternal punishment – might now come away with the notion that the way to salvation was primarily a matter of having the right answers.

Although this wholesale catechizing certainly subordinated ordinary laity to the religious elite in the short run, the persecutions of the later seventeenth century meant that clergy found themselves no longer imposing their theological system upon the unenthusiastic, but rather celebrating the faithfulness of the godly. We should not be surprised that godly layfolk took from the experience a heightened sense of their own agency in maintaining purity in polity and doctrine. I call this sort of popular investment in the failed political project of the Covenanters – rule by the godly, rather than by the well-born, the well-heeled and the well-read – the 'old leaven',[16] to distinguish it from the 'new leaven' which emerged around 1740 in forms such as *pietismus*, awakening and

13 Marsden, *Fundamentalism and American culture*, esp. pp 14–16, 110–16. 14 George M. Marsden, *The evangelical mind and the New School Presbyterian experience: a case study of thought and theology in nineteenth-century America* (New Haven, 1970), p. 39. 15 Margo Todd, *The culture of Protestantism in early modern Scotland* (New Haven, 2002), pp 1–126. 16 There was, of course, also an English 'old leaven' – the politicized enthusiasms of the 1640s and 1650s whose suppression was a primary purpose of the British confessional state of the eighteenth century.

Methodism. I use the terms old and new 'leaven' to refer to popular religious practices, in contrast to the well-known (albeit confusing) terms Old Light and New Light which describe specific doctrinal products on offer from the religious professionals.[17] The Old Light was orthodox Calvinism as represented in the Westminster Confession; 'New Light' was a term coined around 1720 to refer to ministers in the Belfast area who declined to subscribe to the Confession and who at that time seem to have held Arminian views.[18]

Around the same time as the emergence of the new leaven, the old leaven acquired an institutional stronghold when a number of clergy and their congregations seceded from the Church of Scotland in protest over the dominant Moderate party's relatively relaxed attitude toward deviations from confessional orthodoxy and its connivance in the government's enforcement of the unpopular practice of lay patronage – the laird's assertion of a right to appoint the minister without the consent of the congregation.[19] Very soon the Seceders were successfully erecting new congregations in Ulster, sometimes by providing services in Scottish settlements remote from Presbyterian meeting houses, but often by competing with mainstream General Synod congregations for adherents who suspected their ministers of New Light tendencies. They were the growth sector of Ulster Presbyterianism, and they were joined in their opposition to the General Synod by the less numerous Reformed Presbyterian ministers (the 'strict Covenanters'). In Scotland and its diaspora the Secession was loosely analogous to Methodism within England and the English diaspora. However, the matter in contention between the Seceders and General Synod was not conversionist spirituality but conformity to seventeenth-century Scottish Presbyterian standards of doctrine and church-state relations.[20] As a means for fostering serious religion on the part of lay folk, it was an entirely viable alternative to the 'new leaven' of the Methodists, whose successes in Ulster tended to be confined to areas in which English, rather than Scottish, settlers predominated (see figure 1).

Although its lack of established status spared the mainstream Synod of Ulster

17 Patrick Griffin, *The people with no name: Ireland's Ulster Scots, America's Scots Irish, and the creation of a British Atlantic world, 1689–1764* (Princeton, 2001), pp 37–124, argues that Ulster-Scot settlers in Pennsylvania insisted on subscription as a claim for the kind of local established status which they had tried to maintain in Ulster. While this argument is convincing, it is also important to understand that the popular 'old leaven' attitudes which underlay it outlasted any serious prospect for the kind of political recognition which they desired either in Ulster or in Pennsylvania. 18 I.R. McBride, *Scripture politics: Ulster Presbyterians and Irish radicalism in the late eighteenth century* (Oxford, 1998), p. 45; A.W. Godfrey Brown, 'A theological interpretation of the first subscription controversy (1719–1728)', in *Challenge and conflict: essays in Irish Presbyterian history and doctrine* (Antrim, 1981), pp 28–45. 19 Andrew L. Drummond and James Bulloch, *The Scottish church, 1688–1843: the age of the Moderates* (Edinburgh, 1973), pp 25–63. 20 For an excellent treatment of the place of Seceders and Covenanters within eighteenth-century Ulster Presbyterianism, see McBride, *Scripture politics*, pp 62–83.

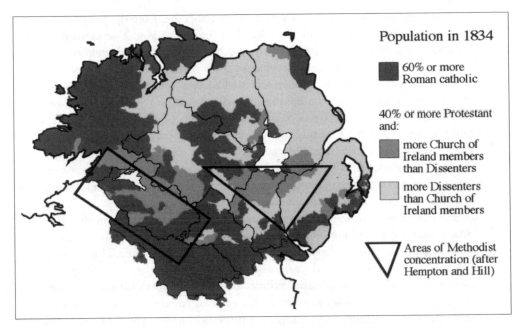

Population in 1834

60% or more Roman catholic

40% or more Protestant and:

more Church of Ireland members than Dissenters

more Dissenters than Church of Ireland members

Areas of Methodist concentration (after Hempton and Hill)

Figure 1. Sectarian zones in 1834. This map first appeared in Jim Smyth (ed.), *Revolution, counter-revolution and union: Ireland in the 1790s* (Cambridge University Press, 2000).

from the Scottish spectacle of riots to prevent unpopular ministers from gaining access to their new pulpits,[21] its ministers had to face suspicions of their orthodoxy by their congregations, frequently exploited by Seceding clergy. The Presbyterian process for calling a minister permitted quite impecunious folk with a smattering of 'ink divinity'[22] to challenge the opinions of their betters. We should think about this practice of the literate but often unreflective countryfolk, grilling the well-read, perhaps even well-born, ministerial candidate[23] as a peculiarly Scottish ritual of social inversion. Less colourful than its southern European counterpart, carnival,[24] it was no less a means of sustaining the social order by turning the world upside down, if only for a day. Related rituals of social inversion included registering complaints about a minister at periodic presbytery visitations of the congregation, attending the outdoor sermons of an

21 Kenneth J. Logue, *Popular disturbances in Scotland, 1780–1815* (Edinburgh, 1979), pp 168–76. 22 The term is John Bossy's in *Christianity in the West, 1400–1700* (Oxford, 1985), p. 103. 23 H.G. Graham, *The social life of Scotland in the eighteenth century*, 4th ed. (London, 1937), pp 366–71. On the origins of lay-clerical relations in Presbyterianism, see Todd, *Culture of Protestantism*, pp 361–70. 24 Emmanuel Le Roy Ladurie, *The peasants of Languedoc*, trans. John Day (Urbana, IL, 1976), pp 192–7. Peter Burke, *Popular culture in early modern Europe* (New York, 1978), pp 185–91.

itinerant Covenanting minister, or withdrawing altogether from the pastoral care of one's minister to join a nearby Seceding congregation. The concept of 'inversion of authority' is used effectively by Nathan Hatch to characterize the conversionist revivals of early nineteenth-century America,[25] but Ulster already had its own social inversion ritual which worked very well indeed. Why bother to listen to an itinerant Methodist preacher denounce your minister as unconverted when you and your peers enjoyed so much latitude to take such matters into your own hands? Ultimately the various means by which lay folk could call their minister to account ensured that elite values were balanced by popular norms in the community's culture and contributed to the unstated assumption, implicit also in the sectarian tensions which permeated Ulster life, that salvation is mostly a matter of having the right answers.

There was more to the old leaven than haggling. Popular religion in Ulster Scot communities had not only a ritual of social inversion, but also a ritual of social integration: the outdoor festal communion or 'holy fair'. The Scottish Covenanters' practice of conducting worship in secret locations to evade persecution evolved into a unique ethnic eucharistic form. Two or more congregations would gather at a remote site once or twice a year for several days of prayer and preaching, culminating in communion around rustic tables. Leigh Eric Schmidt, who has brilliantly analyzed this phenomenon in Scotland (though not in Ulster), points out that in such sacramental occasions the ecstasy reported by communicants was understood not as a once-for-all conversion, but as a recurring annual experience. Its function was 'to rejuvenate those who were already God's people as much as to convert the unregenerate'.[26] The use of tokens from local kirk sessions to certify the worthiness of communicants at the 'fencing of the tables' did certainly draw a boundary around the godly, but a penumbra of the less devout who attended the event mainly in the interest of sociability, refreshment and dalliance ensured that, in Ulster at least, these occasions functioned to affirm an ethno-religious community which transcended godliness. Furthermore, the liminal potentiality of such a ritual, involving travel to a remote site and interaction with those outside one's usual face-to-face relationships, invites comparison with pilgrimages to holy wells and 'patterns' – festal observances of patron saints' days – which played a prominent role in the folk religion of the Roman Catholic neighbours of Ulster Presbyterian folk.[27]

25 Nathan O. Hatch, *The democratization of American Christianity* (New Haven, 1989), pp 44–6.
26 Leigh Eric Schmidt, *Holy fairs: Scottish communions and American revivals in the early modern period* (Princeton, 1989), pp 153–8.   27 Gwen Kennedy Neville offers a provocative analysis of Protestant outdoor festivity as an antitype or inversion of Roman Catholic pilgrimage in *Kinship and pilgrimage: rituals of reunion in American Protestant culture* (New York, 1987), pp 13–27.

TRANSITION TO MODERN PRESBYTERIANISM

The relationship between the old leaven and the new in particular geographic settings depended, of course, on social and political contingencies. The period from the 1790s to the 1860s began with political upheaval in Ulster and religious commotions in America and ended with religious commotions in Ulster and political upheaval in America. Although Ulster and American Presbyterianism took radically different paths during that period, the outcome was two religious systems so similar that the authors of a recent study of the period 1840–60 could plausibly analyze a phenomenon which they called 'Ulster-American religion'.[28]

Now to understand the development of modern Presbyterianism in transatlantic perspective, we must turn to the phenomenon which became, especially in America, the signature ritual of the new leaven: the revival. Outdoor festal communions were a regular part of the life of Scottish and Ulster-Scot settlements in North America in the late eighteenth century, and Presbyterians sometimes retrospectively referred to these events as 'revivals', a usage which was not invented until around 1800,[29] during the so-called 'Great Revival' on the American frontier. At this point the festal communion was already being transformed into the non-sacramental 'camp meeting'.[30] In some areas, especially in the South, reluctance to lower educational standards for clergy meant that the Great Revival immediately drew off a substantial share of the non-elite Presbyterians to Baptist, Methodist and other less ambivalently conversionist denominations, including such offshoots of mainstream Presbyterianism as the Cumberland Presbyterians and the Campbellites.[31] Western Pennsylvania seems to have been a special case in which Ulster Scots were so thick on the ground that pietist Presbyterian clergy were able to weather the frontier phase of settlement (about 1780–1820) without losing their lay constituency. Mainstream clergy, led by the redoubtable John McMillan, generally associated themselves with revivals which their Seceder counterparts condemned.[32]

The experience of Presbyterianism in Ulster during this period was very

---

28 David N. Livingstone and Ronald A. Wells, *Ulster-American religion: episodes in the history of a cultural connection* (Notre Dame, IN, 1999). 29 In all the *Oxford English Dictionary*'s eighteenth-century quotations illustrating usage of 'revival' to mean a religious reawakening, the word is followed by a modifier such as 'of religion.' Only from 1818 does the *OED* document the elliptical usage which we now take for granted: 'The Methodists of Cincinnati are very zealous and have what they call "a revival" in the country.' However, a search of a large on-line database of published books (WorldCat) reveals a spate of titles containing this elliptical usage beginning in 1801. 30 Conkin, *Cane Ridge*, pp 166–7. 31 See, e.g., H. Tyler Blethen and Curtis W. Wood, Jr, 'Scotch-Irish frontier society in southwestern North Carolina, 1780–1840,' in H. Tyler Blethen and Curtis W. Wood, Jr (eds), *Ulster and North America: Transatlantic perspectives on the Scotch-Irish* (Tuscaloosa, AL, 1997), pp 219–20. 32 Peter Gilmore, 'Seemingly revolutionary physician: Thomas Ledlie Birch and cultural conflict in the Pennsylvania backcountry,' a paper delivered at the fifteenth Ulster-American Heritage Symposium, Rock Hill, SC, June 2002.

different. In contrast with those parts of Scotland and its diaspora where the festal communion had evolved into the revival, no evidence of Ulster Presbyterian festal communions turning into revival-like occasions has come to light for the entire eighteenth century.[33] Indeed, in the latter half of the eighteenth century the festal communion seems to have been maintained in Ulster primarily by those special guardians of the old leaven, the Seceders.[34] The 1798 rebellion, in which many Presbyterians and Catholics were briefly allied in opposition to the government, nudged the established Church of Ireland toward the new leaven at least partly in the interest of better securing the loyalty of the small Anglican lower class. The political excitements, however, prompted little or no change in the religious life of Ulster Presbyterians[35] (although the festal communion was probably already declining and continued to do so). The haggling rituals, however, were alive and well, for a number of presbyteries of the General Synod had become lax in their enforcement of subscription to the Westminster Confession and some New Light clergy had moved toward Unitarianism. In the 1820s an Old Light minister of great oratorical (some would say demagogic) skill, Henry Cooke, took advantage of the popular suspicion that New Light clergy were especially supportive of the restoration of political rights to Roman Catholics to gain dominance of the Synod and undertake a crusade to impose subscription upon all ministerial candidates.[36] In

---

33 Marilyn J. Westerkamp, *Triumph of the laity: Scots-Irish piety and the Great Awakening, 1625–1760* (New York, 1988), p. 134. Westerkamp probably means that such Irish Presbyterian revivals did not happen in the 1740s, but no evidence of any such events between then and 1859 seems to have come to light.   34 A famous 1759 attack on rustic communion practice in Scotland by 'A Blacksmith' was rebutted in a 1761 pamphlet by 'A Presbyter of Ireland', who was apparently a minister of the mainstream General Synod of Ulster. *The modes of Presbyterian church-worship vindicated in a letter to the Blacksmith by a Presbyter of Ireland* (2nd ed., Dublin, 1763). The catalogues of the National Library of Ireland and the Library of Congress attribute this pamphlet to Thomas Vance, who was born in County Donegal and served as minister of the Usher's Quay Presbyterian Church in Dublin. In 1853 W.D. Killen alluded with disapproval to the Seceders' 'habit of collecting immense audiences at sacramental seasons' in the late eighteenth century. James Seaton Reid and W.D. Killen, *History of the Presbyterian Church in Ireland* (new ed., Belfast, 1867), iii, 376. Volume 3 was written by Killen and first appeared in 1853. Henry Montgomery, the leader of the liberal bloc which withdrew from the General Synod in 1829, recalled festal communions, known as 'Lyle Fair,' outside the meeting house of Isaac Patton, Seceding minister of Lyle-Hill, County Antrim, whose academy Montgomery had attended as a youth at the turn of the century. Classon Porter, *Ulster biographical sketches* (Belfast, 1884), p. 39. In a 1796 polemic against Seceders who opposed him for his advocacy of equal rights for Catholics, Thomas Ledlie Birch, the radical minister of Saintfield, County Down, offers a colourful description of Seceding sacramental festivals. *Physicians languishing under disease: an address to the Seceding, or Associate Synod of Ireland, upon certain tenets and practices alleged to be in enmity with all religious reformation*, reprinted in Thomas Ledlie Birch, *The causes of the Rebellion in Ireland (1798) and other writings*, Brendan Clifford ed. (Belfast, 1991), pp 53–6.   35 David W. Miller, 'Irish Christianity and revolution,' in Jim Smyth (ed.), *Revolution, counter-revolution and union: Ireland in the 1790s* (Cambridge, 2000), pp 195–210.   36 Cooke claimed to

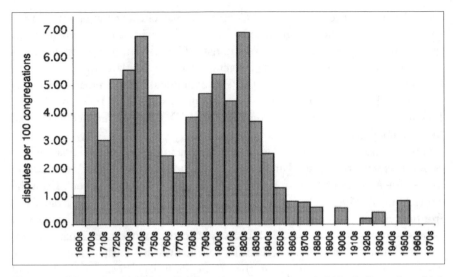

Figure 2. Dissension in Ulster Presbyterian congregations (within judicatories which became the General Assembly in 1840), by decade.

1829 he succeeded in forcing the nonsubscribing minority out of the General Synod, thereby smoothing the way to its union with the Seceding Synod to form a General Assembly in 1840. Once all ministerial candidates were certifiably orthodox, there was little further occasion for lay contention on the subject, as can be seen from figure 2.[37]

Calvinist orthodoxy was a unifying factor in Ulster Presbyterianism in this period; the excluded nonsubscribers were a tiny group compared with the combined General and Seceding Synods. Calvinist orthodoxy was a major source of division, however, in American Presbyterianism. By the 1830s mainstream clergy in western Pennsylvania, having co-opted and tamed revivalism on their own turf, were scandalized by the fact that the 'Plan of

be favourable toward Catholic relief and complained that he was being attacked by fellow clergy for telling a royal commission the simple truth that most of the 'less informed' Presbyterians opposed it. J.L. Porter, *The life and times of Henry Cooke*, 2nd ed. (London, 1871), pp 74–9. Taking his career as a whole, however, it is difficult to avoid the conclusion that much of his popular support rested on the perception that he could be relied upon to oppose concessions to Catholics.   37 The data in figure 2 were drawn from the congregational histories in *A history of the congregations in the Presbyterian Church in Ireland, 1610–1982* (Belfast, 1982). Only disputes which seem to have involved popular participation (as opposed, for example, to disputes solely between a minister and a higher judicatory) are included. Disputes which involved two or more congregations (e.g. those which resulted in formation of a second congregation) are counted only once. The analysis is limited to disputes originating in congregations in Ulster which, at the time of the dispute, were affiliated with the General Synod, the Burgher Synod, the Antiburgher Synod, the Secession Synod or the General Assembly.

Union' between Presbyterian and Congregational churches adopted in 1801 sometimes placed them in ministerial communion with clergy who declined unconditional subscription to the Westminster Confession, by the compromises with Calvinism being proposed by conversionist New England theologians, and by the 'new measures' adopted by the 'Presbygational' revival preacher Charles Grandison Finney in the religious hothouse of upstate New York. In 1837 the Presbyterian Church split into confessionalist 'Old School' and conversionist 'New School' general assemblies.

There was a strong tendency for Presbyterians in the areas of original Ulster-Scot settlement (represented on figure 3 by David Hackett Fischer's delineation of settlement areas of 'British borderers'[38]) to opt for the Old School. Even the aging John McMillan, champion of revivalism when western Pennsylvania was frontier territory, was retrospectively reported to have endorsed the regional Old School consensus before his death in 1833.[39] In the looming sectional conflict, western Pennsylvania Presbyterianism was awkwardly located north of the Mason-Dixon line, but south of the ethnic boundary between English and Scottish post-puritan migration streams across the antebellum North (see figure 3). The Irish General Assembly regarded the Old School as their natural partner in the US, but the Old School General Assembly apparently tired, by the early 1850s, of being lectured on the sin of slaveholding and broke off fraternal correspondence with its Irish counterpart. Significantly, the Irish General Assembly struck up friendly correspondence not with the New School, but with other confessionalist bodies in America, most importantly the United Presbyterian Church which was founded in 1858 by the union of various geographically dispersed Seceder synods.[40]

The major problem faced by the Irish General Assembly in the mid-nineteenth century was the fact that the relatively homogeneous ethnic community in which the old leaven had previously sustained their religious system was becoming a more stratified industrial society. Though there were still virtually no Presbyterian landlords, the denomination included a wealthy and

38 David Hackett Fischer, *Albion's seed: four British folkways in America* (New York, 1989), p. 637. I have some misgivings about Fischer's lumping together of emigrants from Ulster, the north of England and Scotland in his analysis, but his map of settlement by these 'British borderers' gives a reasonably satisfactory representation of Ulster-Scot settlement in the mid-Atlantic and southern backcountry. 39 Joseph Smith, *Old Redstone, or, Historical sketches of western Presbyterianism: its early ministers, its perilous times, and its first records* (Philadelphia, 1854), p. 205. 40 Presbyterian Church in Ireland, *Minutes of the General Assembly*, i, (1841) 83–4, (1842) 161–2, (1844) 345–50, (1846) 507–11, (1847) 621–6, (1848) 700–6, (1850) 864–7, ii, (1851) 59–60, (1852) 133–6, (1854) 301–5, (1855) 385–7, 390–4, (1856) 478–81, (1859) 785, 807–8, iii, (1863) 295–8, (1864) 416–17, (1865) 563–5, (1866) 705. For an interesting treatment of the United Presbyterian Church as an ethnic denomination, see William Lyons Fisk, *The Scottish high church tradition in America: an essay in Scotch-Irish ethnoreligious history* (Langham, MD, 1995).

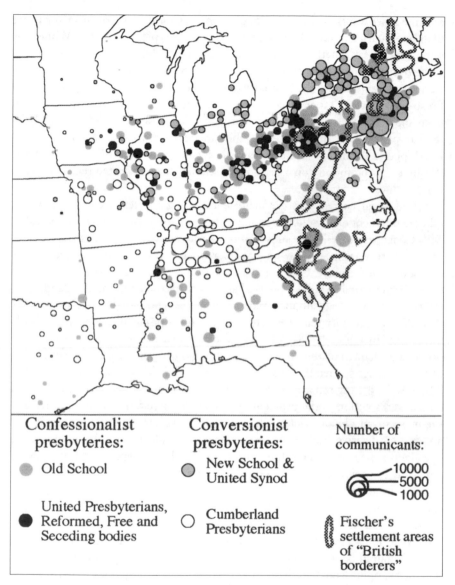

Confessionalist presbyteries:

- Old School

- United Presbyterians, Reformed, Free and Seceding bodies

Conversionist presbyteries:

- New School & United Synod

- Cumberland Presbyterians

Number of communicants:

- 10000
- 5000
- 1000

Fischer's settlement areas of "British borderers"

Figure 3. American Presbyterianism, 1859–60

assertive Presbyterian middle class as well as both an industrial working class in Belfast and a growing deskilled underclass in districts where domestic textile manufacture had once flourished. Ulster Presbyterian clergy, like their counterparts in industrial Britain, were becoming increasingly aware of the lapse of many of the less affluent of their traditional ethnic constituency. By around 1840 it appears that about three-quarters of the nominal Presbyterians in Ulster were in some sense affiliated with a particular congregation, but that probably fewer than one-quarter attended worship services on a typical Sunday.[41] While it is impossible to say whether these figures represent a decline in Sunday church-going over the preceding century or so, by the 1830s outdoor festal communions were largely extinct and the Sunday worship service was increasingly the central Presbyterian ritual. It took place in a meeting house which might be quite distant from the residences of the poorest (probably horseless) Presbyterians, and its regular participants dressed respectably and expected the same of their co-worshippers. Plain folk found it hard to act out their identification with the Presbyterian community on a seasonal timetable which reflected the rhythms of agrarian life.

While social change was gradually eliminating the festal communion, the other component of the old leaven – haggling – suffered a fatal blow (ironically) with Cooke's victory in the subscription controversy of the 1820s. As figure 2 shows, there was little room for haggling once every minister was certifiably orthodox. Furthermore, Cooke undermined his own leadership of the clergy by trying in the 1830s to build a political alliance with the Church of Ireland. This effort cost him crucial support among colleagues who took the old leaven view that differences between Presbyterianism and Episcopalianism were vitally important. In the early 1840s his failed effort to use his Tory connections to broker a settlement of the Scottish Church crisis over the classic old leaven issue of lay patronage spelled the end of his dominance of the Irish General Assembly. There was no clear replacement of his leadership in the succeeding decade. A new leaven solution to the problem of lapsed Presbyterians – that is, a revival – might seem an obvious policy choice. As I argue elsewhere, however, in the absence of decisive leadership several essentially old leaven alternatives were tried before the new leaven solution presented itself, so to speak.[42] Meanwhile, in America, the revival, even under the leadership of Finney, developed into a much more orderly phenomenon, while even strict confessionalist clergy were careful not to rule out the possibility of a 'pure' revival whose origins in provi-dential action, not in popular frenzy, would be attested by decorous devotion. That criterion seemed to have been met in the so-called 'businessmen's revival' which began in New York city in 1857, and as this revival spread to other cities it gained support from Old School men, whose earlier misgivings were paralleled by similar concerns among Irish Presbyterian clergy.[43] Support for revival in

41 The data on which these calculations are based are found in *First report of the commissioners of public instruction, Ireland*, H.C. 1835, xxxiii, and in the National Archives of Ireland, Presbyterian Certificates, 1841, Room VI, 3/372; VIC/15/5. 42 David W. Miller, 'Did Ulster Presbyterians have a devotional revolution?' in James H. Murphy (ed.), *Evangelicals and Catholics in nineteenth-century Ireland* (Dublin, 2005). 43 R. Laurence Moore, *Selling God: American religion in the marketplace of culture* (New York, 1994), pp 71–8. Kathryn Teresa Long, *The Revival of 1857–58: interpreting an American religious awakening*, (New York, 1998), pp 11–18.

Ulster was probably already growing because a non-sacramental open-air preaching campaign during the preceding several summers – an apparent effort to recover something of what had once 'worked' for the traditional Presbyterian constituency – had produced little if any embarrassing religious behaviour (though it did trigger some sectarian rioting in Belfast).[44]

In the spring of 1859 the American spiritual embers burst into flame in mid-Antrim, a district north-west of Belfast with a large underclass of nominal Presbyterians and a few pro-revival ministers. Within a few weeks the revival was transmitted to Belfast, and from there it spread quickly throughout the province. Far from businesslike, revival participants fell into trances, saw apparitions, even exhibited stigmata – in short they displayed all the American behaviours, and perhaps more, that had made revivals so suspect a generation earlier. Popular opinion attributed to converts who had experienced bodily manifestations and altered states of consciousness an access to the supernatural superior to that of the ministers themselves. Perhaps more urgent was the revival's affront to the respectability and scientific thinking espoused by the middle class upon which the ministers, especially in Belfast, were increasingly dependent. Ministers worked tirelessly for about six months to reinterpret lay understandings of the revival and to ensure, insofar as possible, that in the written narratives of these events the operations of the supernatural were confined to the internal world of the individual's psyche. Presbyterian clergy did succeed in the short run in making the revival palatable to many of their respectable middle-class laity, but they probably did not expunge from the consciousness of mill girls and farm labourers the conviction that supernatural power had palpably intervened not just in their souls but in their external world. The revival provided little if any permanent growth in membership, and over the succeeding decades there was a tendency for those who identified with what the revival represented to drift into Methodism and smaller conversionist sects.[45]

MODERN POPULAR PRESBYTERIANISM

The Ulster revival of 1859 meant that once the dust had settled a few years later from the American Civil War the two Presbyterianisms – Ulster and American – had a comparable set of experiences of popular religiosity. Ulster clergy had finally confronted revivalism in its starkest form and come to terms with it. In the United States, the acceptance of a tamed revivalism by the Old School in 1858 could not yield institutional reunion until after the War, but in 1869 the New School and the northern component of the Old School formally ended

44 Janice Holmes, 'The role of open-air preaching in the Belfast Riots of 1857', *Proceedings of the Royal Irish Academy* 102/C (2002), 47–66.   45 Miller, 'Did Ulster Presbyterians have a devotional revolution?'

their schism. In both America and the British Isles revival became routinized as a schedulable event within the local church or in carefully staged appearances by the likes of Moody and Sankey, typically arranged months in advance with serious efforts to secure the support of local Protestant clergy.[46] The spontaneous 'excesses' which so offended the respectable were largely eliminated. In the Ulster case this process was facilitated by the gradual disappearance of plain folk from the typical Presbyterian congregation; in America, with the exception of western Pennsylvania, plain folk had long since deserted mainstream Presbyterianism for the most part. Inward experience became a polite desideratum – important to the individual, but part of his or her private spiritual life, not a proper subject for public display.[47] A tamed conversionist spirituality had acquired a secure and largely noncontroversial place in both Presbyterianisms.

It was confessionalism, however, not conversionism, that forged the strongest links between Ulster and American Presbyterianism. The intellectual lodestar of Ulster Presbyterianism was shifting from the Scottish universities to Princeton, whose president from 1868 to 1888, the Revd James McCosh, had spent sixteen years as professor of logic and metaphysics at Queen's College, Belfast. Though located in the North, Princeton Seminary maintained strong ties with the southern component of the Old School (now happily divested of the slavery issue), which as the 'Presbyterian Church, US' maintained a separate General Assembly until 1983. Nevertheless, the American (northern) and the Irish General Assemblies came to be influenced by new trends in biblical scholarship and experienced fundamentalist-modernist conflicts which both culminated in colourful confrontations in the 1920s in which the fundamentalist side seemed to be defeated.[48]

Like popular conversionism, popular confessionalism could be adapted to a middle-class constituency. There was, of course, little further occasion for plain folk to turn the little world of their parish upside down for a day by taxing the learned ministerial candidate with his possible heresies. The practice, however, could easily be redirected from the face-to-face community of the village to the imagined community of a translocal cosmopolitan society. It is in just such a context that Marsden locates the rise of fundamentalism as a reaction against dismaying cultural change in the early twentieth century.[49] Marsden finds the intellectual origins of the theology of fundamentalist clergy in Scottish

---

46 Janice Holmes, *Religious revivals in Britain and Ireland, 1859–1905* (Dublin, 2000), pp 52–3, 60–98. William Warren Sweet, *The story of religion in America* (Grand Rapids, 1950), pp 346–7. Bernard A. Weisberger, *They gathered at the river: the story of the great revivalists and their impact upon religion in America* (Boston, 1958), pp 207–10. **47** On the interaction between middle-class values and revivalism see Moore, *Selling God*, pp 72–8, 177–8. **48** Loetscher, *Broadening church*; A.A. Fulton, 'Church in tension – in the twentieth century – mainly' in *Challenge and conflict*, pp 149–88; Livingstone and Wells, *Ulster-American religion*. **49** *Fundamentalism and American culture*, esp. pp 153–64.

Common-Sense philosophy. I am suggesting that those intellectual origins were complemented by social origins in the Presbyterian ritual of lay harassment of clergy who disdained to give *the right answers*. Confessionalist appeals to the laity have seldom, if ever, been about the whole theological system of the Westminster Confession. Henry Cooke was mainly concerned with the Confession's christology (his stick to beat the Unitarians) and was prepared to tolerate a variety of casuistical evasions of issues in the Confession which troubled other clergy (so long as they could be concealed from the laity).[50] And although the right answers may remain more or less the same over time, the questions certainly do change.[51] The ability of clergy to exploit lay confessionalist tendencies rests on the fact that even an educated lay person usually lacks the theological training to grasp the broad sweep of the history of doctrine and tends to perceive change only over the interval since his or her own catechetical instruction.

A sociologist considering schism and reunion in Presbyterianism might well conclude that they were not dysfunctions, but a central mechanism by which it works. To an Irish historian (even one raised a Presbyterian) the distinction between mainstream Presbyterian clergy and those in fringe Presbyterian bodies – strict Covenanters plus two different varieties of Seceders in eighteenth-century Ulster, or Orthodox Presbyterians, Reformed Presbyterians and the Presbyterian Church of America in the twentieth-century US – looks less like the boundary between separate 'denominations' than like the Roman Catholic distinction between the secular and the regular clergy. The congregant of a General Synod minister in the 1780s who went to listen to an itinerant Covenanting preacher in a field thought that he or she was hearing a *more* Presbyterian message than had been preached in his or her own meeting house on Sunday, not a less Presbyterian one. Similarly, many mainstream Ulster Presbyterians today probably do not think of the Revd Ian Paisley as a spokesman for a religion different from their own, despite the insistence of their own clergy that Paisley's Free Presbyterian Church is not really a Presbyterian church at all.

Within this complex and long-standing system, it is routine for confessionalist clergy to appeal to the anxieties of layfolk over social or political change to advance their theological agenda. Clergy who take this path may themselves be members of the mainstream church, as when Cooke appealed to fears of Catholic political power in the 1820s and 1830s or the clerical leaders of 'renewal' movements of our own day appeal to concerns over issues of sexuality.

---

50 *Belfast News-Letter*, 12 Aug., 16 Aug. 1836.   51 The five 'essential' points of doctrine which fundamentalists persuaded the General Assembly to adopt in 1910 (inerrancy of scripture, virgin birth, substitutionary atonement, bodily resurrection, authenticity of the miracles) and the three 'essential' points for which the Confessing Church Movement seeks support (singularity of Christ, infallibility of scripture, exclusive sanctity of heterosexual marriage) are very different from the five points of the Synod of Dort (total depravity, unconditional election, limited atonement, irresistible grace, perseverance of the saints).

Alternatively, such appeals may originate in one of the fringe bodies such as the Orthodox Presbyterian Church, formed in the aftermath of the fundamentalist–modernist conflict in the 1920s within the (northern) Presbyterian Church USA. During the generation after the 1954 Supreme Court decision in the *Brown vs. Topeka* case there was considerable anxiety over racial desegregation in (southern) Presbyterian Church US congregations in Mississippi. Such anxieties were exploited to place a number of graduates of the Orthodox Presbyterian Church's Westminster Seminary of Philadelphia in Mississippi pulpits.[52] But one cannot understand how and why such things happen without coming to terms with the long continuities in the Ulster-American religious system, and the most important of those continuities runs not through the history of theology but through the structures through which religious professionals interact with ordinary folk. It is no accident that a chief redoubt of the confessionalist party today is the Pittsburgh suburbs nor that its principal organ, lavishly distributed without charge to friend and foe alike, is entitled the *Layman*.

52 R. Milton Winter, 'Division and reunion in the Presbyterian Church, US: a Mississippi retrospective,' *Journal of Presbyterian History*, 88 (spring 2000), 67–86.

Reflections on '59: local social contexts of religious revival in Ulster

K.J. JAMES

The religious revivals that animated Protestant Ulster in the spring and summer of 1859 have attracted considerable scholarly attention and sustained popular interest. In part this is because they are reasonably well documented in a range of contemporary sources; more importantly, though, it is because they remain a touchstone for Protestant identity and historical memory in Ulster.[1] Centred on rural Presbyterian areas of the province, they began in the region surrounding the town of Ballymena. At their heart were purportedly spontaneous and lay-directed forms of popular worship, characterized by emotional intensity and frequent expressions of individual religious 'enthusiasm'. In the charged atmosphere of revival, crowds gathered in streets and on farms to hear lay and licensed preachers and to witness and experience acts of personal 'conviction'. As news of the progress of the revivals spread throughout the townlands, villages and urban districts of the province, observers and participants also engaged in heated debates over the character and consequences of this 'renewal'.[2] Many historians have concluded that the revivals contributed to a degree of coherence in 'Protestant Ulster'. They are divided, however, over the extent to which new social alliances and cultural identities that subsumed powerful divisions of gender, sect and class were forged from disparate elements of the Protestant population.[3]

1 For a discussion of religion in contemporary Ulster Protestant culture, see Duncan Morrow, 'Suffering for righteousness' sake? Fundamentalist Protestantism and Ulster politics,' in Peter Shirlow and Mark McGovern (eds), *Who are 'the people'? Unionism, Protestantism and loyalism in Northern Ireland* (London, 1997), pp 55–71. 2 Contrasting views on religious convictions are found in two works: Revd William Gibson, *The year of grace: a history of the Ulster Revival of 1859* (Edinburgh, 1860) and Revd Isaac Nelson, *The year of delusion: a review of The Year of Grace, nos. I–XII. 3rd ed.* (Belfast, 1861). 3 S.J. Brown, 'Presbyterian communities, transatlantic visions and the Ulster Revival of 1859,' in J.P. Mackey (ed.), *The cultures of Europe: the Irish contribution* (Belfast, 1994), pp 87–105; David Hempton and Myrtle Hill, *Evangelical Protestantism in Ulster society, 1740–1890* (London, 1992): see especially chapter eight, 'Ulster awakened: the 1859 Revival', pp 145–60; Myrtle Hill, 'Assessing the Awakening: the 1859 Revival in Ulster', in Ingmar Brohed (ed.), *Church and people in Britain and Scandinavia* (Lund, 1996), pp 197–213, and 'Ulster awakened: the '59 Revival reconsidered,' *Journal of Ecclesiastical History* 41:3 (1990), 443–62; David Miller, *Queen's rebels: Ulster loyalism in historical perspective*

Only a few historians have attempted to reduce such events to the status of mere barometers of underlying economic changes. Instead, most would heed David Hempton and Myrtle Hill's cautionary remarks on the intricate relationship between individual behaviour and cultural patterns, and the complex interactions between religious beliefs and socio-economic structures.[4] Even those who may search for a 'crisis' in the social or economic order to explain religious revival must acknowledge the independent influence of cultural and intellectual developments, such as doctrinal changes, which contribute to creating a receptive climate. Still, one of the most influential accounts of the 1859 revivals, written by Peter Gibbon thirty years ago,[5] attempted to analyze the revivals exclusively within the framework of wider socio-economic processes. It remains one of the most ambitious syntheses of economic, social and political development in nineteenth-century Ulster. Audacious in its claims and explicit in its identification of social and economic 'roots' of revival, Gibbon's work is as provocative and challenging as it is dogmatically wedded to Marxist analysis – then much more fashionable than today.

Gibbon's efforts to delineate a theoretical framework within which to under-stand Ulster's experience in the nineteenth century and to examine economic, social and religious developments in both rural and urban Ulster have helped to focus the attention of a generation of scholars on 'uneven development' and industrial capitalism's distinctive path in Ireland.[6] How did a working class marked by deep and enduring confessional loyalties emerge in Ulster? How did a political climate develop in which class seemed to be subsumed by sectarian identities and conflicts? What role did the revivals play in this process? In formu-lating his responses to these questions, Gibbon looked to rural Ireland for major influences on subsequent urban social, economic and political developments. He subscribed to the derivative character of religious experience; revivals could only be understood with reference to underlying economic and social transforma-tions. They occurred at a crucial point at which Ulster's rural population

(Dublin, 1978) and 'Presbyterianism and "Modernisation" in Ulster,' *Past and Present* 80 (1978), 66–90; Janice Holmes, 'The "World turned upside down": women in the Ulster Revival of 1859,' in Janice Holmes and Diane Urquhart (eds), *Coming into the Light: the work, politics and religion of women in Ulster* (Belfast, 1994), pp 126–53, and *Religious revivals in Britain and Ireland, 1859–1905* (Dublin, 2000); Norman Vance, 'Presbyterian culture and revival,' *Bulletin of the Presbyterian Historical Society in Ireland* 22 (1993), 16–19.   4 Hempton and Hill, p. 160.   5 Peter Gibbon, *The origins of Ulster unionism: the formation of popular Protestant politics and ideology in nineteenth-century Ireland* (Manchester, 1975).   6 Most scholars have focussed on Gibbon's analysis of *urban* industrial, social and political developments, from the earliest reviews of his work (Henry Patterson, 'Refining the debate on Ulster,' *Political Studies* 24 [1976], 205–8), to more recent studies of urban religion and sectarianism (Janice Holmes, 'The role of open-air preaching in the Belfast Riots of 1857,' *Proceedings of the Royal Irish Academy* 102/C [2002], 47–66, and Catherine Hirst, *Religion, politics and violence in nineteenth-century Ireland: The Pound and Sandy Row* [Dublin, 2002]).

expressed a 'superstructural' response to social and economic transformations which they had been experiencing for decades. In 1859 they crystallized new social relations which were shaped by what Gibbon characterized as the 'second great mutation of structural determinates of social relations in the countryside between 1780 and 1880'[7] – the demise of domestic industry and small manufacture, a 'social crisis' among the rural weaving population, and the 'creation of a mass urban proletariat.' The revivals, in his view, were simply diagnostic of these underlying changes in socio-economic structures and relationships.

The rural setting was especially salient to understanding these events, as in the mid-nineteenth century Gibbon detected the decisive proletarianization of a linen weaving workforce which had once enjoyed relative commercial and cultural autonomy. He argued that Ulster's revivals redirected Presbyterian politics in some traditional weaving districts away from late-eighteenth century 'democratic radicalism' associated with the independent farmer-weaver class toward an 'ethnocentric Conservative regionalism'.[8] This ideological reorientation was an outgrowth of the eroding position of the independent, middling farmer and his social proximate in such areas, the autodidact-weaver.

Upon close inspection, the conclusion that the revivals were mere 'superstructural' expressions of changes in social relations of production seems untenable. This is especially true for the mid-Antrim district which Gibbon identified as being at the core of the revivals. This paper examines some central propositions in the 'Gibbon thesis' by scrutinizing evidence he used in his discussion of social and economic structures and changes. It is clear that in seeking to develop a broad and ambitious schema of industrial, social and cultural development in Ulster, he presented a narrative premised on economic homogenization and social differentiation in rural Ulster. Yet the authority of his sources – and the uses to which they were put – is highly questionable. By exploring some of these methodological and analytical problems, and by deflating some of Gibbon's grander claims, we can develop a more nuanced understanding of the social, economic and cultural fabric of a remarkably complex rural society.

Most scholars of religious revivals have been interested in elucidating the social profile of the 'revived community'.[9] Unfortunately, though, the sources tell us little about the occupational profile of those who participated in the 1859 revivals. To get round this problem, Gibbon turned to revival accounts, claiming that they represented a broad range of authorities, while cautioning that such literature was 'written not only by the faithful but for the faithful as well'.[10] Straight away, he ran into conceptual difficulties. Most contemporary accounts

7 Gibbon, p. 45. 8 Gibbon, p. 51. 9 A classic account of American revivalism is Paul E. Johnson, *A shopkeeper's millennium: society and revivals in Rochester, New York, 1815–1837* (New York, 1978). 10 Gibbon, p. 44.

of the 1859 revivals, attributed to local and visiting clergymen, conformed to conventions of a genre which was also employed in documenting contemporaneous revivals in such places as Scotland and America. The narratives often include embedded quotations – both attributed and unattributed – which were largely reproduced from other accounts.[11] The language, style and structure of many accounts are remarkably similar, with descriptions of local events linked together, often quite loosely, by an overarching narrative of the 'progress of the revival' throughout Ulster.[12] They form a kind of accreting narrative in the style of mediaeval annals or chronicles. They are replete with anecdotes, some seemingly reproduced word-for-word, that generally describe anonymous men, women and children experiencing intense religious conviction in a particular town or townland.[13] These were pre-eminently polemical documents, written by observers and pamphleteers whose interest in promoting or undermining the revivals was often undisguised. Their polemical character does not negate their value to us as historical sources – they offer a rich base to study the revival narrative as a genre – but it does place limits on their value for deriving the kind of data which Gibbon sought.

Surveying these accounts and detecting a broad consensus in their interpretations of events on the ground, Gibbon argued that although the population most 'moved' by the spirit of revival was in dispute, it was clear that the revivals encountered resistance from large tenant farmers. He further contended that a marked division emerged between these farmers (who were skeptical of these events and unmoved by the fervour which they unleashed) and other sections of rural society. Of course, this fits neatly with his analysis of transformations in rural society; specifically, the rural weavers' progressive proletarianization and the eclipse of rural production.

Gibbon argued that the revivals occurred during a period of social upheaval and dramatic reorganization of local textile production and commerce. These

---

11 See Gibson, pp 430–7; George Macauley, *Times of revival, or 'The natural desirableness and means of revival in religion'* (Edinburgh, 1858 [?]) – see especially his discussion of Ballymena (pp 80–6); William Arthur, *The Revival in Ballymena and Coleraine* (London, 1859).   12 Among the local discussions of the revival in Ballymena are Arthur, *The Revival in Ballymena* and *The Revival in Ulster: Ahoghill and Ballymena* (London, 1859), *Beginnings of a great revival: the awakening in Ulster: Connor* (London, 1859); Revd D. McMeekin, *Memories of '59 or the revival movement* (Hull, 1908), Revd S.J. Moore, *The history and prominent characteristics of the present revival in Ballymena and its neighbourhood* (Belfast, 1859). A good example of a revival account which strings together many separate accounts is James William Massie, *A visit to the scenes of revival in Ireland: the origins, progress, and characteristics of the work of 1859*, parts II and III of *Revivals in Ireland* (London, 1859). The press, especially the Presbyterian *Banner of Ulster*, also reported the revival by aggregating individual reports in a section with an overarching title such as 'Present religious movement in the North' (see, for instance, 7 July 1859).   13 For an example of such an exercise, drawing on first-hand accounts of participants, see Ned Landsman, 'Evangelists and their hearers: popular interpretation of revivalist preaching in eighteenth-century Scotland,' *Journal of British Studies* 28 (1989), 120–49.

Table 1: 'X' marks instead of signatures in marriage registers for selected occupations, First Presbyterian Church, Ballymena, 1857–67

Groom's occupation	N.	Marked 'x' (%)
Farmer	89	16
Labourer	49	49
Weaver	86	43

Source: Marriage Register of the First Presbyterian Church, Ballymena, PRONI, Belfast, MIC/1P/114/1.

changes, he maintained, resulted in new rural social divisions in regions once associated with independent weavers and small farmers. The middling stratum of farmers declined, and relations became polarized between impoverished, land-poor or landless cottars on one hand, and a small group of substantial farmers on the other.[14] There is some evidence that supports his claims of significant differentiation between weavers and farmers. But there are also indications that rural society was more complex than Gibbon realized.

Church records are useful sources for investigating these claims; they can be used to explore some characteristics of local populations, although they have pronounced limitations in yielding information about women. These records indicate that there was indeed a degree of differentiation between males enumerated as farmers and those listed as weavers and labourers. One differentiating characteristic was literacy; male weavers and labourers did not sign Presbyterian marriage registers as frequently as farmers, instead marking an 'x.' This suggests lower levels of education compared to the farmers and a more proximate relationship between labourers and weavers (as Gibbon contended).

Another indicator of rural stratification yields similar results. Those men recorded as farmers were more likely to marry within their cohort; well over two-thirds of farmer-grooms married the daughters of farmers in local Presbyterian congregations. Weavers displayed a less marked propensity toward endogamy, while labourers showed a very limited tendency. See table 2.

Here we see a complex rural society in which endogamy and status were heavily conditioned by gender. Women's occupations were seldom enumerated in these records, but those of their fathers were listed. Farmers' daughters often married into the weaving population, but male farmers exhibited a high level of endogamy by marrying daughters of men from their own rank. This does indicate that the farming 'class' or status group had some distinctive character-

14 Gibbon, pp 51–4.

Table 2: Occupations of grooms and brides' fathers from First Presbyterian
Church, Ballymena marriage registers, 1857–67

| Groom's occupation | N. | Bride's father's occupation | | | |
		Farmer %	Labourer %	Weaver %	Other %
Farmer	89	72	1	12	15
Labourer*	49	33	27	33	8
Weaver	86	26	15	50	9

Source: Marriage Register of the First Presbyterian Church, Ballymena, PRONI, Belfast, MIC/
1P/114/1.
*Total does not equal 100 due to rounding.

istics and that social boundaries had developed between male farmers and other
rural workers (who exhibited a much lower level of endogamy). It offers support
for the levels of rural social stratification which Gibbon identifies. But it also
suggests that females from farming families found boundaries between the
farming, weaving and labouring households more permeable. Their experiences
of social mobility within rural society appear to diverge from those of males.
They testify to the salience of gender in social stratification and deserve greater
attention.

There is a critical methodological issue associated with Gibbon's use of a
conventional data set – the printed census. Gibbon argued that religion furnished
an outlet for the social/psychological instability that was already present in the
community because of profound structural adjustments. Let us turn to his most
controversial claim – that hysteria associated with the revivals can be attributed
to changes in the rural sexual balance and the increasing average age of marriage
of young women. In short, Gibbon's argument is that psychic trauma associated
with delayed marriage and social adjustments to new economic circumstances
found legitimation as expressions of intense piety. He saw this development as
an outgrowth of the collapse of cottage industry in rural areas of Ulster.
Historians may take umbrage at his characterization of women's fragile psychological condition in the face of transitions to new demographic regimes, but even
those who may cling to Freudian explanations will find little support for his
claim. Gibbon cited census data for County Antrim (reproduced in table 3)
which suggested that there was a substantial and growing imbalance between
males and females between 1841 and 1851.[15]

But Antrim was a large county, embracing highly urban regions, including
most of Belfast, vast rural areas, coastal and inland districts – all encompassing
a variety of economic and social organization. And in the region which he

15 Gibbon, p. 59.

Table 3: Balance of sexes in County
Antrim, 1841–61

Year	Number of females per male
1841	1.12
1851	1.18
1861	1.21

Source: Gibbon, p. 59.

Table 4: Balance of sexes in Connor parish, 1841–61

Year	Number of females per male
1841	1.04
1851	1.02
1861	1.05

Sources: 'Report of the Commissioners of the Census of Ireland, 1841' [504], HC 1843, vol. xxiv; *Census of Ireland, 1851*: Pt. VI: General Report [2134], HC 1856, vol. xxxi; *Census of Ireland, 1861*: Pt I: Area, Population, and Number of Houses, by Townlands and Electoral Divisions, Province of Ulster [3204], HC 1863, vol. lv.

identified as being at the centre of the revivals, and therefore at the core of his analysis, we see no such sexual imbalance emerging. See table 4. Local data suggest something markedly different from aggregate county data and cast another tenet of Gibbon's thesis in doubt.

If this is one of the weakest points of his argument, Gibbon's understanding of the provincial linen trade constitutes perhaps the most flawed element of his interpretation. It underpins his analysis of rural Ulster's 'proletarianization.' With the decline of the farming-weaving class, Gibbon argued, came the erosion of the vibrant, autonomous culture of the weavers, personified by the autodidactic weaver-poet. 'As the status of the weaving population declined,' he wrote, 'and its economic independence became eroded, so the culture which had supported the bards also suffered decline.'[16] He argued that this development set the stage for an ideological reorganization of the countryside, in which sectarianism (confessional insularism associated with a belief in ethnic purity) was harnessed by a new political alliance of urban workers and industrialists.

16 Gibbon, p. 55.

Underpinning this claim is a grossly exaggerated reading of conditions in the Irish linen trade in the nineteenth century, which was far from exclusively urban even three decades after 1859.

Weavers had suffered a decline in earnings during a long period of depression in the trade in the 1820s and 1830s. This led the Hand-Loom Commissioners in the 1830s to declare that the 'Golden Age' of the weaver-farmer had long since disappeared.[17] But the decline of weavers' independent activity in the market had been uneven, and in the 1830s there were still several major centres of the trade in which such activity was widespread. Gibbon's periodization of hand-loom weavers' commercial 'subordination' and eventual extinction is inaccurate. There is very little evidence to support his claim that the dispersed rural industrial labour force became extinct during the 1850s and 1860s – or to support his periodization of its prior commercial subordination. Indeed, he reduced its complex and varied development to a narrative of homogenization and urbanization. Yet both the underlying structure of the linen trade, and its many hand-loom workers, remained remarkably diverse.[18]

According to Gibbon, the emergence of power-loom weaving resulted in the urbanization of the linen industry. These developments in the production end of the sector, he argued, followed the extinction of traditional commercial systems in the trade. This was, he believed, particularly the case in County Antrim, which, in contrast to County Armagh's weaving district, had escaped proletarianization in the late eighteenth century. Gibbon further contended that power looms displaced domestic production in regions where cottage industry or the putting-out system predominated (effecting a preliminary 'proletarianization') and drew the remaining hand-loom weavers into the orbit of the urban factory. Rural hand-loom weaving subsequently faded away as power looms emptied the countryside and factory production attracted rural migrants. The setting for Ulster's grand sectarian and industrial struggles then shifted to urban space (where Gibbon's analysis shifts as well, following his discussion of rural transformations).

But is that what actually happened? In fact, there is little evidence to suggest heavy out-migration from the district as a response to the severe adjustments that Gibbon outlined. Indeed, as we turn once again to local data, we find remarkable demographic stability in the 1850s in the parish of Connor, a weaving district that lay at the heart of the revivals.

If we look more closely at the economic profile of the region, we find further evidence that one cornerstone of the rural economy – hand-loom weaving – remained strong during this period. Gibbon claimed that hand-loom weaving in

17 *Royal Commission on hand-loom weavers*, Commissioners' Reports, pt. III (Yorkshire, West Riding; Ireland) (43–II), HC 1840, vol. xxiii, Report of R.M. Muggeridge, pp 703–4.   18 See K.J. James, 'The hand-loom in Ulster's post-Famine linen industry: the limits of mechanization in textiles' "Factory Age,"' *Textile History* 5:2 (2004), 178–91.

Table 5: Population of the parish of Connor, 1841–61		
Year	*Population* *(N.)*	*Population change* *(%)*
1841	8,272	
1851	7,843	−5.19
1861	7,928	1.08

Sources: 'Report of the commissioners of the census of Ireland, 1841' [504], HC 1843, vol. xxiv; *Census of Ireland, 1851*: Pt. VI: General Report [2134], HC 1856, vol. xxxi; *Census of Ireland, 1861*: Pt I: Area, population, and number of houses, by townlands and electoral divisions, Province of Ulster [3204], HC 1863, vol. lv.

the district was being rapidly extinguished. He argued that the development of 'mechanical weaving' dealt a death-blow to the open market and to hand-loom producers in the 1840s and 1850s.[19] But this was not the case; capital investment in power-loom weaving was very limited in the 1850s. It expanded greatly in the 1860s, during the American Civil War, but even then only in a limited number of branches. While in percentage terms the growth in power looms was spectacular in the 1850s, they remained a very small proportion of the looms employed in the trade, and were limited to weaving coarser linen cloth.[20] See table 6.

For a variety of reasons, most linked to improved technology and favourable commercial conditions, the number of power looms in Ireland increased in the 1860s. There was a remarkable regional variation in mechanization, which advanced in a profoundly uneven fashion during the 1860s and afterward. The adoption of the power loom in the 1850s was constrained by a number of factors, including limits in technology and instability of demand in many markets, so that only some 3,633 were in use by the end of the decade, most in the regions of Bessbrook, Lurgan and Belfast.[21] As in the British silk and cotton industries, the development of power looms did not herald their full-scale adoption in the Irish linen industry for many decades.[22] Moreover, the district in which the 1859

19 Gibbon, p. 52. 20 James, 'The hand-loom in Ulster's post-Famine linen industry.' 21 Andrew Ure, *The philosophy of manufactures, or, An exposition of the scientific, moral, and commercial economy of the factory system of Great Britain by the late Andrew Ure*, 3rd edition, *continued in its detail to the present time, by P.L. Simmonds* (New York, 1861), p. 584. 22 For other trades in Britain, about which much has been written, see S.R.H. Jones, 'Technology, transaction costs, and the transition to factory production in the British silk industry, 1700–1870,' *Journal of Economic History* 47:1 (1987), 71–96; John S. Lyons, 'Family response to economic decline: Handloom weavers in early nineteenth- century Lancashire,' *Research in Economic History* 12 (1989), 46–91; Geoffrey Timmins, *The last shift: the decline of handloom weaving in nineteenth–century Lancashire* (Manchester, 1993).

Table 6: Linen power looms in Ireland, at various years,
1850–81

Year	Looms	Year	Looms
1850	88	1872	18,169
1856	1,871	1873	19,155
1859	3,633	1874	19,331
1861	4,933	1875	20,152
1864	8,187	1877	20,958
1866	10,804	1879	21,153
1868	12,969	1880	21,177
1871	14,834	1881	21,779

Source: Flax supply association annual report 1904 (Belfast: Hugh Adair,
1905), p. 17.

revivals were centred was a region in which extensive hand-loom production
continued long after the 1850s. In this area, weavers generally specialized in fine
shirting linen and worked for several manufacturers. Although these weavers
were not directly employed by any one manufacturer, their status had changed
from the days when they were independent actors in the local market. Now they
were contracted to weave by manufacturers who supplied them with yarn. This
system had been gradually gaining ground since the 1830s in many centres of
rural production, and in mid-Antrim it was the primary means of organization.
The large rural hand-loom trade in which thousands of weavers were engaged
continued into the last quarter the century, contracting markedly in the 1890s.

Gibbon's analysis of the linen trade fails to account for these developments.
In 1862, five years after the revivals, William Charley endorsed the view of the
Linen Trade Circular that the supply of hand-loom cloth was diminishing and
argued that 'there are many circumstances which would seem to indicate, that
while the days of progress in power-looms have unquestionably set in, those of
decadence in hand-loom weaving give warning of approach'. Still, he noted that
the hand loom was better suited for finer sets of goods.[23] This was to be the case
for several decades, with the mid-Antrim hand-loom weavers developing a
specialization in so-called 'Ballymenas' – a light yard-wide shirting made by
hand. The local hand-loom weaving labour force's experience was one of
remarkable persistence – not dramatic decline. Here is another feature of the
locality which demands closer attention and suggests that by imposing a unity of
experience on disparate regions, economies and populations, Gibbon's grand

23 William Charley, Flax and its products in Ireland (London, 1862), p. 89.

account of social and economic transition, like the grand narrative of religious revival, obscures profound local differences.

Historians who look primarily at cultural forces as agents of historical change have long had serious reservations about Gibbon's work and the general approach to the study of the past on which it is premised. Yet thirty years on, Gibbon's analysis of rural society and its connection to political realignments in Ulster remains important for the sheer scale of its ambitions – one seldom attempted before or since. Even historians who assert the primacy of socio-economic structures find much that is problematic in this bold synthesis. Gibbon's 'clarification' of the structural pillars of nineteenth-century rural society is a shaky analysis of demographic, industrial and social change in rural areas of Ulster, relying on broad generalizations and selective evidence. The rural transformations he outlines serve as a foundation for his subsequent analysis of social, economic and political developments in urban Ulster. He has left scholars of rural Irish society with a far-reaching but flawed analysis and with a challenge to consider socio-economic factors in Ulster's political and cultural development in the later nineteenth century.

An examination of local environments should lead us to question the extent to which the putatively province-wide, inter-denominational 'revival' effected a high degree of cultural cohesion, given the profoundly varied regions in which these events occurred. In mid-Antrim, much of the evidence outlined in this paper suggests a community experiencing relative stability and not enduring a traumatic transformation. Can the revivals there be seen as expressions of the strength and power of the laity in a region of relative demographic, social and economic stability? In this district, a more plausible premise for exploring these events might rest on the *absence* of pronounced disruptions, even during such a watershed in Irish history as the 1850s. Perhaps as the revivals spread through regions of the province, their social consequences were as varied as the populations and districts in which they were experienced. If so, they are not amenable either to the sweeping claims made by contemporary chroniclers of a general re-awakening throughout the province, or to Gibbon's equally bold narrative of progressive social and economic homogenization. Attention to diverse demographic, social and economic conditions in rural and urban areas of the province offers the potential to yield insight into varied cultural and political developments in a markedly and durably heterogeneous 'Protestant Ulster'.

'Stupid Irish teagues' and the encouragement of enlightenment: Ulster Presbyterian students of moral philosophy in Glasgow University, 1730–1795

MARK G. SPENCER

Scholars have begun to note bits and pieces of an Ulster contribution to the Enlightenment. The life and writings of the Ulster-born John Toland (1670–1722), for instance, have been better documented in an Enlightenment context in recent years.[1] So, too, have a select few other seminal thinkers with Ulster origins, such as John Abernethy (1680–1740) and James Arbuckle (d. 1742).[2] Even some lesser-light figures from Ulster, such as Samuel Haliday (1685–1739) and James Kirkpatrick (d. 1743), have been noted for their enlightened tendencies.[3] More attention has fallen on Francis Hutcheson (1694–1746), although his Ulster roots are not always acknowledged or fully explored.[4] Indeed, Hutcheson is illustrative of a difficulty that is part and parcel

1 See, for instance, Justin Champion, *Republican learning: John Toland and the crisis of Christian culture, 1696–1722* (Manchester and New York, 2003).   2 M.A. Stewart has written entries on Abernethy and Arbuckle in John W. Yolton, John Vladimir Price and John Stephens (eds), *Dictionary of eighteenth century British philosophers* (Bristol, 1999). Also useful are Richard B. Barlow, 'The career of John Abernethy (1680–1740), father of Nonsubscription in Ireland and defender of religious liberty,' *Harvard Theological Review* 78 (1985), 399–419; A.W.G. Brown, 'John Abernethy, 1680–1740: scholar and ecclesiast,' in G. O'Brien and P. Roebuck (eds), *Nine Ulster lives* (Belfast, 1992), pp 127–47; W.R. Scott, 'James Arbuckle and his relation to the Molesworth-Shaftsbury School,' *Mind* 8 (1889), 194–215; and M.A. Stewart, 'Rational dissent in early eighteenth-century Ireland,' in Knud Haakonssen (ed.), *Enlightenment and religion: rational dissent in eighteenth-century Britain* (Cambridge and New York, 1996), pp 42–63.   3 See, for instance, Ian R. McBride, *Scripture politics: Ulster Presbyterians and Irish radicalism in the late eighteenth century* (Oxford, 1998), esp. pp 44–8, 70, 92, 95; see also my entries on Haliday and Kirkpatrick in Thomas Duddy (ed.) *Biographical dictionary of Irish philosophy* (London and New York, 2004).   4 An exception to that trend is M.A. Stewart's entry on Hutcheson in Alan Charles Kors (ed.), *Encyclopedia of the Enlightenment* (4 vols, New York, 2003), where Hutcheson is considered as an 'Ulster–Scots philosopher and educationist'. Of the many works on Hutcheson, also useful are William Robert Scott, *Francis Hutcheson: his life, teaching and position in the history of philosophy* (Cambridge, 1900; reprinted New York, 1966), Thomas P. Miller, 'Francis Hutcheson and the Civic Humanist Tradition,' in Andrew Hook and Richard B. Sher (eds), *The Glasgow Enlightenment* (East Lothian, 1995), and Daniel Carey's entry on Hutcheson in Yolton, Price and Stephens (eds), *Dictionary of eighteenth-century British philosophers*. For an early attempt to see Hutcheson as part of a 'connected' Ulster-Scots intellectual circle see Caroline Robbins, *The eighteenth century Commonwealthman: studies in the transmission, devel-*

of approaching the Enlightenment from the perspective of 'national context.'[5] To which national Enlightenment did Hutcheson belong? Born in County Down, Hutcheson was raised in Armagh. His earliest education was in Ireland, but his formative years were spent in Scotland, especially at Glasgow where Hutcheson was a student in the university from 1710 to 1717. Professor of moral philosophy in the University of Glasgow from 1730 to 1745, Hutcheson is frequently considered to be the 'Father of the Scottish Enlightenment,' in a large measure because of his impact on students.[6] Yet Hutcheson's intellectual development was shaped not only in the Ulster of his birth and youth and the Scotland of his university training but also in Dublin, where he lived and wrote as a young man from 1719 to 1730.[7] Moreover, Hutcheson's subsequent influence can be traced far beyond the Enlightenments of Scotland or Ireland. Some scholars have argued that Hutcheson's most significant impact was felt not in any of the European Enlightenments, but across the Atlantic, where his writings encouraged enlightenment in America.[8] In recent decades scholars have better illuminated other Ulster connections with the Enlightenment, especially those between Ulster Presbyterian radicalism and eighteenth-century Scottish political thinkers.[9] Taken together, all of this scholarship contributes to a developing image of Ulster's place in the Enlightenment, although no systematic attempt has yet been made to bring those parts together.[10] Given this developing historiography, it is

opment and circumstance of English liberal thought from the Restoration of Charles II until the war with the Thirteen Colonies (1959; reprinted New York, 1968), esp. pp 167–76. **5** The approach has also had its rewards, however. See, for instance, Roy Porter and Mikuláš Teich (eds), *The Enlightenment in national context* (Cambridge and New York, 1981). **6** See, for instance, T.D. Campbell, 'Francis Hutcheson: "father" of the Scottish Enlightenment,' in R.H. Campbell and A.S. Skinner (eds), *The origins and nature of the Scottish Enlightenment* (Edinburgh, 1982), and Jane Rendall, *The origins of the Scottish Enlightenment, 1707–1776* (London and Basingstoke, 1978), esp. pp 74–95. **7** On Hutcheson's Dublin context see Michael Brown, *Francis Hutcheson in Dublin, 1719–30: the crucible of his thought* (Dublin, 2002). **8** On Hutcheson's American impact see David Fate Norton, 'Francis Hutcheson in America,' *Studies on Voltaire and the Eighteenth Century* 154 (1976), 1547–68; Caroline Robbins, '"When it is that colonies may turn Independent": an analysis of the environment and politics of Francis Hutcheson (1694–1746),' *William and Mary Quarterly*, series 3, 11 (1954), 214–51; Robbins, *The eighteenth-century Commonwealthman*, esp. pp 185–99. **9** See, for instance, S.J. Connolly, 'Ulster Presbyterians: religion, culture, and politics, 1660–1860,' in H. Tyler Blethen and Curtis W. Wood, Jr. (eds), *Ulster and North America: transatlantic perspectives on the Scotch-Irish* (Tuscaloosa and London, 1997), esp. pp 34–8; Ian McBride, 'William Drennan and the Dissenting Tradition,' in D. Dickson, D. Keogh and K. Whelan (eds), *The United Irishmen: republicanism, radicalism and rebellion* (Dublin, 1993), pp 49–61; E.W. McFarland, *Ireland and Scotland in the age of revolution* (Edinburgh, 1994), passim; P. Tesch, 'Presbyterian radicalism,' in Dickson et al. (eds), *The United Irishmen*, pp 34–48; and Kevin Whelan, 'The United Irishmen, the Enlightenment and popular culture,' in Dickson et al. (eds), *The United Irishmen*, pp 269–96. **10** Perhaps that is why 'Ulster' and 'Ulster-Scots' go without entries in Kors (ed.), *Encyclopedia of the Enlightenment*, where neither term even rates an entry in the index.

also interesting to note that professors of the Enlightenment in Scotland sometimes took note of their students from Ulster.

Newly appointed as professor of moral philosophy in the University of Glasgow in 1764, Thomas Reid (1710–96) was one Scot who noticed his students from Ireland. Writing to his friend, Dr Andrew Skene of Aberdeen, Reid remarked that 'near a third' of the students at Glasgow were 'stupid Irish teagues who attend classes for two or three years to qualify them for teaching schools.'[11] And Reid was not the only professor of moral philosophy at Glasgow to dismiss his Irish students in that way. A generation earlier Hutcheson himself wrote to his fellow Ulsterman, the Revd Thomas Drennan (1696–1768),

> Our countrymen very generally have such an affectation of being men and gentlemen immediately, and of despising every thing in Scotland, that they neglect a great deal of good, wise instruction they might have here. I am truly mortified with a vanity and foppery prevailing among our countrymen beyond what I see in others; and a softness and sauntering forsooth which makes them incapable of any hearty drudgery at books. We had five or six young gentlemen from Edinburgh, men of fortune and fine genius at my class ... our Irishmen thought them poor book–worms.[12]

While Hutcheson in 1741 and Reid in 1764 dismissed their Irish students, historians ought not to write them off so quickly. If we want to understand more fully the contributions of Ulster to the Enlightenment, we ought to consider not only seminal thinkers, such as Toland, Abernethy, Arbuckle, Hutcheson and others of their ilk, but also the relatively obscure boys from Ireland who attended the University of Glasgow. They too were agents of the Enlightenment, and they belong to that history. These students helped disseminate Enlightenment tendencies in the eighteenth–century Atlantic world and their presence at the heart of the Glasgow Enlightenment mattered in other ways, as we will see.

The case for broadening Enlightenment studies to approach the social history of ideas is strengthened in this case when we consider Reid's own goal as a teacher of moral philosophy. In a convincing summary of Reid as enlightened instructor, Knud Haakonssen has argued that Reid's primary aim in the classroom went beyond achieving narrow academic goals. Rather, Reid was concerned most of all with teaching his students how to live. That was arguably part of a tradition stretching back to Glasgow's first professor of moral philosophy, Gershom Carmichael (1672–1729).[13] As Haakonssen put it, 'the

---

11 Thomas Reid to Andrew Skene, 1 November 1764, in William Hamilton (ed.), *The works of Thomas Reid, D.D., now fully collected, with selections from his unpublished letters* (2nd ed., Edinburgh, 1849), pp 40–3.   12 Francis Hutcheson to the Revd Thomas Drennan, 1 June 1741, in James McCosh, *The Scottish philosophy, biographical, expository, critical, from Hutcheson to Hamilton* (London, 1875; reprinted Hildesheim, 1966), p. 464.   13 On Carmichael see James

moral philosophy [Reid] professed was only part of a wider concern with human knowledge, aimed as much at the formation of character as at the imparting of knowledge'.[14] Who were the 'stupid Irish teagues' whose characters Reid aimed to form?

II

Anyone concerned with students at Glasgow University during the Age of Enlightenment will want to begin with the research of W. Innes Addison.[15] Addison, who was from 1887 the matriculation officer at Glasgow, published in 1913 his transcriptions of the matriculation albums of the University of Glasgow.[16] These records covered the 130 years from 1728 to 1858. As Addison admitted in his preface, the albums were not a complete record of the students attending Glasgow University for 'it was impossible, earlier than 1843, to make up a complete list of *alumni*, or to say, from an inspection of the records, that any one person was *not* a student of Glasgow'.[17] The reason for this is that not all students who attended classes at Glasgow matriculated. Matriculation was only compulsory for arts students who intended graduating. It was not compulsory, that is, for students in the faculties of law, medicine or theology. Most students in law and theology, however, first took a preparatory arts course before taking up their specialized studies. That was especially so in the eighteenth century.

Since Addison's *Matriculation Albums* is the most thorough record we have of students at Glasgow University, it is not surprising that scholars have referred to his work often. Indeed, various aspects of Addison's *Albums* have been analyzed by historians over the years. Two historians have used Addison's *Albums* in a way that is of particular interest to the present study. The first wrote almost forty years ago, in 1966; the second, much more recently, in 2002. But in both cases

Moore, 'Natural sociability and natural rights in the moral philosophy of Gershom Carmichael,' in Vincent Hope (ed.), *Philosophers of the Scottish Enlightenment* (Edinburgh, 1984). See also James Moore and Michael Silverthorne (eds), *The writings of Gershom Carmichael* (Indianapolis, 2002). **14** See Knud Haakonssen (ed.), *Thomas Reid: Practical ethics; being lectures and papers on natural religion, self-government, natural jurisprudence, and the law of nations* (Princeton, 1990), p. 3; see also Dugald Stewart, *Account of the life and writings of Thomas Reid, D.D. F.R.S. Edin., late professor of moral philosophy in the University of Glasgow* (Edinburgh, 1803), 50f. On Hutcheson in a similar context see Miller, 'Francis Hutcheson', p. 47, who points out that Hutcheson wrote at the outset of his *A system of moral philosophy* that 'The Intention of Moral Philosophy is to direct men to that course of action which tends most effectually to promote their greatest happiness and perfection ...' **15** On historians' general neglect of the Enlightenment in Glasgow, see R.H. Campbell, 'Scotland's neglected Enlightenment,' *History Today* 40 (1990), 22–8. In the 'Introduction,' p. 2, to Hook and Sher (eds), *The Glasgow Enlightenment* the editors remark that 'the Glasgow Enlightenment as such has been virtually ignored.' **16** W. Innes Addison (ed.), *The matriculation albums of the University of Glasgow: from 1728 to 1858* (Glasgow, 1913). **17** Addison, *Matriculation albums*, p. xi.

the place of Ulster students at the University of Glasgow has been discounted in curious ways.

In 1966 W.H. Mathew published, in the journal *Past & Present*, an essay entitled, 'The Origins and Occupations of Glasgow Students, 1740–1839'.[18] Drawing his evidence from Addison's *Matriculation Albums*, Mathew argued that 'Irish students were especially numerous' in Glasgow 'in the eighteenth century.'[19] Even more interesting, given the focus of the volume to which this essay belongs, Mathew suggested that these Irish students came 'predominantly from tenant farming families in Ulster'.[20] To help illustrate the argument of his text, Mathew drew up a table which he called 'Geographical Origins of Matriculated Students.' Unfortunately, in that geographical table Mathew did not differentiate students from Ulster. His essay – which despite my criticism is a fine piece in other respects – was intended to show the prominence of students from 'West Central Scotland', a region which was granted its own category in the table. Grouped together in another column were students from the rest of Scotland, in a third those from England and Wales and, finally, all students from any part of Ireland. So, for instance, in the decade following Reid's arrival at Glasgow, from 1765 to 1774, Mathew found that 47.7 per cent of matriculated students were from 'West Central Scotland', 21.3 per cent were from the 'rest of Scotland,' 7.8 per cent were from 'England and Wales', and 21.6 per cent were from 'Ireland'. The ratio of Irish students is not quite the third about which Reid complained, but a fifth is a significant proportion.[21] Mathew's essay is interesting for other reasons as well. He concluded, for instance, that 'the sons of merchants, artisans and small farmers' were attracted to the university in large numbers in part because of the 'general, liberal, useful education' they found there.[22] In other words, students were often drawn to Glasgow University for the very sort of teaching Haakonssen argued Reid – and the tradition to which he belonged – aimed to provide.

A more recent example of a historian who has looked to Addison's *Matriculation Albums* is Michael Brown in his book *Francis Hutcheson in Dublin, 1719–30*.[23] In that book Brown included an appendix which purported to summarize, in the form of a table, the origins of Hutcheson's students as recorded in Addison's *Albums*.[24] Brown's categories on first appearance are more differentiated than were Mathew's. Brown listed students under five main categories:

---

18 W.M. Mathew, 'The origins and occupations of Glasgow students, 1740–1839,' *Past & Present*, 33 (April 1966), 74–94.   19 Mathew, 'Glasgow Students,' 76.   20 Ibid.   21 See also I.M. Bishop, 'The education of Ulster students at Glasgow University during the eighteenth century' (MA thesis, the Queen's University of Belfast, 1987), whose findings are reproduced in McFarland, *Ireland and Scotland in the Age of Revolution*, p. 5.   22 Mathew, 'Glasgow students,' 93.   23 See note 7 above. See my review of Brown's book in *The British Journal for Eighteenth-Century Studies*.   24 See Brown's 'Appendix: Matriculation records for the class of Francis Hutcheson,' p. 182.

'Scottish', 'Scot-Hiberno (Scots-Irish)', 'Hiberno (Irish)', 'Anglo (English)' and 'Anglo-Hibernian or (Anglo-Irish)'. Within those categories Brown tabulated that 51.9 per cent of Hutcheson's matriculated students were 'Hiberno', or Irish, but that only 3.8 per cent were 'Scot-Hiberno', or Ulster-Scots. A closer look at Brown's tabulation process, however, reveals that only those few students who were identified in the Glasgow matriculation albums specifically as 'Scoto hibernus' find their way to Brown's column for the Scots-Irish. But almost all of Hutcheson's Ulster-Scot students were registered in the *Albums*, not as 'Scot hibernus', or variations thereon, but simply as being from one of the nine counties of Ulster in Ireland.²⁵ To appreciate the Ulster students among Reid's 'stupid Irish teagues' we ought to look at them more closely than Mathew's study allowed and with a more nuanced approach than that employed by Brown in his analysis of Hutcheson's students. We ought also to consider the eyes through which Reid perceived his students from Ireland.

III

Thomas Reid was born in 1710 in Kincardineshire, Scotland, where his father was a minister of the Kirk. Reid's own college education was at Marischal College in the University of Aberdeen, where his regent was George Turnbull (1698–1749). Having graduated in 1726, Reid studied theology for five years before he accepted, in 1733, a post as librarian of Marischal College. In 1737 he entered the ministry, near Aberdeen. Reid continued to dabble in philosophical problems, however, and in 1752 he was appointed professor of philosophy at King's College in Aberdeen, a post he held until 1764. That is the year in which Reid was appointed professor of moral philosophy at the University of Glasgow, in part with the assistance of Henry Home, Lord Kames. We see then, that before his Glasgow appointment, Reid's background was centred on the northeast of Scotland, and on Aberdeen in particular. There, Reid would have seen few Irish students, a fact that may help explain his being struck by their much larger presence in Glasgow, the largest city in the west of Scotland.²⁶

Glasgow was tempting to Irish students both because it was closer to home

25 Brown is not the only one to have fallen into that trap. See, for instance, Ian McBride, 'William Drennan and the dissenting tradition,' in Dickson et al. (eds), *The United Irishmen*, p. 51, 'An analysis of the matriculation albums of Glasgow reveals that 16 per cent of those who signed the register between 1690 and 1820 identified themselves as *Scotohiberni*.' The actual percentage of Ulster-Scots was much higher, as will be shown below.   26 On Reid's life and writings see, besides relevant sources discussed in the notes above, Knud Haakonssen's entry on Reid in Yolton et al. (eds), *Dictionary of eighteenth-century British philosophers*; Alexander Broadie, 'Reid in context,' in Terence Cuneo and René van Woudenberg (eds), *The Cambridge companion to Thomas Reid* (Cambridge, 2004), pp 31–52. There is no entry on Reid in Kors (ed.), *Encyclopedia of the Enlightenment*, a curiosity that reviewers have noted.

than were the other Scottish universities, and also because it was less expensive.[27] As Reid wrote to Skene, 'thirty' of the university's Irish students had come 'over lately in one ship, besides those that went to Edinburgh. We have a good many English, and some foreigners. Many of the Irish, as well as Scotch, are poor and came up late to save money.'[28] Scholars have long appreciated that large numbers of the boys from Ireland who came to study in Glasgow were Ulster Presbyterians reading for the ministry. As Caroline Robbins put it, 'The liberal Presbyterians [of Ulster] might almost be described as a colony of the city of Glasgow whose university most of them had attended.'[29] In Ireland they were barred from Trinity College Dublin, and the Presbyterian College of Ireland in Belfast was not established until 1810. Many of these students eventually returned home to Ulster, where they had a significant impact on the church and culture of Ireland, as David A. Wilson and others have argued.[30] Consulting the matriculation albums more closely shows that at least forty-five of Reid's matriculated students can be positively identified as boys from Ulster who later made livings in the Presbyterian church, and it is likely that more research will show that others did as well.

While many Ulster boys came to Glasgow with Presbyterian church livings in mind, not all did. At least one of Reid's Ulster students found a living in the Catholic church. Andrew Allen matriculated in 1771, was granted a Glasgow MA in 1773, LLD in 1795, and was later chancellor of the diocese of Clogher, in Ireland, as well as vicar general, official principal, and commissary of the lord bishop of Clogher.[31] But many of Reid's students found miscellaneous livings outside the church. George Nixon was a justice of the peace and then, from 1785, high sheriff of County Fermanagh.[32] Others, such as John Caldwell, went on to receive the degree of MD, in Caldwell's case at Edinburgh University in 1780.[33] In other cases, in the church and without, students' post-Glasgow careers were such that they ranged far and wide throughout the eighteenth-century Atlantic world.[34]

One of Reid's Ulster students with a prominent transatlantic career was

---

27 See McFarland, *Ireland and Scotland in the age of revolution*, p. 5.   28 McCosh, *Scottish philosophy*, p. 203.   29 Robbins, *Eighteenth-century Commonwealthman*, p. 168.   30 See, for instance, David A. Wilson, *United Irishmen, United States: immigrant radicals in the early Republic* (Ithaca and Dublin, 1998), p. 114: 'Closely associated with the New Light, liberal-rationalist wing of Presbyterianism, Glasgow University sent a steady stream of students back into Ulster's Presbyterian church. Known as the "young fry," these Glasgow-educated ministers gradually effected a kind of quiet revolution in the Synod, which became increasingly New Light in character toward the end of the century.'   31 This information comes from Addison, *Matriculation albums*, 95.   32 Georgius Nixon matriculated in 1772.   33 Johannes Caldwell matriculated in 1773.   34 Scholars of Reid's influence would do well do consider the dissemination of his thought through these students alongside the influence of Reid's writings discussed in works such as Benjamin W. Redekop, 'Reid's influence in Britain, Germany, France, and America,' in Cuneo and Woudenberg (eds), *Cambridge companion to Thomas Reid*, pp 313–39.

Thomas Ledlie Birch. Birch, a Presbyterian minister and United Irishman, matriculated from Reid's class in 1770. Birch's interesting American sojourn has been traced elsewhere.[35] But other of Reid's students whose lives spanned the Atlantic, such as James Harper and William Bingham, have been less well remembered.[36] These sorts, too, may have helped to spread the ideals of the Scottish Enlightenment to American shores, even though scholarship on the American Enlightenment has overlooked them. Bingham, for instance, did not even rate an entry in the *Dictionary of National Biography*, although he is mentioned briefly in the entry for his grandson, another William Bingham. Unfortunately, Bingham did not find a home in the new *American National Biography* either, and this time around his grandson was also omitted.[37] Addison recorded that Bingham was born in County Down in 1754 and traced his post-Glasgow career back to County Down and then to North Carolina, where he established and was then headmaster of the Bingham School. One of the few modern biographical notes on Bingham is an entry by Bennett L. Steelman in the *Dictionary of North Carolina Biography*. There, Steelman introduced an interesting puzzle when he wrote that 'Robert Bingham states that his grandfather left Ireland to avoid arrest because of his membership in the United Irishmen ... Bingham arrived in Wilmington early in 1789. Standard sources, however, date the United Irishmen's founding as 1791, so it appears that Bingham must have emigrated at a later date, or for other reasons.'[38] Addison dated Bingham's emigration to 1793, a fact which, if it is true, may support the case for Bingham's connections with the United Irishmen. But whether or not Bingham was connected to the radical United Irishmen, his American school was an important one.

First located in Wilmington, it later moved to Pittsboro, and then to Hillsboro, and finally to Mount Repose, which is where Bingham lived until his death in 1826. Bingham's high reputation as a schoolmaster can be traced in various nineteenth and early twentieth-century sources, such as county histories. His contemporary fame as a teacher was based, in a large measure, on the general, liberal, useful education he provided for his students.[39] In June 1795, Bingham's

35 See, for example, Wilson, *United Irishmen, United States*, esp. pp 114–32, and Peter Gilmore, '"Minister of the Devil": Thomas Ledlie Birch, Presbyterian rebel in exile' in this volume. 36 Jacobus Harper matriculated in 1766; Gulielmus Bingham in 1774. 37 See Allen Johnson and Dumas Malone (eds), *Dictionary of national biography* (1928–36, revised edition, New York, 1958) and John A. Garraty and Mark C. Carnes (eds), *American national biography* (New York and Oxford, 1999). 38 See Bennett L. Steelman, 'Bingham, William,' in William S. Powell (ed.), *Dictionary of North Carolina biography* (Chapel Hill, 1979), i, 159–60. 39 See, for instance, William Henry Foote, *Sketches of North Carolina, historical and biographical, illustrative of the principles of a portion of her early settlers* (New York, 1846), p. 179, where Bingham is described as a teacher who 'attained great excellence and éclat,' and p. 517, where Bingham's school is described as 'flourishing.' See also Charles Lee Smith, *The history of education in North Carolina* (Washington, 1888), p. 131: 'The Bingham School stands pre-eminent among Southern

school was discussed in the *North Carolina Journal* as 'one of the four schools preparing students for admission to the upper classes at the University of North Carolina.' From 1801 to 1805 Bingham himself was professor of ancient languages in the University of North Carolina, resigning, says Steelman, because of tensions caused by the 'trustees' dissatisfaction with Bingham's extreme Jeffersonian political opinions'.[40] No doubt further study of Bingham's life would be rewarding, but enough is known to assert that he was one 'stupid Irish teague' whom Reid clearly underestimated. The same is true of James Harper.

Harper, another boy from County Down, was a Seceder whose ministry was at Knockloughrim. Harper was noted for his 'sympathy with the United Irishmen and with the Rebellion of 1798', for which he was 'arrested, court-martialled but not proved guilty.' Before emigrating to America, Harper was involved in a broil with the Revd Adam Boyle of Boveedy, whom Harper accused of 'perjury and persecution'. Boyle was acquitted of perjury by the Synod, but was found guilty of 'unfriendly and unfeeling behaviour toward Mr Harper'. Harper's few remaining years proved unsettled ones. He 'acted as stated supply of Abingdon, Beaver Creek, Silver Springs and Forks of Holestone, Va., from 1799 until he died on 5 Sept. 1802'.[41] It is not known in what ways, if at all, Reid's teachings impacted the lives of Harper or Bingham, but their Ulster classmates, even the duller ones, ought to figure in the history of the Enlightenment too.

IV

The complete class lists for Reid's classes are not known to exist, but Addison's *Matriculation Albums* give us a telling image of that body. Adding up the names on these lists, one finds that Reid had altogether 217 matriculated students. The place of origin for all of Reid's matriculated students was noted in the matriculation albums. For students from the British Isles, almost all matriculates were identified by the counties in which their fathers lived. A few students came from England; more were from Scotland, although not as many as a reader of Mathew might expect to be the case. The number of Reid's Irish students is striking. So is their geographic origin within Ireland. A handful of Reid's matriculated

schools for boys, and ranks with the best in the Union. It is the oldest, the largest, and the most successful male boarding school for secondary instruction in the South;' and Charles L. Coon, *North Carolina schools and academies, 1790–1840: a documentary history* (Raleigh, NC, 1915), where Bingham's school is described as 'one of the leading schools in the State.'   **40** See also Kemp P. Battle, *History of the University of North Carolina. Volume 1: From its beginning to the death of President Swain, 1789–1868* (Raleigh, 1907), pp 167–8.   **41** I am grateful to David A. Wilson for pointing me to the discussion of Harper in *A history of Congregations in the Presbyterian Church in Ireland, 1610–1982* (Belfast, 1982), on which this paragraph is based.

Table 1: Matriculation records for Professor Thomas Reid, 1764–79

Year	Total matriculates	Ulster matriculates	Ulster matriculates as per cent
1764	18	12	66.7
1765	11	7	63.6
1766	18	15	83.3
1767	9	6	66.7
1768	13	11	84.6
1769	12	10	83.3
1770	18	14	77.8
1771	25	21	84.0
1772	16	14	87.5
1773	17	12	70.6
1774	14	12	85.7
1775	9	7	77.8
1776	8	5	62.5
1777	15	11	73.3
1778	5	3	60.0
1779	9	8	88.9
Totals	**217**	**168**	**77.4**

students were from Counties Louth, Dublin, Limerick and Tipperary. But of Reid's total 217 matriculated students, 168, or 77 per cent, came from Ulster.

As table 1 illustrates, the high percentage of Reid's Ulster students is not the result of a one-off year, or two, of unusual plenty. Across Reid's entire sixteen-year teaching career as professor of moral philosophy at Glasgow, from 1764 to 1779, in each year boys from Ulster made up the bulk of his matriculated students. Ulster boys were never less than 62.5 per cent of the matriculates and sometimes they were as high as 88.9 per cent. The average percentage on a year-by-year basis was 76 per cent and the weighted average was 77.4 per cent. The fact that so many Ulster boys were sitting in Reid's audience may help to explain why he appears to have over-estimated the overall percentage of Irish students at the university.

Identifying the counties whence Reid's Ulster students originated is also revealing of the breadth of Ulster's representation. Surprisingly, for instance, Belfast was not the primary source of students, although County Antrim did account for 15 per cent of Reid's Ulster matriculates. All nine counties of Ulster sent boys to Glasgow where they studied with Reid. There were also regional variations. Least represented were Counties Fermanagh (2 per cent), Cavan (3 per cent) and Monaghan (6 per cent). More significant in their representation

Table 2: Ulster students in the matriculation records: Moral Philosophy
course at Glasgow University, 1730–1796

Professor of Moral Philosophy	Tenure	Total matriculates	Ulster matriculates	Ulster matriculates as per cent
Francis Hutcheson (1694–1746)	1730–45	133	69	51.9
Thomas Craigie	1746–51	46	27	58.7
Adam Smith (1723–90)	1752–63	111	83	74.8
Thomas Reid (1710–96)	1764–79	217	168	77.4
Archibald Arthur (1744–97)	1780–95	62	41	66.1

were counties with higher numbers of Presbyterians: Armagh (8 per cent), Donegal (11 per cent), Londonderry (13 per cent), Antrim (15 per cent), and Tyrone (17 per cent). Most represented of all was County Down; along with Bingham and Harper 24 per cent of Reid's Ulster boys claimed County Down as their home.

While much scholarly attention has focused on the individual professors who held the chair of moral philosophy at Glasgow, the data in Addison's *Matriculation Albums* recommend that historians should not assume it was the particular brilliance of Reid, Hutcheson or any other professorial star whose light Ulster students sought.[42] Tabulating the number and percentage of Ulster students in the moral philosophy classes from 1730 through 1796, from Francis Hutcheson to Archibald Arthur, helps make that point.

These figures suggest that it may not have been particular professors that attracted Ulster boys so much as the moral philosophy course itself. In other words, even mediocre professors of moral philosophy, such as the forgettable Thomas Craigie, attracted a significant number of boys from Ulster. Having picked up sufficient language training in Latin and Greek, as well as logic, at academies in Ireland, their point of entry at Glasgow tended to be moral philosophy. As the table above shows, Ulster students were a significant majority

---

42 That point is supported by an advertisement in the Belfast *Northern Star* for 21–25 September 1793. On page 3 there is an advertisement for the 'ensuing Session' at the 'UNIVERSITY OF GLASGOW.' A noteworthy aspect of the advertisement is that no particular professors' names are mentioned, only the courses that are offered, including the course on 'Moral Philosophy.' Advertisements for other schools, such as the 'SCHOOL OF PHYSIC IN IRELAND' gave more attention to highlighting individual lecturers (see, for instance, 19–23 October 1793).

of all matriculates from 1730 to 1795. As a percentage of all matriculates their presence increased steadily from the 1730s through the 1780s. For the entire sixty-six year period, Ulster students account for 388 of 569, or 68.2 per cent, of those who matriculated in moral philosophy at the University of Glasgow. Surely such a considerable and enduring supply of students from Ulster would have had a role in shaping the course they came to Scotland to consume. At very least their presence would have encouraged the general and useful education for which the University of Glasgow, by Reid's time, was renowned.[43] This short essay has opened more questions about Ulster's contributions to the Enlightenment than it has answered. But enough is known about Glasgow's Ulster Presbyterian students to see that there was some irony in Reid's dismissing them as 'stupid Irish teagues.'

---

43 As Donald J. Withrington, 'Education and society in the eighteenth century,' in N.T. Phillipson and Rosalind Mitchison (eds), *Scotland in the age of improvement* (Edinburgh, 1970), p. 191, has shown, Scottish universities in the eighteenth century were 'nicely sensitive to the educational demands which a changing society was making on them'.

'Minister of the devil': Thomas Ledlie Birch, Presbyterian rebel in exile

PETER GILMORE

Newly exiled in the United States following the 1798 rebellion, the Revd Thomas Ledlie Birch penned a rambling 'letter' to explain the recent 'commotions in Ireland' to Americans.[1] *A Letter from an Irish Emigrant*, published as a pamphlet in Philadelphia the following year, offered a spirited defence of the rebellion, described Birch's own trials and tribulations as 'a marked object'[2] and – adding to a considerable Presbyterian pamphleteering tradition[3] – excoriated the established church. The Church of Ireland, the exiled minister wrote, enjoyed such power over dissenters as to have them legally declared 'out of the pale of the church, and given over to the devil'. Fortunately, Birch concluded, biblical prophecies of Christ's rule on earth would soon be fulfilled, putting an end to 'the tyrants and oppressors' who ruled through the means of religious establishment and sectarian animosities.[4]

Within only a few years of his exile, however, Birch would have difficulty finding the pervasive 'spirit of brotherly love, and general good will to one another' which he associated with the fulfillment of prophecy and with American republican institutions.[5] Instead, he would find himself temporarily forced out of the Presbyterian church[6] and 'given over to the devil.' The émigré rebel was branded 'a minister of Satan' by John McMillan, the politically prominent patriarch of Presbyterianism in Pennsylvania's post-frontier west. In Ireland, Birch had been a political radical and theological conservative; in southwestern Pennsylvania, he became a 'marked object' in the eyes of a Presbyterian clergy who were politically conservative and theologically radical, and whose promotion of religious revivalism contradicted his core beliefs.

---

1 Thomas Ledlie Birch, *A letter from an Irish emigrant to his friend in the United States* (Philadelphia, 1799). 2 Birch, p. 22. 3 For a discussion of this literature, see, for example, Ian R. McBride, *Scripture politics: Ulster Presbyterians and Irish radicalism in the late eighteenth century* (Oxford, 1998), pp 91–6. 4 Birch, pp 53–4. 5 Ibid., p. 54. 6 Birch finally gained admission to the American church as a minister in 1810. The following year he joined the Presbytery of Baltimore. David A. Wilson writes, 'In a highly unusual and controversial move, the Baltimore Presbytery allowed Birch to stay in western Pennsylvania, so that he could preach to his flock in Washington without interference from his old enemies in the district': *United Irishmen, United States: immigrant radicals in the early Republic* (Ithaca, 1998), p. 129.

The tensions in Birch's position propelled him to seek an unlikely alliance with recent Irish immigrants who belonged to the Associate Synod of Ireland, a dissenting movement within Ulster Presbyterianism, and who were known as Seceders. In Ireland, Birch had been one of the Seceders' strongest opponents. His *Letter from an Irish Emigrant* criticized the Seceder clergy for a political conservatism that seemingly repudiated the historic covenanting opposition to 'exclusive prelatic establishments'.[7] A few years earlier, he had subjected Ulster Seceders to a withering condemnation in another pamphlet, *Physicians Languishing under Disease*,[8] in which he accused them of poaching his congregation. Birch's political and religious conflict with earlier Presbyterian settlers in America, and his cooperation with recently arrived Seceders whose politics and practices he had attacked in Ireland, reveal a great deal about the stresses and strains within the transmission of Ulster Presbyterianism to the United States. The transformation of a prominent Ulster minister into a backwoods American 'preacher of Satan' is a moment in the process through which the Ulster Scots became the 'Scotch-Irish'.

Birch was born in County Down in 1754,[9] educated at Glasgow University in the early 1770s and ordained as minister of Saintfield, County Down, in 1776. His was among the largest Presbyterian congregations in Ireland.[10] As an orthodox, 'old side' Presbyterian, Birch appears to have had no direct experience with the kind of revivalism that he would encounter in the western Pennsylvania backcountry. He may have known of the Cambuslang revival in lowland Scotland in 1742; it is much less likely that he would have been aware of the religious enthusiasm that occurred in the Sixmilewater valley, County Antrim, in 1625.[11] However, to his great annoyance, Birch was well acquainted with the behaviour of the Seceders, whose sacramental occasions bore a superficial similarity to American revivals.

The Associate Synod of Ireland represented a naturalization of the 1733

7 Birch, pp 29–30. 8 Birch, 'Physicians languishing under disease,' in Brendan Clifford (ed.), *The causes of the rebellion in Ireland (1798) and other writings by Rev. Thomas Ledlie Birch, United Irishman* (Belfast, 1991). 9 A testimonial from the minister, stated clerk and elders of the Tullylish congregation asserted that Birch was born and educated in that parish. Thomas Ledlie Birch, *Seemingly experimental religion* (Washington, PA, 1806), p. 142. Tullylish is in the barony of Lower Iveagh in County Down and encompasses Gilford and nearby land owned by the Birch family beginning in 1692. Aiken McClelland, 'Thomas Ledlie Birch, United Irishman,' *Proceedings and Reports of the Belfast Natural History and Philosophy Society*, 2nd Series, 7 (1965), 24–5. 10 McClelland, 'Thomas Ledlie Birch, United Irishman,' 24–5, 26. 11 Birch, *Seemingly experimental religion*, p. 142; McClelland, 24–5; David W. Miller, 'Illiteracy, apparitions, stigmata: the 1859 crisis in Irish Presbyterianism' (a paper delivered at the Keough Center for Irish Studies, Notre Dame University, 1 February 2002), p. 7. Miller argues that the 1625 Sixmilewater commotions had been forgotten until mentioned in James Seaton Reid's *History of the Presbyterian Church in Ireland*, published in 1834. However, those events are cited in a pamphlet published in Washington, PA in 1805 by 'A Presbyterian' which refuted criticism made by five Seceder ministers of contemporary revivals in the United States.

Secession from the Church of Scotland. The principal issue that spurred dissension within Scotland's General Assembly, the lay patronage of ministers, had little relevance in Ireland given the relative paucity of Presbyterian landlords. But the evangelical Seceders, with their adherence to a hyper-confessionalist[12] strain of Presbyterianism, found a ready audience in the areas of heaviest Scots settlement in Ulster. The Associate Synod offered Ulster Scots tenant farmers and weavers a familiar alternative to the more urbane 'New Light' theology which gained in influence in the middle decades of the eighteenth century. The Seceders had particular success in those areas that appeared to be underserved by the mainstream General Synod of Ulster and in territories of later Scots settlement.[13] The Seceders became, as David Miller has remarked, Ulster Presbyterianism's 'growth sector' in the century's second half.[14]

In keeping with their traditionalist Presbyterianism, the Seceders embraced large, open-air sacramental festivals that invited comparison to the American revivals of the early nineteenth century in their crowds, excitement and carnival atmosphere. But American revivals, which arose out of similar outdoor celebrations of the Lord's Supper among Presbyterians, were explicitly encouraged by clergy imbued with a differing conception of evangelicalism. Ulster Seceders, writes Peter Brooke, 'did not trust an enthusiastic preaching that seemed to offer grace as an emotional moment experienced under the influence of powerful preaching'. Their theology of grace, he adds, 'was a matter of doctrine, not a matter of highly charged emotional experience'.[15] Sacramental festivals among Ulster Seceders may have attracted the sacrilegious as well as the saintly, but not with quite the same goal (or identical conclusion) as those of similarly rambunctious events in the United States.

In his thunderous broadside against the Seceders, Birch denounced the

---

12 The term, for which I am indebted to David W. Miller (private correspondence), suggests extreme loyalty to what are perceived as the fundamental tenets of a denomination. William Lyons Fisk regards the Seceders as representing the 'Scottish High Church Tradition,' while the Associate and Reformed Presbyterian (Covenanter) churches may also be identified as the 'Scottish Dissenting' tradition within Presbyterianism. See Fisk, *The Scottish high church tradition in America: an essay in Scotch-Irish ethnoreligious history* (Lanham, MD , 1995); Reid W. Stewart and Basil G. McBee, *A history of the Associate Presbyterian Church in North America* (Apollo, PA, 1983). 13 Myrtle Hill, 'The religious context: Protestantism in County Down in 1798' in Myrtle Hill, Brian Turner and Kenneth Dawson (eds), *1798 Rebellion in County Down* (Newtownards, 1998), p. 63. 14 Miller, 'Illiteracy, apparitions, stigmata,' p. 9. Miller elsewhere observes that 'Three Presbyterian sects, the Reformed Presbyterians and the Antiburgher and Burghter Seceders ... in the latter half of the eighteenth century seem to have erected about 90 congregations in Ulster.' 'Radicalism and ritual in East Ulster' (a paper presented at a bicentennial conference on the 1798 Rebellion, Dublin and Belfast, May 1998), p. 9. John M. Barkley has demonstrated that the Burgher wing of the Secession enjoyed rapid growth in Ulster in the second half of the eighteenth century. See Barkley, *A short history of the Presbyterian Church in Ireland* (Belfast, 1959 [?]), pp 69–70. For an explanation of the Burghers, see note 33. 15 Peter Brooke, *Ulster Presbyterianism: the historical perspective, 1610–1970* (Dublin, 1987), pp 100, 103.

excesses of the way in which they observed communion and enumerated the vices of their *'noisy, drunken idolatrous feast'* – tippling, courting, dancing, quarrelling and fornication. 'Your *sacrament is a place* where no person, who wishes well to the increase of Presbyterians in this kingdom, respects character, or even common decency should ever shew his face!' Birch declared. Here, he said, was a scene deserving of a satire by Robert Burns, whose poem, 'The Holy Fair,' lampooned the excesses of contemporary sacramental festivals in Scotland.[16] Birch accused the Seceders of seeking 'large collections' at these events, and even argued that this was their primary aim.[17] But the main point of his pamphlet *Physicians Languishing under Disease*, published in 1796, was not to excoriate the Seceders for apparent abuse of ritual. Rather, it was, in the first instance, a highly personal counterattack, as the Seceders had set themselves up in direct competition with Birch in Saintfield. Further, Birch seized this opportunity to publicly rebuke the Associate Synod for its reactionary politics.

Addressing himself to 'the most worthy Seceding members (both clergy and laity),' Birch largely avoided criticism of the Associate Synod on theological grounds. Birch did not fault the Seceders' professed orthodoxy – particularly their adherence to the National Covenant of 1638, the Solemn League and Covenant of 1643 and the Westminster Confession of Faith – but clearly regarded their presence in Ulster as both unhelpful and unneeded. His strategy was to oppose the recent reckless behaviour of Seceder ministers in County Down with the covenanting principles of the *'old Presbyterians'*. He argued that their conduct revealed the offending Seceders as *'arch-apostates*, even from the *original practices of Seceders'*.[18] Birch acknowledged the legitimacy of the Secession from the Church of Scotland but questioned the relevancy of the movement in Ireland, where 'all Presbyterian congregations have the free choice of their clergyman.' This allowed him to attribute the erection of a separate denomination to 'pride' and 'fortune-hunting'.[19] Here he unfavourably contrasted the Seceders' practices with those of the small Reformed Presbyterian body in Ulster, 'who do not debase themselves for the sake of a little sordid gain, by making their congregations become the receptacles of the out-casts of every society'. Birch accused the Seceders, to their shame, of encouraging the malcontents who refused to pay ministers' salaries and submit to church discipline.[20] Implicitly Birch defended the quasi-established status of General Synod and proclaimed the orthodoxy of both the Presbytery of Belfast and the Saintfield congregation (and its minister).

16 Birch, *Physicians*, pp 55, 53, 54–5. Emphasis in original. (All references to *Physicians* are from the Clifford edition.) For another contemporary description of 'Lyle Fair' in County Antrim, see David Stewart, *The Seceders in Ireland* (Belfast, 1950), p. 254. 'The Holy Fair' appeared in Burns' first collection of poetry, published in 1786. 17 Birch, *Physicians*, pp 53–4, 48. 18 Ibid., pp 39, 45, 44. Emphasis in original. 19 Ibid., p. 46. 20 Ibid., pp 48, 49. Ironically, charges laid by Birch against Seceder ministers are reminiscent of those brought against him by American clergy less than a decade later: that they flouted the constituted authority of the church, fomented division and accepted other congregations' outcasts. (Birch, pp 44, 45, 48.)

The attention Birch gives to the Scottish covenants reveals both his points of agreement with the Associate Synod and most fundamental disagreement of principle. As observed above, he had no quarrel with the Secession's fealty to the covenants and Westminster Confession; he noted favourably that 'The original Seceders in Scotland, held frequent renewals of their covenant.'[21] However, Birch objected to the Seceders' abandonment of the political obligations of the Solemn League and Covenant; for Birch, like the Covenanters, Christ's authority extended over state as well as church.[22] Birch implicitly accepted (as proposed by a twentieth-century historian) that '[b]y standing firm for Presbyterian ideals, one became an instrument of divine purposes and potentially of dramatic providential intervention in the external world'.[23] This was the source of his political radicalism, which was inextricably bound up with his theologically conservative (if not old-fashioned) Presbyterianism; it is because of this interconnected set of beliefs that he so readily conflated religious and political reform. Birch preached a revolutionary doctrine, 'setting forth from Scripture prophecy the extension of the Redeemer's kingdom over the whole earth'.[24] His reading of scripture and theological interpretation of contemporary events led him to a millenarianism in which reformation of church and state were one project, linked to the 'final overthrow of *the Beast*'.[25] Birch believed the End Times had begun; he identified the Antichrist as the church establishment and found Babylon in London, the centre of the British Empire.[26] Birch called upon Christians to be soldiers in the apocalyptic struggle to pull down 'that mongrel authority of *church and state*' – and found the Seceders wanting. 'You are,' he told them, 'amongst the principal *opponents* in this kingdom, in the way of a *general reformation*.'[27]

Saintfield's minister strongly rejected the Seceders' interpretation of their covenant obligations with respect to opposition to Catholicism and episcopacy. Birch interpreted the requirement of the Solemn League and Covenant 'to extirpate Popery and Prelacy' as signifying 'every rational, gospel attempt' to ensure the spread of Presbyterianism and to prevent popery or prelacy from 'acquiring an *ascendancy, or dominion, over the Presbyterian church;* as being an usurpation of *Christ's headship over his church*'. This did not mean, he insisted, engaging in unchristian behaviour to those of other faiths or rooting out popery and prelacy by fire and sword. The Seceders' anti-Catholicism fell into

21 Ibid., *Physicians*, p. 49.   22 Ibid., p. 52. Ian McBride has observed that by the 1790s, the Seceders no longer saw the state 'as a vehicle for reformation' (105). Birch, p. 52.   23 David W. Miller, *Queen's rebels: Ulster loyalism in historical perspective* (Dublin, 1978), p. 83.   24 Birch, *A letter from an Irish emigrant*, p. 22, note. Here Birch described how his preaching and prayers had been characterized by his opponents.   25 Thomas Ledlie Birch, 'The obligations upon Christians' in Clifford (ed.), p. 36. Emphasis in original.   26 Birch, *Seemingly experimental religion*, pp 15, 17. (All subsequent references to *Obligations* are from this edition.) This characterization represents a departure from the historic Protestant identification of the pope and Roman Catholicism as the Antichrist.   27 Ibid., p. 15; *Physicians*, p. 59. Emphasis in original.

categories of '*superstition, falsehood,* and *mental tyranny*', conditions contrary to divine requirement of true reformation. Birch suggested that 'the original Seceders (though, perhaps, mistaken in some things) appear to have been men of real piety, who wished to help forward a *reformation.*' But contemporary Seceders in Ireland, he declared, 'oppose all *reformation* for worldly purposes!'[28]

Those organizing the Seceder congregation had labelled him '*a friend to Roman Catholics*', Birch said, presumably on the basis of his public advocacy of civil rights for the island's majority. He acknowledged that friendship in *Physicians Languishing under Disease* and decried the Seceders' perceived complicity in 'the revival of the old game, of fighting the Presbyterians of the North against the Roman Catholics of the South.'[29] According to a historian of the Seceders in Ireland, the Saintfield congregation reportedly harboured 'considerable dissatisfaction' with Birch because of his 'political sympathies'; if the Seceders were not encouraged by the local power elite to disrupt Birch's congregation, anti-Catholicism proved to be sufficient to the task.[30]

Birch reminded his foes that in the 1780s, when the Irish Parliament received petitions for reform from twenty-eight of Ireland's thirty-two counties, Seceding ministers signed a counter-petition originating in County Down. This show of political conservatism secured for the Associate Synod a share in the *regium donum*, the state support granted Presbyterian clergy, despite their status as 'dissenters' from the established church. The Seceders had thus accepted the '*wages of prostitution*'.[31]

The Seceding ministry's share in the royal bounty had been proposed by Lord Downshire, a determined advocate of the status quo who saw the Secession as a conservative counterweight to an Ulster Presbyterianism perceived as inclined to radicalism.[32] Nicholas Price, a local landowner whom Birch regarded as his chief antagonist, permitted the Seceders to raise their meeting house on his estate.[33]

For all of the force of this public outcry, Birch nonetheless dismissed as only

---

28 Birch, *Physicians*, pp 50–1, 50, 59–60, 49. Emphasis in the original.   29 Ibid., pp 57, 58. For Birch's position on Catholic emancipation, see 'Letters from Saintfield' in Clifford, pp 22–3. 30 Stewart, *The Seceders in Ireland*, p. 343.   31 Birch, p. 51. (Emphasis in the original.) Birch signalled his distaste for the proceedings by renouncing his share of the royal bounty and declaring his opposition to state support of religion in general – a stance likely made easier by the size of his congregation.   32 Hill, p. 63.   33 The Burgher meeting house was built on the estate of Nicholas Price. A.T.Q. Stewart writes that Squire Price 'was making a reputation as the scourge of all suspected rebels in this part of Down, and he was now [following publication of *Physicians languishing under disease*] determined to rid Saintfield of its radical pastor.' *The summer soldiers: the 1798 Rebellion in Antrim and Down* (Belfast, 1997) p. 181. Rodgers Dickie, 'Presbyterianism in Saintfield – a brief note,' in *Saintfield Heritage Number Five*, 28–9; Birch, *Letter*, pp 36–7. A dispute within the Scottish Secession over the burgher's oath led to the new denomination's division in 1747 into Burghers and Anti-Burghers. This Scottish controversy divided Ulster Seceders as well, with the Burghers enjoying greater success in Ireland. The Saintfield congregation organized in opposition to Birch came under the Burgher Presbytery of Down. See David Stewart, pp 65, 126–7, 343–4.

'a few *restless spirits*' those former members of his congregation who encouraged the Seceders in organizing a Saintfield congregation. He contended that his congregation of around 900 families had experienced only minimal losses.[34]

By the time of the Seceders' intervention, Birch had both visibility and stature in the General Synod of Ulster and a well-attested interest in political reform.[35] He claimed to have opposed the 'American war' from the beginning; in 1784 he evinced his admiration for the American Revolution, forwarding an address to George Washington to the *Belfast Mercury* for publication.[36] His political career advanced with his election as chaplain of the Saintfield Light Infantry, a contingent of the Volunteers.[37] Like other Irish radicals, Birch hoped that his country would emulate the examples of the American and French Revolutions. He organized the Saintfield branch of the Society of United Irishmen in January 1792, proselytizing and recruiting among his congregants.[38] Writing to the radical Belfast newspaper *Northern Star* in 1792 from his manse, Liberty Hill, Birch described with satisfaction his congregants' celebration of 'the happy progress of French liberty.'[39]

A sermon Birch preached to the General Synod at its June 1793 meeting in Lurgan, County Armagh, demonstrated how his politics and theology came together in millenarianism.[40] In his address, published as a pamphlet the following year in Belfast, Birch asserted the 'obligations upon Christians' to extend brotherly love toward the nation as a whole and affirmed the ministerial role, through biblical precedent, for restraining 'the corrupt practices of Governors'.[41] Particularly in Ireland, given the intervention of the state into religious matters, ministers were called to witness, according to Birch; in giving unto Caesar, the clergy must 'take care to render to God the things that are God's, by bearing a public testimony against all Rulers who shall presume to infringe upon his sovereign authority'.[42]

Like Birch, a number of Presbyterian ministers of various tendencies saw in contemporary events the realization of biblical prophecy.[43] Their sermons

34 Birch pp 41, 42–3. Emphasis in the original. 35 Birch was nominated, although never elected, as moderator of the General Synod on several occasions and frequently served on the Synod's executive and financial committees. McClelland, 26; *Records of the General Synod of Ulster from 1691 to 1820*, iii, 1778–1820 (Belfast, 1898), pp 171, 177, 179–80, 186, 189, 196, 198. 36 Birch, *Letter from an Irish emigrant*, p. 22; McClelland, 27. 37 McClelland, 27. 38 McClelland, 28; A.T.Q. Stewart, *The summer soldiers*, p. 181; 'Extract of a letter from Saintfield, 25th, Jun 1795,' *Northern Star*, 29 June 1795, in Clifford, pp 25–6; McClelland, 29; Stewart, p. 181. 39 'Extract of a letter from Saintfield' in Clifford, pp 23–4. 40 Birch, *Obligations*, p. 28. Birch had polled second in the balloting for moderator of the General Synod that year. Pieter Tesch, 'Presbyterian radicalism,' in David Dickson, Dáire Keogh and Kevin Whelan (eds), *The United Irishmen: republicanism, radicalism and rebellion* (Dublin, 1993), p. 47. 41 Birch, *Obligations*, pp 30, 31. 42 Ibid., pp 32, 33. 43 Ian R. McBride, '"When Ulster joined Ireland": Anti-popery, Presbyterian radicalism and Irish republicanism in the 1790s,' *Past & Present* (November 1997) (Online version at www.findarticles.p/articles/mi_m2279/is_

display a blending of Enlightenment, and even Paineite, political ideology with traditional Calvinism. Birch took the very fact that his was 'a very advanced and enlightened period of the world' as an indication that the awaited reformation was at hand; as he told the General Synod, 'We must think that the final overthrow of the Beast, or opposing power, is almost at the door.'[44] Peter Brooke has observed how Birch's interpretation of prophecy was similar to that of Covenanter ministers who identified the most closely with Paine's radicalism while at the same time embracing both rigid adherence to the seventeenth-century covenants and dissemination of popular prophecies.[45] Presbyterian millenarians, Birch among them, located the Antichrist and his works in the confessional state. They saw in the French Revolution evidence of prophecy realized, as both Catholic officialdom and state tyranny had come under assault.[46] Birch, as an admirer of the French Revolution, saw the conflict between Britain and France as 'the seemingly literal accomplishment of the prophecy of the Battle of Armageddon'.[47]

With his sense of the revolution's millennial significance, Birch persisted in his admiration for the French despite the outbreak of war in 1793.[48] The scope for dissidence became increasingly constricted, however, and the difficulties confronting Birch became dramatically worse than poaching by the Seceders. In 1797, clandestine organizing by the United Irishmen and a state of martial law together created 'a state of real, though smothered, rebellion' in Ulster.[49] That year, Birch was jailed at the instigation of Nicholas Price, initially facing a charge of high treason; the jury of the Down assizes found the minister not guilty.[50] In April 1798, Birch again came before the Down assizes on charges that included attempted bribery to prevent prosecution of United Irishmen. The charges were dismissed 'for want of prosecution'. Conveniently for the defence, the principal witness had been shot dead on the road to Belfast the previous week.[51]

Two months later, rebellion erupted in two short blazes in Counties Antrim and Down. The minister's exact role in the 1798 rebellion cannot be pinpointed with precision. As the elected chaplain to the United Irish army in County Down, Birch may or may not have taken the field with his men on 9 June, preached to the rebel encampment on Creevy Rocks the following day ('Pike Sunday') or have been with the United Irish army until its 13 June defeat at

n157/ai_2022), 10. **44** Birch, *Obligations*, pp 34, 36. **45** Peter Brooke, 'Controversies in Ulster Presbyterianism, 1790–1836,' PhD thesis (Cambridge, 1980) (Online version at http://web.ukonline.co.uk/pbrooke/p&t/Northern per cent20Ireland/controversies), pp 14–16; McBride, 10–11. **46** McBride, 10; Brooke, p. 18. **47** Birch, *Obligations*, p. 36. **48** At a meeting of the General Synod's Fixed Committee on 27 February 1795, Birch protested a statement expressing support for the appointment of Ireland's new lord lieutenant because of its failure to express '*a Desire for Peace.*' (Emphasis in the original.) *Records of the General Synod of Ulster*, p. 172. **49** W.E.H. Lecky, quoted in A.T.Q. Stewart, p. 35. **50** *Belfast News-Letter*, 17 November 1797. **51** *Belfast News-Letter*, 16 April 1798; McClelland, 30; Wilson, *United Irishmen, United States*, p. 118.

Ballynahinch[52] A troop of light dragoons arrested the minister at Liberty Hill at three o'clock on the morning of 16 June and took him to Lisburn for court-martial.[53] Birch was charged with rebellion and treason, by 'being present at and encouraging the Rebels at Creevy-Rocks', at Saintfield, Ballynahinch and elsewhere during the five days of the rising.[54] Witnesses gave contradictory evidence.[55] Birch, for his part, claimed to have saved the lives and tended to the needs of wounded British troops and to have buried their dead.[56]

In his closing address to the military tribunal, Birch declared, according to a newspaper report, 'He might have done wrong, but it was in error ... He loved his King, he loved his Country, and should ever pray for their prosperity.'[57] If permitted, Birch said, he would gladly remove himself to a country not at war with Great Britain – America, for example.[58] The record is silent as to just what the military tribunal made of this speech, but its decision was clear: 'Evidence is not sufficiently strong to affect the Prisoners Life & therefore acquit him of the Crimes laid to his Charge.'[59] Birch was not found guilty, but he was not regarded as altogether innocent either. In July 1798 he was lodged in a prison ship to await exile; with him were four other Presbyterian ministers and two licentiates who were also implicated in the rebellion.[60]

Less than a month later, Birch stood on the deck of an altogether different ship, the *Harmony* of New Bedford, Massachusetts. He was accompanied by his wife, Isabella, and five children who ranged in age from nine to seventeen. They arrived in New York in September 1798 to a new life in a new world of unanticipated but perhaps not unpredictable controversies.[61]

The exiled minister and his family remained in New York through the end of the year, long enough for Birch to pen his personal account of the rebellion, the 58-page pamphlet *Letter from an Irish Emigrant*. Birch preached from Presbyterian pulpits in New York, where he began to solicit recommendations in hopes of gaining admittance to the American ministry.[62] Birch then moved to

52 McClelland, 30; A.T.Q. Stewart, p. 205; McClelland, 31. 53 McClelland, 31; Birch, *Letter*, p. 22. 54 *Belfast News-Letter*, 22 June 1798. 55 *Proceedings of a garrison court martial held by order of L. Col. Wollaston* ... in Clifford, pp 68–9, 72, 74–6. 56 Birch, *Letter*, p. 22; *Proceedings*, p. 78. 57 *Belfast News-Letter*, 26 June 1798, p. 2; see also, *Proceedings*, p. 78. Birch tempered this profession of loyalty somewhat in *Letter from an Irish emigrant*: 'For he [that is, Birch] prayed that the King's throne might be established in right counsels, in the hearts and affections of his people; that authority might be a terror to evil doers, a praise to them that do well.' He claimed that he went on to say that what he should have done was to pray 'that the King and those in power should ever be victorious over all their enemies.' A member of the court supposedly upbraided Birch, objecting that this, too, would be considered seditious (p. 22). 58 *Belfast News-Letter*, 26 June 1798. McClelland says that Birch owed his life to a loyalist brother with political connections who advised him that the court would acquit if the minister agreed to exile (pp 31–2). 59 *Proceedings*, p. 79. 60 Birch, *Letter*, p. 32; McClelland, 32. 61 Birch, *Letter*, p. 1; P. William Filby with Mary K. Meyer (eds), *Passenger and immigration lists index, 1982–85, Cumulated Supplements*, i, A–E (Detroit, MI c.1985), p. 253; McClelland, 33. 62 Birch was the guest of the Revd Samuel Miller, who, like the émigré, supported the French Revolution, opposed

Philadelphia, headquarters of American Presbyterianism and gateway for Ulster immigrants,[63] where he met with approval from the committee of the Presbytery of Philadelphia responsible for examining the credentials of travelling and foreign ministers. Birch preached for several months in 1799 at the Third Presbyterian in Philadelphia and in East Nottingham, Maryland, garnering another clutch of recommendations.[64]

Despite what (by his own account) appeared to be a promising future on the East Coast, Birch responded favourably to a proposal from Washington County, Pennsylvania.[65] Travelling in the backcountry in early 1800, Birch visited the town of Washington, where he received an invitation from its elders to enter the vacant pulpit. In Washington, he later observed, 'there was a number of my old hearers and neighbours from Ireland'.[66] The Washington session reaffirmed the invitation by a three-to-one vote in the summer of 1800, following Birch's travels elsewhere in the American interior.[67] Birch passed an initial interview with a committee of the Presbytery of Ohio, consisting of the Revd John McMillan, the Revd Samuel Ralston and Elder John McDowell.[68] (The Presbytery of Ohio encompassed what is now the southwestern corner of Pennsylvania, West Virginia and eastern Ohio.)

However, dissension and disappointment quickly clouded the immigrant's incipient ministry. Birch sought admission to the Ohio Presbytery in October 1800. The Presbytery rejected him and did so again in January and March 1801. In May 1801 Birch sought redress from the General Assembly of the Presbyterian Church and received some satisfaction; the following month he was again rejected by the Ohio Presbytery. Half-victory and failure continued to attend Birch's efforts to achieve formal recognition of his ministry and rescue a disintegrating personal reputation. He asked the Ohio Presbytery to censure McMillan, his chief antagonist; that April 1802 effort ended disastrously. Birch lodged another protest before the May 1802 General Assembly. Later in 1802 he applied for admittance to the presbyteries of New Castle in Delaware and Huntingdon in central Pennsylvania; both presbyteries rejected him because of accusations against his character broadcast by the Ohio Presbytery. Birch

Federalist politics and saw the millennium approaching (Wilson, p. 121). 63 McClelland (33) says Birch moved to Philadelphia in early 1799; documents published by Birch suggest November 1798. 64 Birch, *Seemingly experimental religion*, pp 34–6. 65 Ibid., p. 31. 66 Ibid., p. 31. In another connection, a Washington elder, Joseph Wherry, was the son of an East Nottingham, Maryland elder who signed a letter of recommendation for Birch (pp 35–6.). 67 Ibid., p. 64. 68 Ibid., pp 31, 64–5. The Presbytery established this committee in April 1800, which suggests that Birch may have been among the first interviewed. *Minutes of the Presbytery of Ohio* (17 April 1800), p. 58. McMillan, the son of Ulster immigrants, was a founder of and the dominant figure in the Presbytery. Irish-born, McDowell had arrived in Washington County in 1773 and gained prominence in local government. Originally aligned with Pennsylvania's radical party, he had become a Federalist. Ralston, a native of County Donegal, had been educated at Glasgow University and emigrated in 1794.

pleaded his case to the General Assembly a third time in May 1803. Frustrated once again in securing a berth in the American ministry, he angrily walked out of that meeting and was formally read out of the American Presbyterian Church.[69] Birch, in the meantime, had initiated a civil suit against McMillan for defamation of character. Eventually he blasted all those who had opposed his ministry with a densely written 144-page book published in 1806.

How did a respected member of the General Synod of Ulster, who had minis-tered to one of the largest Presbyterian congregations in Ireland, find himself shuttled off the broad avenue of American Presbyterianism into a cul-de-sac of acrimony and bitter disappointment? The opposition to Birch, and his own missteps, derived from several sources. His unabashed radicalism ill-disposed him to membership in a presbytery controlled by conservative clergy. Birch's old-country training and personal theology left him ill-prepared – and unwilling – to embrace the revivalism western clergy believed essential to impose social order and lay a solid foundation for the church. The Presbytery's resistance to Birch became more entrenched with the arrival of carefully nurtured revivals. And, finally, the contention for adherents among tendencies within Presbyterianism, similarly sharpened by the revival movement, exacerbated the division between Presbytery and exiled minister.

To a considerable extent, Birch's predicament in the United States may be assigned to the larger political controversies that caused his exile. In Ireland Birch had belonged to a dissenting church involved in a sometimes turbulent relationship with an Erastian state; he ministered to a population long burdened with civil disadvantages. To Birch, revolutionary politics aimed at asserting a new conception of rights inexorably linked to a religion of revelation. In a new nation without an established church, the Presbyterian clergy of southwestern Pennsylvania laboured in a fluid post-frontier society; prizing maintenance of order, they chose politics of a conservative, if not counter-revolutionary, nature.

Ministers denounced the violent opposition to the federal excise tax among western Pennsylvanian farmers that culminated in the Whiskey Rebellion of 1794, and acted on their disapproval by denying rebels admission to the Lord's Supper. The clergy perceived a particular danger in the spread of deism and radical republicanism.[70] Their fears were not groundless. The Society of United Freemen – a name which suggests conscious imitation of the contemporary Irish organization – assumed a leading role in regional opposition to the federal excise. These 'Jacobins' met in the Mingo Creek Presbyterian congregation's log

69 Birch, *Seemingly experimental religion*, pp 39, 41, 63, 67–71, 73, 100–9, 109–28, 132–6.
70 Leigh Eric Schmidt, *Holy Fairs: Scotland and the making of American revivalism* (Princeton, 2001), p. 199; Paul K. Conkin, *Cane Ridge: America's Pentecost* (Madison, 1990), p. 47; Barbara Christine Gray Wingo, 'Politics, society and religion: The Presbyterian clergy of Pennsylvania, New Jersey, and New York, and the formation of the nation, 1775–1808' (PhD diss., Tulane University, 1976), pp 12–13.

meeting house.[71] The town of Washington likewise boasted a radical society and, during the Whiskey Rebellion, a liberty pole. Judge Alexander Addison lamented that the 'terrible spirit' of 'Jacobinism' could be found in his own Washington town.[72]

With outspoken Federalist John McMillan at their head, the Presbyterian clergy associated their church with a regional elite of merchants, landowners and lawyers who sought the social stability and economic improvements linked to a strong national government. John McMillan became well known for preaching Federalism as well as the gospel to the region's Presbyterians.[73] McMillan actively campaigned for the treaty with Britain negotiated by Chief Justice John Jay on behalf of the Washington administration, a measure strongly supported by the Federalist party and vigorously opposed by Republicans and Irish immigrants.[74]

McMillan's politics are reflected in his close association with Alexander Addison, a Scottish immigrant who realized social and political prominence as lawyer and landowner. McMillan became Addison's mentor once the predecessor to the Ohio Presbytery rejected his application for admission to the ministry in 1785. President John Adams appointed the former ministerial candidate to Pennsylvania's Fifth Judicial District in 1791. Outspoken in his growing concern with the perceived threat to law and order posed by rampant democracy, Judge Addison became a Federalist spokesman locally and nationally. Addison defended the Alien and Sedition Acts and excoriated the French Revolution and pernicious influence of aliens in American life. In an address to the grand jury in December 1800 on the 'Rise and Progress of Revolution', Addison warned of the presence of revolutionary elements in the United States, among them the Society of United Irishmen. According to Russell Ferguson, 'The polemic, delivered under the guise of a charge to the jury, included also the observation that the recent election of [Thomas] McKean as governor of Pennsylvania was the result of the baneful influence of a revolutionary spirit.'[75]

71 Eugene Perry Link, *Democratic-Republican societies, 1790–1800* (New York, 1942), p. 147; Dwight Raymond Guthrie, *John McMillan, the apostle of Presbyterianism in the West, 1752–1833* (Pittsburgh, 1952) p. 163; Thomas P. Slaughter, *The Whiskey Rebellion: frontier epilogue to the American Revolution* (New York, 1986), pp 164–5. *Inventory of the church archives of Pennsylvania churches: Presbyterian churches*, prepared by the Pennsylvania Historical Records Survey, Works Progress Administration, arranged and indexed by Candace W. Belfield (Philadelphia, 1971), 05649–05650. 72 R. Eugene Harper, *The transformation of western Pennsylvania* (Pittsburgh, 1991), p. 98; Slaughter, p. 203; G.S. Rowe, 'Alexander Addison: The disillusionment of a "Republican schoolmaster,"' *Western Pennsylvania History Magazine* 62 (1975), 246. 73 Russell J. Ferguson, *Early western Pennsylvania politics* (Pittsburgh , 1938), p. 123. The term 'Federalist,' originally associated with supporters of the US Constitution (1787), came to be applied to the party in power during the first two American presidential administrations. Federalists supported policies embracing a strong central government, rapprochement with Great Britain and opposition to the French Revolution. 74 Guthrie, *John McMillan*, pp 169–72; Ferguson, p. 136. 75 Rowe, pp 223–4, Guthrie, pp 135, 157 (fn. 100); Ferguson, pp 48, 115; Harper, pp

Democratic-Republican candidate Thomas McKean gained Pennsylvania's governorship in 1799 amid rumours that this son of Ulster immigrants intended to import 'Twenty Thousand United Irishmen' into the state to influence the outcome.[76] The state election that year assumed crucial importance because of its presumed impact on the following year's presidential contest. By gaining a majority in the lower house of the state legislature, Republicans hoped to deliver Pennsylvania's critical eight electoral votes to Thomas Jefferson in 1800. The gubernatorial election saw the participation of Washington Presbyterian elders who provided McKean's opponent with testimonials attesting his religious values; Federalist candidate James Ross was another protégé of the Revd McMillan.[77] McKean's election meant that the tide had turned against the state's Federalists, for whom the town of Washington was increasingly a Federalist island in a Republican sea. With Pennsylvania holding a potentially deciding role in the outcome of the high-stakes presidential election of 1800, voters in the state election on 14 October that year delivered 'a crushing defeat' to the Federalists. Washington and other southwestern counties went overwhelmingly to the Jeffersonian party.[78]

Birch's prospects, then, were not enhanced by his arrival in Washington town during the bitterly contentious election in 1800. General Henry Taylor, an early and prominent Birch supporter, remarked at the time that 'party spirit ran so high' that townspeople lacked their former neighbourliness.[79] As the minister himself noted, 'Parties [were] at that time running high (for purposes not of a religious nature).'[80] Birch was, as he would write later, 'deemed of certain principles', meaning Republicanism.[81] Divisions within the village[82] with regard to Birch's

141–2; Rowe, pp 238–42, 245–6, 247; Ferguson, pp 168, 169. A Federalist-controlled Congress in 1798 enacted a series of laws (collectively known as the Alien and Sedition Acts) designed to reduce the scope of opposition by the Democratic-Republican party of Thomas Jefferson. Immigrant Irish republicans were a special target.   76 Harry Marlin Tinkcom, *The Republicans and Federalists in Pennsylvania, 1790–1801* (Harrisburg, PA, 1950), p. 231; Ferguson, pp 149–50, 150.   77 Tinkcom, pp 234–5; Ferguson, pp 48, 115. Ross had been accused of Deism. Both Ross and Addison, a particularly politically prominent pair, served as McMillan's defence attorneys when Birch brought a suit of defamation against their mentor.   78 Tinkcom, pp 245–6; Ferguson, pp 90, 163. Although Jefferson carried Washington County, the town of Washington was considered a 'center of Federalism,' as was Pittsburgh. (Ferguson, p. 160) The phrase 'Federalist island' is borrowed from Ferguson, who used it with respect to an earlier period. Discussing the debate over the US Constitution in the late 1780s, Ferguson wrote, 'The vote for western Pennsylvania stood seven to two against the Constitution and probably was representative of the sentiment of the region. The townspeople of Pittsburgh and Washington, in Washington County, were assuming an attitude that was more conservative than that of their agricultural neighbors. The two towns were *fast becoming Federalist islands in a sea of democracy'* (p. 60; emphasis added). As the early citation suggests, this tendency grew over the next decade as discrete political parties developed in the region and nationally.   79 Birch, *Seemingly experimental religion*, pp 113–14. 80 Ibid., p. 65. 81 Ibid., p. 89. 82 Washington had 635 residents; Washington County, the most populous in rural southwestern Pennsylvania, had a population of 27,874 in 1800.

ministry seemed to have formed according to political allegiance. Washington could claim several prominent democrats prepared to extend a welcome to a Republican minister.[83] Federalists, meanwhile, immediately indicated their disapproval. The wealthy and powerful John Hoge reportedly told the minister 'that he [Hoge] had marked Birch, from his hearing in the newspapers of his arrival at New York'.[84] Hoge closed the doors of the Washington Academy, the building used by the Washington congregation, to Birch on his first visit to the town.[85] On two separate occasions in 1800, the *Western Telegraphe*, Washington's Federalist weekly, denounced the radical minister, once unsympathetically referring to him as a 'United Irishman'.[86] The Revd Samuel Ralston told Birch that in McMillan's opinion, and his own, 'Birch's politicks were not suited to Washington.'[87] Opposition to Birch within the Washington congregation, the émigré decided, derived from fears that he would obstruct 'their carrying their meeting-house ticket'; that is, that he would undermine the influence of prominent Federalists like elder Andrew Swearingen, one of the area's richest men.[88] Opponents of Birch, men of substance, would deride his supporters as 'riff raff', as artisans, drunks, heretics and aliens.[89] Congregational allegiances mirrored divisions within the village as a whole.[90]

If politics provided a context for how the community divided in its appreciation of Birch, theology alone formed the basis for the Ohio Presbytery's formal

83 Early supporters of Birch included General Taylor, an early (and wealthy) settler and leading Jeffersonian; Dr Absalom Baird, a state senator in the 1790s and respected physician; John Israel, Jeffersonian publisher; the silversmith Robert Anderson; and tavern-keeper William McCammont. Some of these individuals reportedly warned Birch away from Washington in July 1800 on account of his rumoured intemperance; there is no evidence of their later opposition to his presence or ministry in Washington. (It should be noted that Baird and Taylor were both dead by the time the controversy reached its height.) Addison condemned Baird as one 'uniformly among the strenuous opponents and censurers of our government, and has been and yet is of what is called the French party.' (Quoted in Rowe, fn. 54, p. 246.)   84 Birch, *Seemingly experimental religion*, p. 138. Hoge, the town proprietor, was also Washington's wealthiest individual. Harper found that in 1793 Hoge enjoyed far more taxable wealth than any other of the county seat's professional and mercantile elite (p. 102). He was later a Federalist member of Congress. 85 Birch blamed the incident on both Hoge and Samuel Clarke, the latter still 'sore with the wounds of Governor M'Kean's turning him out office'; he alleged that Hoge and Clarke swore that 'any one who opposed the British government, should be kicked out of town'. *Seemingly experimental religion*, p. 138.   86 *Western Telegraphe* (Washington, PA), 3 February 1800; 4 August 1800.   87 Birch, *Seemingly experimental religion*, p. 138.   88 Ibid., p. 56. Swearingen, who at one time served as County Treasurer, ranked number four in taxable wealth in Washington and number one in Chartiers, where McMillan's church was located (for the period 1784–1796). Harper, pp 77, 148.   89 Birch, *Seemingly experimental religion*, pp 96, 112. The 'riff raff' comment Birch attributed to the Revd John Anderson; the catalogue of Birch supporters comes from a paper drawn up by anti-Birch elders.   90 Among those paying pew rental for the Washington Academy, where the congregation met for services, were Federalist publisher John Colerick and the Federalist poet David Bruce, who dedicated his 1801 collection of verse to Alexander Addison. Archives of the Washington Historical Society, A–28, Records of First Presbyterian Church, Washington.

rejection of the exile in October 1800. Following a conversation with Birch 'upon his experimental acquaintance with religion, and soundness in the faith', Presbytery 'did not receive such satisfaction as would enduce [sic] them to take him on any further trial'. An interview at the subsequent meeting in December 1800 and later exchanges similarly failed to satisfy the presbyters.[91]

Unfortunately for Birch, the rules established by the General Assembly of the Presbyterian Church for admittance of foreign ministers had been revised earlier that year to give greater prominence to 'soundness in the faith, and experimental acquaintance with religion.'[92] He was clearly unprepared for the American Presbyterians' emphasis on personal experience of salvation. He seemed to have no idea what they were talking about. As Birch remarked to a Washington elder, 'it was not the fashion in Ireland to examine on experimental religion'.[93] The immigrant minister understood 'religious experience' to mean understanding of doctrine. 'What would have pleased the Presbytery (as I have frequently learned since) was, if I had told them of a certain time and place when I became assured of eternal happiness', Birch wrote in 1806. He objected that there could be no assurance this side of heaven.[94] In Ireland and Scotland such unreliable self-evaluations as sought by American clergy would not be expected from ministerial candidates. 'The Presbyterian Ministers in the old countries never ask candidates concerning the notions they entertain of themselves,' he explained. Further, Birch held that exposition of doctrine was a more reliable test than a pharisaical show of religion. As he had written years earlier in Ireland, 'Man can only observe the outward appearance, God alone can see the heart.'[95]

The life experiences, philosophical assumptions and theological under-standing of Birch and McMillan ran directly counter to each other. Born in 1752 in Lancaster County, Pennsylvania, McMillan was a child of America's Great Awakening. His understanding of Presbyterianism was shaped by the revivalist-inclined New Side which dominated the denomination following a 1741 schism. McMillan studied at two eastern Pennsylvania academies founded by New Side clergymen and at the College of New Jersey, also a New Side institution. The New Side regarded experiential religion as a ministerial requisite; significantly, McMillan had his first profound religious experience in a student revival.[96]

McMillan's pioneering work in organizing Presbyterian congregations in the transmontane frontier did nothing to lessen his commitment to revivalism. On the contrary, the mission of soul-saving became inextricably bound up with both the necessity of gathering in sufficient numbers of communicants to sustain the

91 *Minutes of the Presbytery of Ohio*, i (typescript in the archives of the Pittsburgh Theological Institute), pp 66, 70.   92 *Minutes of the General Assembly of the Presbyterian Church in the United States of America, from its organization A.D. 1789 to A.D. 1820 inclusive* (Philadelphia, 1847), p. 200.   93 *Birch v. McMillan* (Historical Collections, Washington and Jefferson College, Washington, PA; typescript of unpublished court transcript), p. 29.   94 Birch, *Seemingly experimental religion*, pp 37–8.   95 Ibid., pp 37, 48; Birch, *Obligations*, p. 33.   96 Guthrie, pp 66–7.

rapidly proliferating number of congregations and the imperative of achieving social stability. When the Ohio Presbytery was erected in 1793, its five ministers had responsibility for more than twenty congregations.[97] By 1802 the Ohio Presbytery had twenty-one ministers but twenty-seven vacant pulpits.[98] Many congregations lacked the resources to engage a full-time minister. And although ministers' salaries were often paid in kind, congregations were frequently in arrears.[99] Revivals met the urgent goal of 'greatly strengthening the feeble churches', a minister recalled a generation later.[100]

The clergy regarded the 1790s as a period of spiritual deadness among Presbyterians in transmontane Pennsylvania as elsewhere in the western country.[101] This apprehension was clearly related to political and social tensions. Ministers regretted 1799, the year of Republican electoral triumph in Pennsylvania, as a time 'when the graceless became more bold in sin and impiety …, most of the pious became very weak and feeble in the cause of Christ, much buried in, and carried away with the things and pursuits of the world'.[102] The times demanded a revival of religion.

Revivals occurred within some Ohio Presbytery congregations in 1799 and 1800 but the region's largest and most successful occurred following Kentucky's Cane Ridge revival in 1801.[103] As in western Pennsylvania, the Kentucky revivals developed around Presbyterian sacramental occasions. The minister associated with Cane Ridge, James McGready, was a native of southwestern Pennsylvania who studied with McMillan and experienced spiritual rebirth at a Washington County sacramental festival in 1786. He remained in contact with the Ohio Presbytery. The southwestern Pennsylvania clergy looked to the Kentucky experience as a fruitful example of spiritual awakening.[104]

As the pulse of revival in southwestern Pennsylvania quickened, the acrimony between Birch and the Ohio Presbytery intensified. Birch became subject to increasingly harsh personal attacks.[105] McMillan condemned Birch as 'a

---

97 *History of the Presbytery of Washington*, (Philadelphia, 1889) p. 10.   **98** *Minutes of the General Assembly*, pp 186, 240–1. The churches with vacant pulpits in 1802 were found in what is now West Virginia and Ohio as well as western Pennsylvania.   **99** The *Minutes of the Ohio Presbytery* give frequent reports on congregations' inability to fully complete their financial obligations to clergy. Two of the Cross Creek congregation's earliest elders, according to a church tradition, agonized over their inability to scrape together the four or five dollars needed to meet their obligations; one raised the cash by shooting a wolf (for which a bounty was paid). *History of the Presbytery of Washington*, p. 270.   **100** Quoted in William Speer, *The Great Revival of 1800* (Philadelphia, 1872), p. 17. The Revd Joseph Stevenson (1779–1865) graduated from Jefferson College, an institution associated with McMillan, in 1807 and married a daughter of the Revd Thomas Marquis, a prominent revivalist. *History of the Presbytery of Washington*, p. 127. **101** Conkin, *Cane Ridge*, pp 47, 52.   **102** *Western Missionary Magazine*, 292.   **103** Guthrie, p. 68; p. 117; James D. Smith III, 'Kentucky biographical notebook, James McGready, 1797 revivalist,' in *The Filson Club History Quarterly* (Louisville, KY), 71: 4 (1997), 465.   **104** Smith, 464.   **105** The Ohio Presbytery, in part, acknowledged the severity of the invective when Birch brought charges against the Revd McMillan in April 1802. In the end, the Presbytery ruled as

Minister of the Devil' in June 1801, not long after the General Assembly heard the exile's protest. This denunciation came with McMillan's alleged declaration that 'he would do all he could to put [Birch] away'.[106] The Ohio Presbytery had already rejected Birch three times in less than a year for his unfamiliarity with experimental religion when he was castigated by presbyters in July 1801 for 'the general report which prevails with respect to his imprudent and irregular conduct'. After a four-hour deliberation behind closed doors, the assembled ministers and elders announced that 'they would have no farther to do with Mr Birch, as to his trials for the Gospel Ministry'.[107] At its April 1802 meeting, the Presbytery for the first time publicly revealed its case against Birch's personal conduct. McMillan acknowledged he had called Birch 'a minister of the Devil' because of Birch's failure to evince any sign of 'special grace' and his 'excessive drinking and deliberate falsehood'.[108] At this meeting the Presbytery brought forward witnesses to testify to Birch's alleged intemperance, profanity and adultery.[109] Rumours of heavy drinking that had first appeared in July 1800, mixed with fresh allegations, became the Presbytery's justification for resisting the General Assembly's (May 1801) resolution that Birch could be taken on trials by any presbytery.[110] Indeed, the Presbytery's stance may be taken as a rebuff to the General Assembly.

The Presbytery already regarded Birch as unregenerate; following his rejection by Presbytery and General Assembly, he revealed himself an implacable (if not spiteful) opponent of revivalism and revival theology. The depth of Birch's unease with the revival phenomenon allows us to better understand the meaning of McMillan's denunciation of the émigré as 'unconverted.' Birch's argument against revivalism is woven throughout much of *Seemingly Experimental Religion*, his 1806 exercise in self-defence. The secondary titles clearly show his opposition to the Presbytery's project: *Converters Unconverted – Revivals Killing Religion – Missionaries in Need of Teaching – or, War against the Gospel by Its Friends*.

'not supported' the charges that McMillan had defamed Birch and lied to evade church censure. The charge that McMillan had called Birch a 'Minister of the Devil' and had engaged in 'unchristian threats' was ruled 'not fully supported'; the phrase 'Minister of the Devil' was judged 'very harsh and unguarded.' McMillan was admonished. *Minutes of the Ohio Presbytery* (21–22 April 1802), pp 100–2, 103–5; Birch, *Seemingly experimental religion*, pp 103–6; *Minutes of the Ohio Presbytery* (22 April 1802), pp 102–3.   **106** *Birch v. McMillan*, pp 8, 9.   **107** *Minutes of the Ohio Presbytery* (1 July 1801), p. 79.   **108** *Minutes of the Ohio Presbytery* (21 April 1802), pp 99–100.   **109** The charge of profanity seems to have been flimsy at best, the adultery charge frivolous. John Stockton, a Washington congregant and the alleged cuckold, commented derisively in court testimony, 'People often say I keep my wife for the clergy.' (*Birch vs. McMillan*, p. 16.) Intemperance is a culturally relative term. Birch's chief antagonist, McMillan, was not averse to a dram or two.   **110** The General Assembly ruled: 'they find no obstruction against any Presbytery, to which he may apply, taking [Birch] up and proceeding with him agreeably to the rules and regulations.' *Minutes of the General Assembly*, pp 220–1.

Birch derided what his foes called 'religious experience' as merely 'an impudent belief ... that somehow or other we may get ourselves wrought into.' Birch saw only the Pharisee's ostentatious display of faith in the Presbytery's 'societies, monthly and quarterly meetings, attending sacraments, giving experiences'. The County Down-born minister dismissed the exercise of 'getting religion' and the revivals' physicality. He complained that the Washington County revivalists 'far exceed the pharisee in their fallings, accompanied with other gestures, which are reckoned by many, clergy not excepted, the infallible test.' The sudden, mysterious physical collapse of revival participants, the 'falling' so esteemed by the clergy, was little more than an excuse for '[t]he debauching of young women', he charged.[111]

Birch wrote, 'We will not say, with some, that it is a work of the Devil, or even a delusion; but with every respect for the opinion of some, we hope truly religious people, who think favourably of the work, we ask, where is the Divine proof?'[112] Western Pennsylvania's Seceders, who did in fact make the charge that the revivals were a devilish delusion, were asking the same question.

The Presbyterian family in southwestern Pennsylvania in the early nineteenth century comprehended Seceders and Covenanters, organized in congregations of the Associate, Associate Reformed and Reformed Presbyterian churches.[113] Numerous Seceders settled in Washington County following the American Revolution.[114] The Seceders in southwestern Pennsylvania, as in Ulster, may have established congregations in those areas of late Irish and Scots settlement that were perceived as underserved by the mainstream Ohio Presbytery.[115] These

111 Birch, *Seemingly experimental religion*, pp 49, 48.   112 Ibid., p. 135.   113 In 1782, the Associate Presbyteries of Pennsylvania and New York merged with the Covenanters' Reformed Presbytery to form the Associate Reformed Church. However, a minority of Seceders rejected the merger. Their Associate Synod convened in 1801, with four constituent presbyteries: Philadelphia, Kentucky, Cambridge (New York) and Chartiers – the last-named based in the same Washington County township where John McMillan ministered. The Chartiers Presbytery, in turn, consisted of four congregations: Chartiers, Buffalo, Harmons Creek with Mill Creek and Montours with Beaver. As members of the Reformed Presbytery refused to join the 'union church,' there were now three churches. By the summer of 1802, when the revivals encouraged by the Ohio Presbytery finally occurred, these denominations had organized more than thirty congregations in Allegheny, Beaver, Fayette, Washington and Westmoreland Counties in Pennsylvania and in adjacent Ohio County, Virginia. Of those in Beaver, Ohio and Washington Counties, and therefore sharing territory with the Ohio Presbytery, eight were in the dissident Associate Synod and four in the Associate Reformed Synod. William Melanchthon Glasgow, *Cyclopedic manual of the United Presbyterian Church of North America* (Pittsburgh, 1903), p. 10; The Revd John T. Brownlee, *History of the Associate and United Presbyterian Presbytery of Chartiers* (1877, reprinted by Chartiers Presbytery, 1936), pp 4–5; Basil G. McBee and Reid W. Stewart, *History of the Associate Presbyterian Church in North America* (Apollo, PA, 1983), p. 22. Calculated on the basis of information contained in the section 'Congregations' in Glasgow, pp 377–585.   114 Fisk, *The Scottish high church tradition in America*, p. 54.   115 A look at a map of Washington County in 1817 locates the bulk of Associate and Associate Reform congregations in the western half of the county, within townships which tended to be settled later than those along

rival organizations competed for communicants among Ulster Scots and Scots settlers with the mainstream Presbyterian church and with each other. Seceder churches provided an alternative to the innovations of the Great Awakening for those in southwestern Pennsylvania whose Calvinism owed more to old-world religion. For example, mainstream Presbyterian congregations on several occasions protested the introduction of Watts' Psalms by defecting to an Associate or Associate Reformed body.[116] Criticism of the mainstream church levelled by the smaller bodies appears to have been of concern to the Ohio Presbytery, judging by declarations and clarifications of church principle the presbyters felt obliged to make.[117]

The Seceders strenuously criticized the revival movement the Ohio Presbytery vigorously encouraged. According to the Revd John Eagleson (writing in 1860), the Seceders denounced the revival 'as a delusion, as a work of the Devil, and as a judgment sent on the Presbyterian churches for using Watts' Psalms and Hymns'.[118] In a 53-page pamphlet published in Washington, Pennsylvania in 1804, five Associate Presbyterian ministers offered a detailed critique entitled *Evils of the Work Now Prevailing in the United States of America under the Name of a Revival of Religion*.[119] The five divines objected to the unscriptural nature of the revival, its physicality, the public displays of emotion, and teaching and exhorting by those 'without any regular call', as well as the

river valleys.   116 To give one such instance: When their pastor gave one of Watts' Psalms to be sung, congregants of the Three Ridges church in Donegal Township, Washington County, reorganized themselves as a Seceder congregation (*History of the Presbytery of Washington*, p. 279). The hymns of English poet Isaac Watts were in vogue in mainstream Presbyterian churches but rejected by Seceders as unscriptural. Presbyterian minister Adam Rankin, later a vitriolic critic of revivalism, unsuccessfully fought use of Watts' Psalms all the way to the General Assembly before leading his congregation into the Associate Reformed Church. John B. Boles, *The Great Revival, 1787–1805* (Lexington, KY, 1972), pp 98, 22.   117 At its 25 December 1800 meeting, the Ohio Presbytery heard a report that in some congregations without ministers it was rumoured 'that the Presbyterian body have wholly rejected the Book of Psalms together with the five books of Moses; we do hereby declare the above to be a groundless slander.' In a clear response to Seceder criticism of revival practices the Presbytery resolved on 30 June 1802 'that it is improper for this Body, or any of its members to invite any person who is not known to be a regular minister of the Gospel or who is unsound in principle or irregular in practice, to preach in their pulpits, or hold communion with him under the character of a minister.' The Presbytery alluded to another prominent issue of old-world Presbyterian sectarians in declaring that 'the practice of swearing upon and kissing the Bible is an unscriptural and idolatrous mode of swearing, and is such as relic of popery and paganism that we highly disprove of.' The Presbytery pledged to discourage this practice. *Minutes of the Ohio Presbytery*, pp 70, 113, 182.   118 John Eagleson, *A historical discourse delivered in the Presbyterian church of Upper Buffalo* (Washington, 1860), p. 12.   119 The authors, John Cree, John Anderson, William Wilson, Thomas Alison and Ebenezer Henderson, ministered to congregations in Allegheny, Beaver, Westmoreland and Washington Counties in southwestern Pennsylvania. Cree was born in Scotland, Wilson in Ireland and Anderson in England to Scottish parents. The other two were born in eastern Pennsylvania in Scots-Irish enclaves.

'singing of human composures'. Accepting that a spiritual awakening should be welcomed, the authors indicated no objection if such led to increased public and private exercises of divine worship – but cautioned that Satan as well as the Holy Spirit worked on the conscience. The Seceding ministers' objection to revivalism lay in its confusion of means and ends as well as its perceived deviation from a strict reading of scripture. They concluded, 'We would say to our dear brethren: Let it be your exercise at this time, *to ask for the old paths, where is the good way?*'[120]

Birch's critique of revivalism agreed in some essential points with that of the Seceders, even if he did not see a satanic hand in the phenomenon. Like the Seceders, Birch believed the purported revival of religion lacked divine proof of a true transformation.[121] Like the Seceders, Birch excoriated the revivalists' admission to the communion table of the newly converted, based on 'feelings' rather than knowledge, with the result that 'actually persons grossly ignorant are admitted.' The millenarian Birch, who believed the reign of Christ would begin in 1848 in western Pennsylvania, wrote that 'Extraordinary Revivals are indeed expected and earnestly prayed for', but believed that the '*sacramental camp meetings*' did not meet that expectation.[122]

Birch complained that newly ordained ministers, fresh from the humble academies founded by his opponents, lacked the necessary education and training.[123] He believed that ministers in America, and particularly in the backcountry, did not have sufficient qualifications. Quoting the Revd Adam Rankin, a critic of revivalism who left mainstream Presbyterianism to join the Associate Reformed Church, Birch observed that Americans would choose the best lawyer, the best physician, 'but any Quack will do for the soul'.[124]

In *Seemingly Experimental Religion*, Birch appears at times to appeal directly to Seceders and disgruntled 'old country' Presbyterians.[125] He frequently and

120 Ibid., pp 26, 51. Emphasis in the original. 121 Birch, *Seemingly experimental religion*, p. 135. 'But with their hundred fallings [regarded as physical manifestation of divine intervention], it is challenged to produce one Preacher, or faller, to be esteemed as having obtained more truth, honesty, or mercy.' 122 Ibid., pp 134, 135. Emphasis in the original. 123 McMillan was instrumental in the establishment of two academies in Washington County (predecessors to today's Washington and Jefferson College in Washington, PA) which trained young men for the Presbyterian ministry. Of the twenty-one ministers who belonged to the Ohio Presbytery as of June 1801, a little more than half (eleven) had been born in Pennsylvania; four had been born in contiguous states, one in Massachusetts and four in Ireland. Only one had been educated abroad (at the University of Glasgow); only four had received higher education in the United States. Nine had been instructed at a Washington County academy; two appear to have had no other education than studies with local ministers prior to ordination. A majority (thirteen) had been ordained within the past five years. See *History of the Presbytery of Washington; Minutes of the Ohio Presbytery* (30 June 1801), p. 78. By contrast, most of the Seceder ministers at that time were foreign-born and educated abroad. 124 Birch, *Seemingly experimental religion*, p. 53. For Rankin, see note 116. In *The evils of the work*, the Seceder ministers frequently quote from Rankin's pamphlet, *A review of the noted revival in Kentucky*. 125 Birch makes at least seven

respectfully referred to David's Psalms, declaring in one passage that 'it is become fashionable, with late converts, to throw away David's Psalms altogether.' Elsewhere in *Seemingly Experimental Religion* Birch contrasted unfavourably the General Assembly's 'Rules and Regulations for the introduction of foreign Ministers' with 'the cordial reception' given by the Associate Reformed Synod to ministers from Ireland and Scotland. He recalled reverently *'our pious old covenanting forefathers.'*[126] In a curious passage, Birch favourably compared himself to founders of the Associate Synod who, in Birch's interpretation of events, had been 'read out' by the Associate Reformed Church just as he had been by the Ohio Presbytery.[127] Thus, two years after the publication of *Evils of the Work*, Birch had launched his own particular appeal to the immigrant Ulster-Scots community on the basis of similar objections to mainstream American Presbyterianism.

In the light of Birch's withering condemnation of the Seceders in County Down, friendly overtures to them in western Pennsylvania may seem surprising. The robust criticism of revivals in *Seemingly Experimental Religion*, however, is consistent with the condemnation of Irish Seceders' communion excesses contained in *Physicians Languishing under Disease*, published a decade earlier. Further, in that pamphlet Birch commented favourably on the Anti-Burgher Seceders, who seemed to have predominated among the early Associate Presbyterians settled in the United States.[128] And in Washington County, in the absence of a perceived Catholic threat, the complications of Seceder alliances with his political foes and the threatened loss of congregants, neither Birch nor the Associate Presbyterians had cause for hostility or mutual recrimination.[129] The émigré 'Minister of the Devil' found common ground with other recent immigrants on the basis of a shared understanding of their old-country faith.

The congruence of criticism levelled against revivalism by both Birch and the Seceders, together with the actual and perceived threat of membership loss to rival organizations, allows a deeper understanding of the Ohio Presbytery's fears of the immigrant's potentially pernicious effects within its jurisdiction. The

explicit 'old country' references (pp 10, 36, 37, 52, 54, 130, 137).   **126** Birch, *Seemingly experimental religion*, pp 47, 36, 10. Emphasis added.   **127** Ibid., p. 139. In this rather startling passage, he wrote, 'Birch can plead as a precedent, the Apostles and Reformers, the first American settlers, Messrs. Marshal and Clarkson, read out by the Union and formed the Associate body in America.' The reference is to two Scottish-born Seceder ministers, William Marshall and James Clarkson, both of whom objected to the 1782 Seceder-Covenanter union that created the Associate Reformed Church. Marshall served as the first moderator of the Associate Synod in 1801; Clarkson served as moderator the following year. Glasgow, *Cyclopedic manual*, pp 248, 78. **128** Birch, *Physicians*, p. 50. Seceder immigrants in the American colonies decided to abandon the Burgess oath controversy in 1765.   **129** It is worth noting that during the 1790s the Seceder rank and file in Ulster did not always follow the loyalist leadership of their clergy. The exhortations against rebellion by the Revd Francis Pringle of Gilnahirk, writes Ian McBride, 'aroused such hostility that he was forced to emigrate to America.' *Scripture politics*, p. 107.

affinity between Birch and the Seceders seems to have been noted even before the United Irishman relocated to Washington County. A Washington elder reportedly solicited Seceder support for the émigré's ministry, commenting that 'a number of you Seceders think a heap of him.' Immigrant Andrew Nickell, a Seceder who apparently joined Birch's small congregation, confirmed this view with the declaration, 'He is a brave, thundering preacher.'[130]

Early in his disputes with the Ohio Presbytery, Birch met privately with McMillan. The frontier preacher, as Birch recalled the conversation, 'told me he did not see what right I had to come to their Presbyterian body for admittance, as my hearers out of the old country, (some of whom he named in his own bounds) all turned Seceders'. Birch said that as 'an old side Presbyterian' he would be sorry to leave his church. 'But,' he explained, 'there were certain inquiries and modes of Psalmody made use of by some Ministers, very different from those they had been accustomed to, and therefore not pleasing to us old country people, – such preachers they left, and went to Seceders as being most agreeable, to what they were taught to believe as Presbyterians. Mr McMillan said he believed so.'[131]

The Ohio Presbytery apparently regarded Birch as a potential schismatic. An early and continuing complaint of the Presbytery was Birch's insistence on ordaining four elders and administering other ordinances. That most of those elders, in the opinion of the Presbytery, had never been communicants of the Washington church only exacerbated the problem.[132] The original elders objected that 'very few, if any', of Birch's hearers 'ever belonged to the Washington Congregation', a charge that suggests Birch was perceived to be erecting a congregation within an existing one.[133] Indeed, an attorney who defended McMillan in the defamation suit brought against the cleric by Birch insinuated in October 1804 that Birch's congregation was '*independent*'[134] – that is, outside the Presbyterian church.

Writing to a Philadelphia ally in 1803, Birch described his intention to publish a collection of psalmody, 'in where there (is) ground for the happy prospect of the union of Seceders and all orthodox Christians'.[135] In *Seemingly Experimental Religion* he declared: 'Birch's desire is to cultivate peace and goodwill with the truly religious of all professions, and *a connection with old-side Christian Presbyterians, and to form a Presbytery of such* ... supporting covenanting reformation and perpetual testimony to the truth.'[136] Birch, the rebel who desired the end of monarchy, was seemingly prepared to foment revolution within the

130 Birch, *Seemingly experimental religion*, p. 121. Nickell is described as a 'Seceder, of Canton township.' He is also listed among signatories on an appeal to the General Assembly on Birch's behalf (p. 131).   131 Ibid., p. 54.   132 *Birch v. McMillan*, p. 25; *Minutes of the Ohio Presbytery* (22 October 1801), p. 86.   133 From the *Western Telegraphe*, quoted in Birch, *Seemingly experimental religion*, p. 86.   134 *Birch v. McMillan*, p. 42. Emphasis in the original.   135 Quoted in McClelland, 34.   136 Birch, *Seemingly experimental religion*, p. 139. Emphasis added.

Presbyterian church through the creation of a new presbytery, if not an altogether new denomination.

The perception of Birch as an alien rebel dogged his efforts to be accepted by the Ohio Presbytery even as his old-world understanding of theology and church governance condemned him in the eyes of the Washington County clergy. The Presbytery deemed Birch 'an entire stranger to those views which real Christians obtain' and greatly ignorant 'of sound doctrine'.[137] Compounding his undesirability, Birch obstinately insisted on assuming the prerogatives of the ministry. He essentially established a new congregation within an older one, heightening and confirming the fears of those who worried that Birch, like his immigrant former hearers, would join the ranks of schismatics.[138]

Birch's difficulties also lay in his opponents' perception of his eccentricities, his obvious Irishness, his marked contrast to their self-image as frontier missionaries. James Riddle told the court (as part of Birch's defamation suit against McMillan), 'an Irishman then present said, I knew [Birch] is an Irishman, by his *Grace*'. When Birch supporter Andrew McMekan declared, 'I have heard of him in Ireland and never heard but he was a careful faithful minister,' such a testimonial held little value for American-born ministers trained in the expectations of the post-Great Awakening church. The similar affirmation of Birch by Irish Seceder William Bennett was unlikely to have swayed the presbyters, nor would that of Birch elder Robert Anderson, who proclaimed, 'I never saw [Birch] disguised with Liquor, but free, hearty, jolly; too much, I thought for the people of this country; *he could not act the Hypocrite for [them]*.'[139] The young ministers trained in western Pennsylvania openly ridiculed Birch, offering no respect for his Irish pastorate or Glasgow University background. Theirs, after all, was an avowedly *American* Presbyterian church, shorn of connections with Britain and Ireland.[140] In rejecting Birch, the Ohio Presbytery maintained that 'a Minister coming from Europe is no more to be acknowledged as a member of the Presbyterian Church in America, *than if he had come from the Church of Rome*.'[141]

---

137 *Minutes of the Ohio Presbytery* (22 October 1801), p. 86.   138 Contemporary Presbyterianism in western Pennsylvania was a volatile affair. Regular Presbyterians defected to the dissenting bodies; the Donegal dissidents cited above by 1802 had followed their Ulster-born pastor in a further schism to form the Reformed Dissenting Presbytery. Associate minister Robert Laing (who lived near Birch outside Washington, PA) was accused of intoxication; he was acquitted, whereupon members of the session resigned and most of the congregation withdrew and reconstituted itself. The newly reorganized Reformed Presbytery met in Pittsburgh in December 1800, attracting the support of Covenanters dissatisfied with the Associate Reformed Church. Thomas Campbell, a Seceder minister from County Armagh, arrived in Washington County in 1807 and soon laid the groundwork for a new denomination, the Disciples of Christ.   139 *Birch v. McMillan*, pp 39, 8, 21. Emphasis in original.   140 By contrast, the Associate and Reformed Presbyterian churches maintained links to the Irish and Scottish churches.   141 *Minutes of the Ohio Presbytery* (22 October 1801), p. 86. Emphasis added. The *Minutes* noted that the General Assembly had established a relationship with Connecticut's Congregational churches but

Accordingly, when Birch sued McMillan for defamation, McMillan's attorneys based their defence on the exile's lack of standing with the Presbyterian church in the United States.[142]

The Birch affair, in a sense, continued the controversy over vital religion and church governance that consumed American Presbyterianism on the eve of the Great Awakening. The crisis of the 1730s and 1740s revealed two differing visions of Presbyterianism, with the fault-lines more or less dividing old-world from new-world conceptions of the denomination. New Side ministers tended to be American-educated and younger, the Old Side older Irish-born men who were products of Scottish universities.[143]

The New Side insisted on ministers 'such as are experimentally acquainted with the renewing and sanctifying Grace of God in their own souls.' The Old Side tended to look askance at 'spiritual Frenzy' and argued (like Birch) that 'The heart is not under human cognizance; declarations of experience may be, or not be, what men feel.'[144] The two camps differed, too, on the questions of church governance. Old-Side ministers, doubtful of the educational standards of the New Side 'Log College', proposed that the Synod as a whole examine those ministerial candidates lacking degrees from European or New England universities. The New Side countered by insisting that the presbytery, not a higher judicature, was the church's basic unit and alone had the right of ordination.[145] The Ohio Presbytery forcefully reiterated that argument in the Birch case, derailing pro-Birch delegates to the 1801 General Assembly by insisting that presbyteries had the exclusive right to judge whether a candidate 'was acquainted with experimental religion'.[146] In responding to Birch's charges, the Ohio Presbytery maintained the General Assembly had no right to oblige a presbytery to accept a minister. In this conception of Presbyterian federalism, presbyteries alone were the source of church power.[147]

In the Birch case, as in the 1741 schism, the antagonists did not line up neatly into exclusively 'Irish' or 'American' camps. Four Ulster-born ministers were among the ranks of the Ohio Presbytery and Birch's wide range of supporters encompassed the Virginia-born Henry Taylor and Connecticut delegates to the General Assembly. Ultimately, though, the fault-line running through the Birch controversy is the cultural divide separating Old World from New.

dissolved the connection with the Presbyterian churches in Ireland and Scotland, due to the Europeans' 'general departure from soundness of doctrine, and want of vital Godliness.' **142** *Birch v. McMillan*, pp 21, 43. **143** Patrick Griffin, *The people with no name: Ireland's Ulster Scots, America's Scots Irish, and the creation of a British Atlantic world, 1689–1764* (Princeton, 2001), p. 150; Patricia U. Bonomi, *Under the cope of Heaven: religion, society, and politics in colonial America* (New York, 1986), p. 145. **144** Quoted in Griffin, p. 144. **145** Quoted in Griffin, p. 147; Leonard J. Trinterud, *The forming of an American tradition: a re-examination of colonial Presbyterianism* (Freeport, NY , 1970), p. 98. **146** James Carnahan, 'John Watson, 1798–1802' in William B. Sprague, *Annals of the American pulpit*, iv (New York, 1859), p. 209. **147** *Minutes of the Ohio Presbytery* (22 October 1801), pp 87, 86.

The church being built by John McMillan and the young ministers trained in his academies was an American institution constructed on the requirements of American conditions, regardless of these Presbyterians' Ulster roots. Birch embodied for these ministers their suspicions of foreign churchmen. However strongly Birch identified with American republicanism, he was ill-prepared for Americans' declaration of cultural and ecclesiastical independence. The Presbyterianism of post-frontier western Pennsylvania appeared to him unforgivingly unfamiliar, as it did to his 'hearers out of the old country' and recent immigrants of the Seceder tradition. Birch and his Irish-born admirers remained essentially Ulster Scots; further generations of immigrant Presbyterians would have to construct their denominational and ethnic identity anew before all would be retrospectively designated 'Scotch-Irish'.

United Irishmen in the American South:
a re-evaluation

KATHARINE L. BROWN

The political tensions of the 1790s in Ireland and the failure of the 1798 Rebellion caused many United Irish activists and sympathizers to board ships bound for the new American republic, whether under duress or voluntarily. However, the American South has not been perceived as a destination and refuge for these émigrés. An examination of the American activities and contacts of three refugees – the passionate Presbyterian preacher John Glendy, the duelling playwright and historian John Daly Burk and the successful linen merchant James Bones – suggests that there were significant, active and successful communities of United Irish sympathizers in many Southern communities. Through their experiences this essay explores three communities of 1798 Rebellion-era immigrants in a modest effort to counter a firmly entrenched popular impression, abetted by the popular scholarly work of the late James Leyburn, that the immigration of Ulster Scots, or Scotch-Irish, to the South is a colonial frontier phenomenon. That image rarely includes immigration from Ulster to the American South in the years after the Revolution and ignores the role of a new generation of immigrants spawned by the political turmoil in Ireland during the 1790s.

The careers of these high-profile United Irish immigrants provide an entry point to the experiences and attitudes of a larger body of like-minded contemporary immigrants to the South. These new Ulster immigrants not only settled in the Southern backcountry, where their countrymen were thick on the ground, but also expanded into port towns where the Ulster Scots' influence was minimal, thereby increasing the ethnic diversity of the urban South. They brought their United Irish liberal views with them and made themselves at home in Jefferson's Republican party.

One was the superb preacher John Glendy. Ordained in 1778,[1] and the pastor

---

1 James McConnell, compiler, Samuel G. McConnell, reviser, *Fasti of the Irish Presbyterian Church, 1613–1840* (Belfast, 1951), reprinted from *The Genealogist's Magazine* (September and December, 1936), p. 202. Son of Samuel Glendy, a farmer at Faughanvale outside Derry, he studied at the University of Glasgow. Glendy was probably named for his uncle John Glendy, also a farmer at Faughanvale.

of the Presbyterian congregation at Maghera,[2] Glendy was captain and chaplain in a Volunteer unit[3] that in 1792 supported Catholic emancipation,[4] and he served in the same capacity in the Maghera National Guards which emerged from this unit in 1793.[5] A government informer described Glendy as 'tainted with the blackest principles of revolution' and charged that his 'sermons are but discourses containing treason'.[6] Glendy's congregation at Maghera ('a few individuals excepted, on whom the breath of aristocracy has shed its baneful influence') lauded Glendy for the 'public-spirited manner' in which he discerned 'the signal interposition of heaven on behalf of the French Nation and Universal Right of Conscience'. This public political statement was applauded in the *Northern Star,* the United Irish newspaper, in December 1792, in a notice signed by the Maghera session clerk, James Graham.[7] Graham's son, Walter, also an elder at Maghera, was indicted for treason in 1797 and released, only to be executed for his part in the Maghera uprising of June 1798.[8]

Glendy was more fortunate. His house was burned,[9] but his family fled to Derry, seeking refuge with relatives. Accused of being a leader of the abortive uprising in Maghera on 7 June 1798, Glendy went into hiding and then reportedly fled in women's clothing. It is unclear whether he was captured or gave himself up. The Synod of Ulster recorded in August 1798 that Glendy was charged with sedition but was permitted by Colonel Leigh (Leith) to transport himself and his property to America.[10] His was one of many cases in which influential friends and relatives negotiated on behalf of rebels with the impromptu local military

2 S. Sidlow McFarland, *Presbyterianism in Maghera: a social and congregational history* (Maghera, 1985), pp 48–9. Glendy's land, Vesper Hill, was a farm that his father bought for him outside town. In 1785 he led the congregation in building a new meeting house and was active in the presbytery of Route.   3 Maghera sported four units. The earliest were the Maghera Volunteers 1st Company, 1783, 1784, 1793, and the Maghera Volunteers 2nd Company in 1783 and 1793. The Maghera First Company of National Guards was formed in 1792. Pádraig Ó Snodaigh, *The Irish Volunteers, 1715–1793: a list of the units* (Dublin, 1995), p. 59. The 20–23 January 1784 issue of the *Belfast News-Letter* names John Glendy in an article mentioning a parade of the Maghera Company. See *Belfast News-Letter* Index Database.   4 See a notice inserted in the *Northern Star,* 29 December 1792, quoted in S. Ó Saothraí, 'Walter Graham of Maghera, United Irishman,' *Ulster Local Studies* 13 (winter 1991), 44–5.   5 McFarland, p. 49. Glendy cut quite a figure in his green uniform faced with yellow and black, its silver buttons engraved with the harp and shamrock.   6 Ibid., p. 50. McFarland notes that the date of the communication was 13 July 1794. The complaint of James Spottswood of the Salters Company in nearby Magherafelt. 7 *Northern Star,* 12 December 1792.   8 Ó Saothraí, 51–2. Walter Graham attended the General Synod of Ulster at Lurgan in 1793 with Glendy.   9 Information about the burning of Glendy's house comes from the Revd Thomas Witherow, *Historical and literary memorials of Presbyterianism in Ireland* (Belfast, second series, 1880) pp 313–4, as noted in S. Ó Saothraí, 'Walter Graham of Maghera', 50.   10 McFarland, pp 51–2, quotes *Records of the General Synod of Ulster,* p.205; Baillie, *A history of congregations in the Presbyterian Church of Ireland, 1610–1982* (Belfast, 1982), 'Maghera,' p. 620. Joseph Waddell, *Annals of Augusta County, from 1726 to 1871* (2nd ed. Harrisonburg, 1972) p. 374 claims that the sentence was banishment.

tribunals held between 24 May and Cornwallis' arrival as lord lieutenant on 20 June 1798, when a less brutal form of justice was instituted.[11]

Glendy, his wife, two sons and three daughters sailed to Norfolk, Virginia.[12] They remained long enough for Glendy to attract attention by his preaching and to realize that his wife's health could not endure the subtropical Norfolk climate. The family was directed instead to the Shenandoah Valley and, in 1799, settled in Staunton, the county seat of the heavily Scotch-Irish Augusta County. Glendy became stated supply to the Presbyterians in the town and to an older rural congregation.[13]

Local Continental Army officers invited Glendy to deliver an oration for Washington's birthday in February 1800. As the first commemoration since Washington's death the previous December, it was a significant occasion. His address was immediately published in Staunton and was later reissued in Baltimore.[14] Surprisingly, Glendy described himself as 'Little schooled in political researches; a stranger to the din of arms and clangor of war ... a foreigner,

---

11 Thomas Bartlett, 'Clemency and compensation: the treatment of defeated rebels and suffering loyalists after the 1798 rebellion' in Jim Smyth (ed), *Revolution, counter-revolution and union: Ireland in the 1790s* (Cambridge, 2000), pp 105–7. 12 The children were Samuel, William, Eleanor, Jane and Mary. The eldest son, Samuel, was named for Glendy's father. William, Eleanor and Mary were named for his siblings. Samuel was lost at sea en route from Havana in 1818. William became a commodore in the United States Navy. Eleanor remained single. Jane married Dr George Sproston of the US Navy, and Mary married Isaac McCauley and lived in Philadelphia. My thanks to H. Jackson Darst of Charles City County, Virginia, for calling my attention to the excellent genealogical work on the Glendy family in Sanford Charles Gladden, *Durst and Darst families of America: with discussions of some forty related families* (Boulder, CO, 1969), pp 517–40. See also his own study of the family, H. Jackson Darst, *The Darsts of Virginia: a chronicle of ten generations in the Old Dominion with sketches of the Cecil, Charlton, Glendy, Grigsby, Larew, Miller, Trolinger, Welch, Wygal and Wysor families* (Williamsburg, VA, 1972). 13 A stated supply was a temporary minister appointed by the regional presbytery to serve a congregation that had no minister. Herbert S. Turner, DD, *Bethel and her ministers, 1746–1946* (Staunton, VA, 1946), pp 78–80. Dorothy Boyd-Rush and Katharine L. Brown, *The history of First Presbyterian Church, Staunton, Virginia, 1804–2004* (Staunton, VA, 2004), pp 15–18; Glendy's place of preaching was probably the old Augusta parish church, which had no Episcopal clergyman to serve it. He was also supply at Bethel Church, located near the farm of several hundred acres that Glendy bought. 14 John Glendy, *An oration on the death of Lieut. Gen. George Washington, composed on the special request of the commandant and his brother officers, of the cantonment in this vicinity, and delivered at Staunton, on the twenty second day of February last past, 1800* (Staunton, 1800). The second edition was printed at Baltimore by Sands & Neilson, 1835. It was signed by Alexander St Clair, chairman of the committee, and John Coalter, secretary. St Clair was a distinguished local figure. He had been named in an act of the Virginia legislature during the revolution as trustee of a manufactory for sail duck to make sails for the Virginia Navy. In 1793, Coalter had become second clerk of the district court at Staunton and was later its judge. He was eventually a judge of the state Court of Appeals and moved to a handsome seat, Chatham, outside Fredericksburg, where he married a sister of Senator John Randolph of Roanoke. Waddell, *Annals of Augusta County*, pp 341, 382.

yea an alien on your shore.' For one fresh from the political and military misery of Ireland, this was something of an understatement.

Glendy purchased an Augusta County farm in 1803, possibly for family still in Ireland whom he was encouraging to emigrate. By that time, however, wider opportunity beckoned him. Thomas Jefferson, who had heard Glendy preach and was impressed, invited him to address Congress. 'Your kind and benevolent recommendation,' Glendy told Jefferson, 'has raised me very high indeed, in the scale of public estimation.'[15] Jefferson also used his influence with General Samuel Smith, congressman and leader of Baltimore's Republicans, to secure a pulpit for Glendy. As a result, Glendy became the pastor of Baltimore's newly formed Second Presbyterian Church.[16] While in that pastorate, Glendy was invited to serve in 1806 as chaplain to the US House of Representatives, and in 1815 as chaplain to the US Senate.[17]

Glendy once told Jefferson 'my heart bleeds for my devoted[?] Country – ah poor Erin!' and wished that the president 'may long live ye darling of ye People, the father of your Country, the firm friend, and [relentless?] Advocate of civil and religious Liberty'.[18] In 1815, Glendy wrote to Jefferson for help in drumming up a congregation to hear him preach in the courthouse at Charlottesville, and hoped for 'the honor of your sitting under my ministry'. He added that he had dined the previous day 'at the peaceful and hospitable board, of President Madison', along with Secretary of State Monroe, whom Glendy found an 'upright, downright Republican' of 'undeviating patriotism'.[19] Bad weather, alas, caused Jefferson to miss Glendy's courthouse sermon by only an hour.[20]

15 John Glendy to Thomas Jefferson, 5 December 1801. Jefferson Papers, Library of Congress. The bearer of the letter to Jefferson was General Samuel Smith, the 49-year old 'tall, handsome, and popular gentleman-merchant and congressman who led the [Republican] faction' in Baltimore. W. Wayne Smith, 'Politics and democracy in Maryland, 1800–1854,' in Richard Walsh and William Lloyd Fox (eds), *Maryland: a history, 1632–1974* (Baltimore, 1974), pp 239–40. 16 Gladden, *Durst and Darst Families of America*, p. 519. See also McFarland, *Presbyterianism in Maghera*, p. 52, and 'John Glendy of Maghera,' *Ulster Journal of Archaeology*, 2nd series (1907) 101–5. Accounts differ somewhat in the chronology of Glendy's move to Baltimore. For nearly a year after August 1803, Glendy travelled between Baltimore and Staunton. On 9 August 1803, Glendy was admitted to the fellowship of the Presbytery of Baltimore. On 9 May 1804, the records of Bethel Church indicate that Glendy moved permanently to Baltimore, according to a manuscript history of Bethel. In December 1804, a committee was formed at Second Presbyterian in Baltimore to see to erecting a church. It called subscribers together on 19 December 1802. A charter was granted on 4 November 1804 and the church was completed in 1805. Glendy was installed in April 1805 and served until 1823, when old age and ill health forced his retirement. See *One hundred fifty years of Second Presbyterian Church*, pp 7–8. 17 I am grateful to John Odell of the United States Senate Commission on Art for supplying me Glendy's dates of chaplaincy service from the *Guide to Congress*, 174-A and from Robert C. Byrd, *The Senate 1789–1989, Historical Statistics 1798–1992*, Volume Four, Bicentennial Edition, edited by Wendy Wolff, US Senate Historical Office (Washington, 1993), pp 660, 637. 18 John Glendy to Thomas Jefferson, Baltimore, 5 December 1801. 19 John Glendy to Thomas Jefferson, Charlottesville, 28 September 1815. 20 Thomas Jefferson to John Glendy,

Glendy not only formed close links with Jefferson and Madison; he also played a crucial role in bringing other rebels to settle in the South and formed close connections with recent immigrants who may have been United Irish sympathizers. From the strong republican sentiments in his letters, it is clear that Glendy shared his political beliefs with his friends and relatives in America. Although few Glendy papers survive, it is possible to piece together parts of the story. An 1818 document from an Augusta County estate settlement reveals that, in 1804, Glendy had brought over most of his extended family. These included his widowed brother, William Glendy, and his children. Glendy's sister, Nancy, and her husband, Robert Guy, Senior, and their children emigrated and brought Eleanor Glendy, the unmarried sister, as well. All of them had been lifelong residents of County Londonderry.[21]

An Augusta County Chancery Court suit reveals a network of connections between Glendy's Maghera and Staunton congregations. In Maghera, Glendy had as his 'singing clerk' – the man who lined out the Psalms to the congregation – one William Herron, whose father and sisters and their husbands were also in his congregation. An older half-brother had immigrated to Virginia prior to Glendy's arrival. Around 1795, Herron came to Virginia to teach school. When Glendy arrived in Staunton, Herron was already living there, and the two became reacquainted. Herron became singing clerk again and sold a horse to Glendy for £20 on credit.[22]

In 1800, Herron drowned while crossing a river. He left no will. His older half-brother, Thomas Herron, was appointed administrator[23] and approached Glendy to collect the £20 the minister owed for the horse. Glendy testified in a deposition in the case that he urged Thomas to keep careful accounts, as he knew that William's sisters in Ireland would claim the estate. Glendy offered to send an account of the estate to Ireland with the news of William's untimely death.[24] By 1802, one sister, Jane Herron, and her husband, Alexander Campbell, emigrated from Maghera to Augusta County and promptly sued Thomas.[25]

What does all of this have to do with United Irishmen? It is likely that many of these immigrants to the Staunton area between 1795 and 1805 were United Irish sympathizers. Some who arrived after 1798 may even have participated in the Rebellion. Family lore in the Glendy-Guy families claims that Glendy's

Monticello, 22 October 1815. Library of Congress, Jefferson Papers. **21** Sworn testimony, Augusta County Order Book 37:197–199, 23 November 1818. **22** Deposition of John Glendy taken 26 April 1803 at James Edmondson's house, Staunton. *Campbell v. Herron*, Augusta County Chancery Court. William's full siblings were Charity Herron, who married Thomas Kyle, Jane Herron, who married Alexander Campbell, and Mary Herron, who married Thomas Mitchell. Thomas Herron was the older half-brother. **23** Deposition of William Blair, Rockingham County, Virginia, 19 February 1807, *Campbell v. Herron*. **24** Glendy deposition, 26 April 1803. **25** The suit dragged on for several years, requiring numerous depositions, including ones from Glendy in Staunton, and another after he had moved to Baltimore.

brother-in-law, Robert Guy, was a United Irishman who had been pressured to leave Ireland.[26] A December 1792 notice in the *Northern Star* indicates that the majority of Glendy's Maghera congregation shared his enthusiasm for the ideals of the United Irishmen. And they were all horrified when their elder, Walter Graham, was executed for his part in the Rebellion. The arrival in Augusta County of members of the Maghera congregation suggests that they were part of that large body of sympathizers with the lost dream of a united Irish republic.

* * *

Petersburg, on the Appomattox River, was another Virginia collecting point for United Irishmen and sympathizers from Ulster. This inland port to the south of Richmond was far to the east of the Scotch-Irish bastion in the Valley of Virginia. The most visible United Irishman in Petersburg was John Daly Burk, a deist from Cork who may have been related to Edmund Burke, and who became the central figure in an émigré community that consisted mainly of Ulster Presbyterians. Burk has been the subject of several monographs and articles and is featured in most studies of the United Irishmen in America.[27] In Ireland, he had been the quintessential student revolutionary;[28] he wrote for the radical *Dublin Evening Post*, was expelled from Trinity College for advocating deism,[29] wrote a blistering pamphlet about his expulsion and helped to found some of the most extreme underground clubs in Dublin.[30] Faced with charges of treason, Burk escaped with the help of a female bookseller, one Miss Daly –

26 'John Glendy of Maghera, County Derry, Presbyterian minister and patriot, 1798,' *Ulster Journal of Archaeology* (August 1907), 101–5; Darst, *The Darsts of Virginia*, pp 191–3, 218; Waddell, *Annals of Augusta County*, 374n. 27 Among those studies are Charles Campbell, *Some materials to serve for a brief memoir of John Daly Burk, author of a History of Virginia. With a sketch of the life and character of his only child, Judge John Junius Burk* (Albany, NY, 1868); Edward A. Wyatt, IV, *John Daly Burk: Patriot playwright historian, Southern Sketches* Number 7, First Series, J.D. Eggleston, General Editor (Charlottesville, VA, 1936); Arthur Shaffer, 'John Daly Burk's *History of Virginia* and the development of American national history,' *The Virginia Magazine of History and Biography* 77(1969), 336–46; Joseph I. Shulim, *John Daly Burk: Irish revolutionist and American patriot* published in *Transactions of the American Philosophical Society*, New Series, 54 (1964); 'John Daly Burk,' *Dictionary of American Biography*, 2:279; 'John Daly Burk,' *Dictionary of Virginia Biography*, ii (Richmond, VA, 2001); 'John Daly Burk,' *Appleton's Cyclopedia of America Biography*, (New York, 1888), i, 453. 28 John Burk, the son of a Cork schoolmaster, entered Trinity College, Dublin as a scholarship student in 1792. Shulim, p. 5. 29 Ibid., n. 1. Dublin newspapers noted the expulsion. See *Dublin Evening Post*, 12 and 15 April 1794. 30 Nancy J. Curtin, *The United Irishmen: popular politics in Ulster and Dublin, 1791–1798* (Oxford, 1994), pp 147–8. The pamphlet, held in the National Library of Ireland, was *The trial of John Burk, of Trinity College, for heresy and blasphemy, before the Board of Senior Fellows. to which is added, his defence containing a vindication of his opinions and a refutation of those inquisitional charges, in which he shews that his opinions are perfectly consonant to the spirit of the Gospel* (Dublin, 1794). Burk's secret societies had ties to the Defenders. William Lawlor was the informant who told the government about Burk.

hence his newly acquired middle name. In what would become something of a cross-dressing United Irish tradition, he disguised himself in women's clothing and took ship for America, arriving in Boston in 1796.[31]

Burk must have been a dynamic, engaging, charismatic figure and one with no small share of sex appeal, as we shall see. On the high seas he wrote a play, *Bunker Hill*, soon produced to acclaim in Boston and New York. In Federalist Boston he founded the city's first daily paper, the *Polar Star*. The similarity in name to the United Irish paper, the *Northern Star*, is hardly coincidental. In New York in 1798 Burk edited the *Time-Piece*, a Republican paper whose patron was probably Aaron Burr. Burk's criticism of President John Adams led to his arrest for seditious libel at the time of the Alien and Sedition Acts. While awaiting trial in 1799, he published a *History of the Irish Rebellion*. During deportation negotiations, fearing that he would be seized by British spies, Burk skipped to Virginia.[32]

Republican friends there appointed him principal of the new Jefferson College in Amelia County. When a trustee charged Burk with making improper advances to his wife, he left, but not before delivering an oration extolling Jefferson's electoral victory. Failing to gain a much-desired federal appointment through Jefferson, Burk settled in Petersburg, practised law and became an American citizen. His wife died after bearing him a son, so Burk moved into the home of Elizabeth Swail, a respectable midwife and native of Ballynahinch, County Down, the site of an important battle in 1798. Burk's reputation was less respectable, for he was named in a paternity suit filed by an unmarried woman.[33]

In Petersburg, Burk collaborated with another United Irish émigré, John McCreery, to produce a book of Irish airs with American lyrics, many written by Burk himself.[34] Burk's most significant publication, however, was his three-volume *History of Virginia*, the first comprehensive history of the state to appear since independence.[35] When Burr came to Petersburg in 1804, a pariah after killing Alexander Hamilton, Burk entertained him lavishly.[36] Burk's death came in 1808 in a duel with a Frenchman. An elaborate funeral procession and burial on the plantation of a prominent leader attested to the affection many Republicans in his adopted state felt for this Irish rebel.[37]

Burk's partner in the Irish music project, John McCreery, was in Petersburg

---

31 Shulim, pp 7–9.   32 Ibid., pp 11–16.   33 Ibid., pp 30–9. The text of Burk's oration was printed in Richmond's *Virginia Argus*, 15 May 1801.   34 *A selection from the ancient music of Ireland, arranged for the flute or violin, some of the most admired melodies, adapted to American poetry. Chiefly composed by John M'Creery to which is prefixed, historical and critical observations on ancient Irish music* (Petersburg, 1824).   35 John Burk, *The history of Virginia from its first settlement to the present day* (Petersburg, 1804–07). For a consideration of the work, see Arthur Shaffer, 'John Daly Burk's *History of Virginia*', 336–46. As Shaffer indicates, in spite of its polemic weakness and its avowedly Jeffersonian view, the history was an important study in its day.   36 Edward Wyatt, *John Daly Burk*, p. 9, indicates that Burk's 1801 letter to Jefferson asking for a non-government appointment spoke of Aaron Burr as having been to Burk 'in the place of a friend and father.'   37 Shulim, pp 48–52; Wyatt indicates that the burial was at Cedar Grove, the plantation of Revolutionary War general Joseph Jones, pp 12–13.

by late 1797, advertising for sale dry goods just imported from Europe. While McCreery is a name of County Tyrone origin, records have not been found to indicate whether John McCreery was an Ulster Presbyterian. Little is known of him, but he appears not to have attained a reputation for fiscal responsibility, much less financial success. When his children received a $2,000 legacy in 1815, it was to be administered, not by their father according to common custom, but by their mother, Mary McCreery, by instruction of the testator, George Magee. The connection with Magee may explain why the United Irishman McCreery came to Petersburg in the first place. Magee was brother-in-law to McCreery's wife. He was a successful Petersburg merchant specializing in tea, raisins, sugar, china, fabrics, Irish whiskey and fiddles.[38] Another Magee brother, Andrew, was also a Petersburg merchant, while a third, John, remained at home in Killegordon townland, Donaghmore parish in the barony of Raphoe, County Donegal.[39] The family names are strongly Protestant and that area of Donegal was still heavily settled with Presbyterians. It would be interesting to investigate whether these Magees were related to John Magee, editor of the pro-United Irish *Dublin Evening Post* for which Burk had written in his student days at Trinity College, Dublin.

Elizabeth Swail, the midwife with whom Burk boarded, is an important link in the Ulster United Irish community in Petersburg.[40] One of her clients was a young woman from Lisburn, County Antrim, Mary Craig Cumming; she was married to William Cumming, a Petersburg merchant who dealt in brown and white Irish linen.[41] In December 1811, soon after her arrival, Mary wrote to her father, Andrew Craig, the Presbyterian minister in Lisburn, that 'Mr Cumming has begun to read [Burk's] the "History of Virginia" to me, I like it very much.'[42] By then, John Daly Burk was three years in his grave, but the new bride had surely heard many tales of his time in Petersburg. When Mary Cumming had a baby in 1812, Elizabeth Swail was the midwife. Her husband wrote to Mary's

38 See ad in the *Petersburg Intelligencer,* 21 January 1803; will of George Magee, 6 June 1815, Petersburg Will Book 2: 114.   39 Killegordon (Killygordon) was a town (not a townland) in Donaghmore parish in the barony of Raphoe, near Stranorlar. *General alphabetical index to the townlands and towns, parishes and baronies of Ireland,* (Baltimore, 2000), p. 578. John received £500 at George's death. Will of George Magee, 6 June 1815. Will Book 2: 114.   40 Suzanne Lebsock, *The free women of Petersburg: status and culture in a southern town, 1784–1860* (New York and London, 1984), pp 73–4, 169. Lebsock, in her pioneering study of Petersburg women, noted the importance of Mrs Swail and her daughter, Ann, as independent women earning their living. 41 See notice of dissolution of partnership between James Cumming (the uncle) and William Cumming in October 1802, with William taking over the business from the uncle. *Petersburg Intelligencer,* January 1803.   42 Mary Cumming to the Revd Andrew Craig, Lisburn, County Antrim, Ireland, 6 December 1811. Mary Cumming letters. The Public Record Office of Northern Ireland, t 1475/2/41–11. Accessed from Emigration Database, Ulster-American Folk Park. The manuscript at PRONI is a typed transcript also available on Virginia Colonial Records microfilm, SR07110, reel #850, University of Virginia Special Collections.

sister in Lisburn, 'Mrs Swail, formerly of Ballynahinch, attended her, she is a great favourite among the ladies here.'[43]

When Elizabeth Swail died in 1813, she left her entire estate to May Leed and Jane Swail of County Down, to Junius Burk, the son of John Daly Burk, and to Valentine Swail of Telecarner in the county of Down.[44] Elizabeth Swail had a possible brother-in-law in Petersburg, Simon Swail, whose 1799 will left 'fifty pounds to my brother Vallentin's son Vall'.[45] William McComb's account of the battle of Ballynahinch refers to Dr Valentine Swail of that town who was an adjutant under the ill-fated commander, Henry Munro. Swail may have been a Volunteer officer prior to that and was apparently a respected local figure. Swail is said to have urged Munro to attack the British forces at night when they were drunk, probably his only chance of victory; Munro refused the advice.[46] A.T.Q. Stewart maintains that following the battle, Swail hid out on the Montalto demesne for several weeks where a servant took him food, and that he eventually received government permission to emigrate with his family for America.[47]

There are numerous others in Petersburg with Ulster backgrounds. That does not guarantee United Irish affiliation or even sympathy, but the likelihood is strong and, when combined with other evidence, becomes even stronger. That it was a tight community is testified by the extent to which its members served as witnesses for wills and as executors and securities for each other's estates. Petersburg residents from Ulster who can be identified through wills include:

43 William Cumming to Margaret Craig, 2 May 1812. Mary Cumming letters. PRONI T1475/2/70–71. These letter have been published. Jimmy Irvine (ed.), *Mary Cumming's letters home to Lisburn from Americas, 1811–1815* (Coleraine, N. Ireland, 1982).   44 Will of Elizabeth Swail, 9 October 1813, proved 2 November 1813. Petersburg Will Book 2: 90. Wills, Petersburg, Virginia, Book 1 and Book 2. Telcarner could not be located in the townlands index, but Tullycarnan, a townland in Ardglass parish in County Down is most likely the location. *General alphabetical index to the townland and towns, parishes and baronies of Ireland*, p. 883. Although Jane Swail cannot be identified for certain, she may have been the Jane Swail who was buried in the Saul parish church in August 1849, age 56. She would have been the right age to be a niece of Elizabeth Swail. Her brother Simon Swail was buried there as well in 1856 at age 75, adding to the likelihood that Simon Swail of Petersburg was a kinsman. Jane was the daughter of John Swail of Bishops Court and his wife, Mary Norris Swail. One might conjecture that the May Leed also mentioned in Elizabeth Swail's Petersburg will was a nickname for Mary Swail Leed, a married sister of Jane. See Volume 7, *Old families of Downpatrick & district* in the County Down Gravestones series.   45 Will of Simon Swail, 3 June 1799. Petersburg Will Book 1, 285. This is probably the extended family of Valentin Swail of Ballynary who died in 1726, age 69, and is buried in the graveyard of Saul Parish Church outside Downpatrick. There, a large raised horizontal stone memorializes Swails of Ballynarry and Bishops Court, a townland in nearby Dunsfort parish. Christian names engraved on the stone, which covers burials between 1726 and 1785, are Valentine, Ada, Ann, John, James and Elizabeth.   46 Kenneth L. Dawson, 'The military leadership of the United Irishmen in county Down, 1796–1798,' in Hill, Turner and Dawson, *1798 Rebellion in County Down*, p. 34. Dawson cites the *Belfast News-Letter*, 12 June 1782 and William McComb, *McComb's guide to Belfast* (Belfast, 1861), p. 138.   47 A.T.Q. Stewart, *The summer soldiers: the 1798 rebellion in Antrim and Down* (Belfast, 1995), p. 220.

Mary Dunn Fleming of County Londonderry, in trade in Petersburg with Thomas Dunn, possibly a brother; Richard Stewart of Armagh; John McConnell; James Cuming and his brother William; John Johnston and his brother Hugh Johnston; Patrick White; William Haxall; Robert Moore and his brother William; James Campbell; William Bowden; Hector McNeill; and Dr Thomas Robinson.[48] Although more work needs to be done on each of these figures, it is clear that Petersburg was an important Southern centre of United Irishmen and that Ulster Presbyterians formed a substantial section of this vibrant community of émigrés.

* * *

Several hundred miles south of Petersburg is Augusta, Georgia, site of another significant colony of United Irishmen and their sympathizers. The most exotic United Irish figure in the town was the radical deist editor Denis Driscol, who had been a Roman Catholic priest and then a Church of Ireland curate in the Old Country. But Driscol was a loner who has left few traces of his links to the wider community to which he belonged. A less well-known United Irishman, the Ulsterman James Bones, merits study precisely because of his connections to a large and influential circle of Ulster Presbyterians in the town. Bones, a farmer and linen bleacher from Duneane parish near Randalstown, married Mary Adams in 1790. Her father, John Adams, came from the Ballymoney area; he was a linen industry innovator who manufactured a blue and white check cloth using a factory system.[49] Bones probably met Mary through her uncle Thomas Adams, a Randalstown merchant.[50]

How and when James Bones and his brother Samuel became United Irishmen

---

48 The identifications of all of these except Robinson are made through Petersburg wills naming parents and siblings in counties of Ulster.   49 James Bones was born in 1767, the third of five sons and one daughter of John Bones, a successful Presbyterian farmer in Duneane Parish near Randalstown, and his wife, Elizabeth Scott of Ballygarvey near Ballymena. Henry Carmichael, 'History of Bones Family,' unpublished typescript, 1949, provided courtesy of two family members, Blanchard and Mary Smith of Alexandria, Virginia, and Robert Roy Goodwin II of Evans, Georgia. Loughguile Parish, where Ballyweeny townland and John Adams' home Chequer Hall are located, was a centre of the linen industry. Lewis, *Topographical atlas of Ireland*, p. 315. Euell Dunlop, compiler, *S Alex Blair's County Antrim characters: 'Portraits from the past' which first appeared in the Ballymena Guardian* (Mid-Antrim Historical Group, 1993), pp 28–30. 50 Randalstown, seventeen miles NW by W from Belfast, was a market town, post-town, and until 1801, an Irish parliamentary borough in the parish of Drummaul and barony of Upper Toome. It was situated on the River Maine at the junction of two mail coach roads to Belfast. The town, a former iron foundry centre, had a bleach green and became a centre of cotton spinning and calico weaving. The mills employed more than 600 in the early nineteenth century. As late as 1830, it had only 618 persons in 113 houses 'neatly built and of pleasing appearance.' Lewis, *Topographical atlas*, i, 484. In the 1830s, the owner of one of those mills was James Black, a man who had strong ties in Augusta, Georgia and Charleston, South Carolina and who visited there in 1837–8.

is unclear, but one of the first societies outside Belfast was in Randalstown.[51] We do know that James was marked on a 1797 list of County Antrim jurors as 'bad in every sense of the term'.[52] Another radical in the family circle was the Revd William Staveley, the father-in-law of Mary Bones' sister. Staveley, who had been active in the Volunteer movement, was minister of the Reformed Presbyterian (Covenanter) congregation at Knockbracken, County Down. In June 1797, when General Lake was suppressing the United Irishmen in Ulster, a cavalry unit raided the Knockbracken meeting house on suspicion of an arms cache and arrested Staveley. He was released from a Belfast prison on lack of evidence of his involvement in hiding arms.[53] Two months later, when it was time for the young United Irish leader, William Orr, to be hanged for treason, Staveley accompanied the young rebel to the gallows outside Carrickfergus.[54] Following the battle of Ballynahinch in June 1798, British troops raided Staveley's meeting house, burned and sacked his house and arrested him. Staveley spent four months on a prison ship in Belfast Lough before the authorities released him for lack of proof.

In June 1798, when the Rebellion broke out in Ulster,[55] the Bones brothers were among the first to march into Ballymena. James was a member of the rebels' republican government there.[56] Both were captured. Samuel was lashed and James was imprisoned. Family tradition tells of a dramatic escape and

51 Local societies met monthly, usually on Sunday evening, and collected a shilling dues from each member, most of which went to superior committees in the structure to pay for printing, for arms and for legal fees. Nancy J. Curtin, 'The United Irish Organization in Ulster: 1795–8.' Dickson et al., *The United Irishmen*, pp 210–12. 52 James B. Hamilton of Ashleigh, Ballymoney to Harvey W. Moore, Concord, NC in 1948, quoted in Carmichael typescript. According to Hamilton, this would mean that he was known to be 'against the government' and would be excluded by the crown prosecutor from any jury in trials of disaffected persons such as United Irishmen. 53 W.D. Bailie, 'Presbyterian clergymen and the county Down rebellion of 1798,' in Myrtle Hill, Brian Turner, Kenneth Dawson (eds), *1798 Rebellion in County Down* (Newtownards, 1998), pp 178–80. 54 Euell Dunlop, compiler, *S Alex Blair's County Antrim characters (3): Final 'Portraits from the past' which first appeared in the Ballymena Guardian.* Mid-Antrim Historical Group 36 (Ballymena, 1997), p. 65. Staveley's wife's farm was beside Orr's farm; the families were neighbours and friends. The brutal hanging took place on Gallows Green, an open plain south of Carrickfergus between the Belfast Road and the lough. Cavalry, infantry and artillery were on hand to keep the peace. Staveley prayed at the foot of the stone gallows as Orr ascended the ladder. Stewart, *The summer soldiers*, pp 40–5. 55 Rebels took Randalstown and sent their Duneane troops to destroy the bridge across the River Bann at Toome, the only link between east and west Ulster. This action lives on in the ballad/folk song about Roddy McCorley, who was hanged on the bridge at Toome in 1799. The Bones brothers may have sat at worship in the Presbyterian meeting house at Duneane with Roddy McCorley when he was a lad. Curtin, 'United Irish organization in Ulster,' 218–19; Stewart, *The summer soldiers*, pp 102–21, 153–6. 56 Stewart, pp 102–21, 129–31. Much of what is known about their participation comes from a statement by another member of the Committee of Safety, Robert Swan of Mount Pleasant, Ballymena, like Bones, a farmer and linen merchant. Some of the references to Bones come from Swan's statement regarding his own conduct on June 7,8,9, to be found in McCance MSS PRONI D 272/31.

sojourn in Jamaica[57] before James returned to Ulster to farm the Ballyportery land of his father-in-law, John Adams, and to bleach linen.[58]

In 1810, after John Adams died, James and Mary Bones sold their inherited farm and took their capital and nine children to Winnsboro, South Carolina, as late Rebellion emigrants.[59] Winnsboro, in the middle of the state, would seem an odd choice of relocation and shows the strength of the family ties that drew them there. Bones' only sister, Jane, and her Antrim-born husband, Andrew Crawford, had settled there around 1795, joining other Ulster immigrants. Family tradition holds that Crawford left Ireland for political reasons, so he too may have been a United Irishman.[60] After James Bones' father died in 1799, his mother joined her daughter in South Carolina.[61] Three other Bones siblings immigrated to South Carolina: Robert, the rebel Samuel, and William, the youngest, who became a successful merchant in Augusta and Charleston.[62]

57 Documentary evidence about James has been hard to find. A note in the McCance papers at PRONI indicates that he was imprisoned in Ballymena. Family tradition has held that he was sentenced to be shot, but that sympathetic guards, on seeing his wife and babe visit, allowed him to escape. An alternate version holds that a friend visited him in prison, exchanged clothes with Bones, and enabled him to escape. A bizarre addition to the escape story is that, on the way to the port, he stopped to get a stone from the Giant's Causeway to take with him into his exile. This, no doubt, explained the presence of such a stone at James Bones' home at the end of his life. There are many other ways the stone could have reached America's shores, as the remainder of this story will make clear. Carmichael typescript.   58 Ballyportery was actually two townlands, probably adjacent, in County Antrim, in the barony of Upper Dunluce and the parish of Loughguile, the same parish in which Chequer Hall was located. Ballyportery North had 345 acres, and Ballyportery South had 272. There is no indication in which the James Bones family lived, or what the size of their farm was. *General alphabetical index to the townlands and towns, parishes and baronies of Ireland based on the census of Ireland for the year 1851* (originally published Dublin, 1861; reprint, Baltimore, 1992), p. 120. John Adams' account books for Chequer Hall show James Bones carrying out linen bleaching and washing activities through the year 1806. PRONI.   59 Last Will and Testament of John Adams Ballymoney in the Parish of Loughgeel and County Antrim Chequer Manufacturer, transcribed in Carmichael transcript. The last of the Adams daughters at Chequer Hall, Anne, died in 1860. See also the Inventory of the Chattel Property of the late John Adams of Chequer Hall PRONI D/1518/2/14.   60 Genealogy of Andrew Crawford and Jane Bones provided by John Foster JCF456@aol.com and by Jim Taylor. Andrew and Jane Crawford apparently lived at Castle Dawson before emigrating.   61 Jane Scott Bones, mother of James, William, Robert, Samuel and Jane, was buried at the Old Brick Associate Reformed Presbyterian Church at Fairfield, South Carolina. This denomination is the representation of the Covenanters (Reformed Presbyterians) and Seceders (Associate Presbyterians) in the Southern states. *The centennial history of the Associate Reformed Presbyterian Church, 1803–1903, prepared and published by order of the Synod* (Charleston, SC, 1905), pp 333–4, 500–1.   62 Rootsweb World Connect Project contains material about Robert Bones, his wife Elizabeth Young, and their daughter Melinda Bones in genealogies posted by Blanchard and Mary Smith and by Elizabeth DuBois Russo. http://worldconnect.genealogy.rootsweb. Family legend recalls that in Winnsboro he encountered a childhood friend, James Adger, from Duneane, and decided to go into business with him in Charleston as Bones & Adger. Locals called the firm 'Bones & Ankle.'

Commercial opportunities in Augusta soon drew the young adults among the Bones children into the town.

For several decades from the early 1790s there was a close-knit Ulster community in Augusta. Its members forged business and marital ties that enabled them to attain economic, political and social influence in Augusta and environs. That some of these members can be clearly identified as sympathetic with, or even participating in, the United Irishmen and the Rebellion of 1798 suggests that the Augusta Ulster community in general shared a broad political outlook that was strongly democratic-republican. When members of the Bones family moved to Augusta, they were incorporated quickly into that community of like-minded persons.

The Ulster community in Augusta coalesced initially around two dynamic young cousins who arrived in the 1790s, John Clarke and John Campbell from Killead parish near Randalstown. Their siblings who remained in Ulster intermarried, providing an extended family pool that would be drawn to Augusta over the next three decades. Whether Clarke and Campbell were United Irishmen or sympathizers remains to be seen. In Augusta, as in Petersburg, uncle-nephew relationships in the mercantile community were often more significant than father-son ties. This was certainly the case from the late 1790s to the 1830s in two large Ulster family circles in Augusta: the Campbell-Clarke-Harper-Bryson network, and the Bones-Adams-Brown connection.

William Bones, the youngest brother of the rebels James and Samuel Bones, was a partner in Augusta of John Campbell from Killead, tying the two family circles together. In 1811, he invited James Bones' eldest son, John, to join him in his fine Irish linen business, which he advertised in the *Augusta Chronicle*, whose editor was the United Irishman Denis Driscol.[63] As time went on, John Bones became a business mentor to his own younger brothers and then eventually to their sons and to younger relatives from Ireland. John Campbell, William Bones' former partner, brought over the three sons of his sister Ellinor from near Randalstown to train as merchants in Augusta. In time, they started their own businesses in the community.[64]

Many in the Ulster community in Augusta became wealthy and took on various leadership roles in town. That was certainly true of banking. In 1822, for example, six of the fifteen directors of the Bank of Augusta were Ulstermen with ties to the Bones circle. Five Antrim men were directors of the Augusta Banking and Insurance Company.[65] A number of Ulster immigrants owned fine

63 *Augusta Chronicle*, 1 January 1813. 64 John Campbell, Augusta, to Thomas Allen, Belfast, 5 April 1820, PRONI T/3597/4 Emigration Database #930022. 65 *Augusta Chronicle*, 18 April 1822; 29 April, 1 November 1828. John Moore, John Carmichael, John Bones, Hugh Nesbitt, John Campbell and John Clarke were Ulstermen, and all but Moore from Antrim. The other bank directors included Samuel Clarke, John Bones, William Bones, James Harper and William Harper.

townhouses and plantations. In the 1820s, John Bones purchased Cedar Grove in Edgefield County, South Carolina, as a gift for his parents, James, the United Irishman, and Mary Adams Bones. In antebellum Augusta, as in Petersburg, Virginia, plantations and fine townhouses meant slave ownership. As David Wilson observed in *United Irishmen, United States,* the radical egalitarianism of United Irishmen and their sympathizers who settled in the South was never understood to extend to African Americans. Driscol, the United Irish editor of the *Augusta Chronicle,* opposed slavery when he arrived in America but soon began to adopt mainstream Southern white views on the subject.[66]

Many members of the Antrim circle in the Augusta area held slaves. James Bones' son Thomas owned fifteen slaves when he died in 1822.[67] Descendants of William Bones still sang a lullaby in the 1950s handed down in the family from a slave nurse who was purchased at Savannah directly off the ship from Africa.[68] There were, nonetheless, several in the Ulster community in Petersburg whose wills manumitted slaves and provided for their support and care. Richard Stewart from County Armagh freed 'my mulatto girl Eliza' in his 1797 will.[69] George Magee provided that his slave Jack would be freed when his brother Andrew no longer needed him.[70]

The family networks and marriage patterns that emerged among the Ulster Scots in Ulster contradict James Leyburn's contention that these later Ulster immigrants operated as individuals rather than as a self-conscious ethnic group and his view that they quickly blended into their adopted culture.[71] In fact, most of them married other Ulster immigrants or children of immigrants, while others returned home to Ireland to claim brides. Those who married American men and women without Ulster roots selected them from a narrow circle of business associates and church members with whom the Ulster community mixed.

The length and strength of ties to the homeland is another measure of adaptation. Surviving correspondence from Petersburg, especially from Mary Cumming to her Craig family in Lisburn and from members of the Bones, Brown, Campbell and Moore families in Augusta, suggests that these Ulster immigrants maintained strong ties to Ireland. For half a century, little took place in Augusta or Petersburg that was not broadcast within weeks in the environs of Randalstown, Ballymoney, Lisburn or Maghera.[72]

---

66 Wilson, *United Irishmen, United States,* p. 9.   **67** Thomas Bones inventory and appraisement of the estate in Oglethorpe County, 1822. Richmond County Probate Court, Book C, 150–152. **68** 'Tales retold by Margaret Jordan Johnson and Floride Cantey Johnson, September 1953.' Typescript circulated among family members. The version I used was #32 of a limited mimeograph edition of fifty given to the Duke family by Margaret Johnson, one of the compilers, and lent to me by Jinx Duke of Atlanta.   **69** Will of Richard Stewart, 31 January 1797. Petersburg Will Book 1.   **70** Will of George Magee, 6 June 1815. Will Book 2: 114.   **71** Leyburn, 270, 318–9.   **72** For examples of letters back home from these families see John Bones, Augusta to the Revd William Staveley, Ballybollan, Ballymoney, 5 April 1815. PRONI D1835/27/1/2; John Moore, Augusta, to Eleanor Wallace, Newtownards, 8 April 1843. PRONI D1558/1/2/42.

Some immigrants returned occasionally to Ireland, stopping first in Liverpool to select merchandise for their stores or to sell cotton or tobacco. One of the earliest return visits for which evidence survives is also one of the most touching; it occurred in 1822 and is documented in stone. Just inside the gate at Duneane parish church is a lone headstone to John Bones, father of the United Irishmen Samuel and James, and of the successful Charleston merchant, William. John Bones died in 1799 at the age of sixty-six.

> *As a tribute of filial gratitude*
> *To one of the best of Parents,*
> *This stone is erected by an affectionate*
> *Son, who, after a long absence from*
> *His native country, visits the*
> *Grave of his Father with feelings*
> *Of undiminished regret.*
> *1st Septr. 1822*

Even for those who could not return to Ireland, there were many means of maintaining ethnic identity. With the United Irishman Denis Driscol as its editor until 1820, the *Augusta Chronicle* carried considerable Irish news, poetry and stories, some reprinted from other Irish-American papers. Such articles were also the focus of newly established Irish-American newspapers such as the *Irishman and Charleston Weekly Register*, a paper said to be 'Tolerant in its principles' and which was heavily promoted in Augusta in 1829.[73] Examples of reprinting Irish-American material can be found in the *Augusta Chronicle* at least as late as 1829, long after Driscol's departure from the paper.[74]

Another expression of ethnic identity was the Saint Patrick's Day celebration, which reached back to at least the 1790s in Augusta and which attracted both Presbyterian and Catholic Irish immigrants. Typically, a few days before 17 March, instructions appeared in the newspaper for members of the Irish Volunteers militia unit to convene at their usual parade ground on Green Street at nine o'clock fully equipped. In 1828, for example, plans called for the company to march to the Catholic church, 'where an oration appropriate to the occasion will be delivered by Alexander Mackey, Esq., a member of the corps'.[75]

Emigration Database #9803625, Ulster-American Folk Park, Centre for Migration Studies; Henry Moore, Augusta to W.J.C. Campbell, Belfast, 11 May 1835. PRONI 1558/1/1. See also miscellaneous entries in the James Black of Randalstown diary. 1837–1844. PRONI. For Mary Cumming see Mary Cumming, Blandford, Virginia, to Margaret Craig, Strawberry Hill, Lisburn, 2 January 1814, reprinted in Kerby A. Miller, Arnold Schreier, Bruce D. Boling, David N. Doyle, *Irish immigrants in the land of Canaan: letters and memoirs from colonial and revolutionary America, 1675–1815* (New York, 2002), pp 369–75. **73** *Augusta Chronicle,* 3 June, 6 June 1829. **74** *Augusta Chronicle,* 4 April 1828. **75** *Augusta Chronicle,* 14 March 1828.

The fact that an Ulster Presbyterian (for such Mackey almost certainly was) would deliver his speech at the Catholic church indicates a significant degree of cooperation between the Ulster Presbyterian and Irish Catholic immigrant groups in Augusta and suggests that the United Irish emphasis on national commonalty rather than religious difference was stronger in Augusta than it was becoming in Ireland.

Plans for the patron saint's celebration in Augusta for 1829 were especially elaborate. The Irish Volunteers held their usual morning parade and muster for the general public. The evening program featured a dinner at the Mansion House, a leading Augusta hotel, whose proprietor, Mr Shannon, may have been Irish. The *Augusta Chronicle* reported that those giving toasts were Edward J. Black, Colonel McGran, John Moore, John Bones, the Revd J. McEnroe, Samuel A. Plummer, Samuel Rea, William Wallace, George Dunbar, William Logan and Colonel Gould. The list included most of the leaders of the Ulster business community in Augusta. But it is especially important to note that among those offering toasts was the Revd J. McEnroe, the local Catholic parish priest.[76]

A Saint Patrick's Day celebration had also long been held in Charleston, where the Hibernian Society had a handsome Greek Revival temple in which to meet. When James Black, a cotton manufacturer from Randalstown with business and family ties in Charleston and Augusta, visited Charleston in March 1838, he recorded that 'the 17th being St Patrick's day I dined at the Hibernian Society with 85 and had a very pleasant time, fine music and singing, band and piano and singers from the Theatre. S. Clarke and Jno. [Bones?] of Augusta came all the way to join us'.[77]

Given the strong United Irish presence in Augusta, it is not surprising that the town became a centre of support for Daniel O'Connell's Catholic Emancipation campaign. In 1827, Augusta's Friends of Civil and Religious Liberty appointed a committee to prepare an address of solidarity with the Catholic Association of Ireland. That committee included two leaders of the Ulster community, the brothers-in-law John Moore and John Bones.[78] The *Augusta Chronicle* gave considerable space to the parliamentary debate over the Catholic Emancipation Bill in 1829 and expressed its pleasure when O'Connell took his seat in the House of Commons.[79]

Just as the sons were following in their United Irish fathers' footsteps by supporting Catholic Emancipation, they also carried on the traditions of the Irish Volunteers and United Irishmen by enrolling in local militia units. It is no

76 *Augusta Chronicle*, 21 March 1829.   77 James Black diary, 19 March 1838. PRONI.
78 *Augusta Chronicle*, 7 April 1827. The address, presented in April 1827, is remarkable for its peculiarly Southern slant on the Irish problem. It answered the oft-voiced criticism of Southerners for practising slavery by hastening to tell the Irish Catholic world that poor Catholic tenants in Ireland had fewer religious rights than slaves in America.   79 *Augusta Chronicle*, 22 April, 29 April, 6 May 1829.

coincidence that one of Augusta's militia companies called itself the Irish Volunteers or that John Bones' first appearance in the public record was in connection with militia duties in the defence of Savannah as the war of 1812 loomed.[80] After watching a militia muster in Augusta in November 1809, Driscol wrote that 'If an Irishman was there, to be sure the cockles of his heart would not be raised to see Americans march to Irish music!'[81]

The United Irish immigrants in the three communities examined here maintained a lively interest in public affairs, as the letters and orations of Glendy, Burk and the Bones family attest. The commitment to Jefferson of the United Irish sympathizers who had come to America around 1800 was strong, as David Wilson has made clear. There are also examples of that commitment from a later period. One comes from the *Augusta Chronicle* of 12 July 1826, which reported on the city's celebration of the fiftieth anniversary of the Declaration of Independence. A great crowd that assembled at City Hall to honour Jefferson was made aware of the former president's 'pecuniary embarrassment', and appointed a committee to send contributions to him. John Bones, the son of an imprisoned United Irishman and old enough to remember the Rebellion of 1798, was named to the committee.[82] The action was too late, of course, for as the Augusta citizens assembled at their City Hall, the author of the Declaration of Independence lay dying at Monticello. In the black-bordered issue of 15 July the editor wrote of Jefferson: 'A mighty spirit of the age – great in life and glorious in death – has winged its flight to eternity.'[83]

This brief foray to three Southern communities into which United Irishmen immigrated and eventually integrated suggests that this may be the proverbial tip of the iceberg. A more systematic and detailed study of a larger number of Southern communities, both on the coast and in the backcountry, linking American sources and records in Ireland, should lay to rest the idea that Scotch-Irish in the South derive almost entirely from colonial immigrants who were farmers. Such a study is likely to show a more complex and sophisticated economic network and should also illuminate our understanding about politics and acculturation in the early republic. Not every immigrant with a United Irish link will be as dramatic or vocal a figure as John Glendy or John Daly Burk. But each story will widen our perspective on this remarkable group of immigrants in the young republic and modify and refine our understanding of the Scotch-Irish community in the American South.

80 *Augusta Chronicle,* 24 July 1812. 81 Wilson, *United Irishmen, United States,* p. 111.
82 *Augusta Chronicle,* 12 July 1826. 83 *Augusta Chronicle,* 15 July 1826.

John Caldwell's memoir: a case study in Ulster–American radicalism

DAVID A. WILSON

In 1849, John Caldwell, the veteran Irish-American radical whom Lord Castlereagh once described as 'the Chancellor of the Exchequer' of the United Irishmen, decided to write his autobiography. His close friends and the younger cousins of his extended American family had long been urging him to record the stories that he told, and he had made intermittent attempts to accede to their wishes. Now, approaching his eightieth birthday, he must have been conscious that time was running out. And so, he cast his mind back to his early days in Ballymoney and Belfast, his education at Bromley Academy in England, his activities with the United Irishmen, his arrest, imprisonment and exile to the United States, and his new life in the new republic. Gathering together the memoranda, letters and diaries that he had brought to his home in Salisbury Mills, New York, he sat down at his desk and put pen to paper. Thus began his 'Particulars of History of a North County Irish Family', one of the most illuminating, perceptive and engaging accounts of middle-class Ulster Presbyterian radicalism that has ever been written.[1]

The timing of his memoir was not only related to his age and the encouragement of his family; it was also connected to the immediate political context of 1849. Since the previous autumn, a stream of revolutionary refugees from the Young Ireland Rising of 1848 had been pouring into New York, the heartland of Irish-American nationalism. From their American base, they attempted to continue the struggle for Irish independence. Some talked about avenging Ireland by invading Canada, while others emphasized the importance of sending moral and monetary support to the secret revolutionary cells that still existed in and around Dublin. All of them harboured a deep hatred of England, which was only equalled by the intensity of their mutual recriminations for the humiliating fiasco of their failed rebellion.

---

1 John Caldwell, 'Particulars of history of a north county Irish family,' Public Record Office of Northern Ireland (henceforth PRONI), T 3541/5/3, 1, 99, 153. This is a 162-page typescript of the original document. The memoir includes family correspondence dating back to 1760; it also draws on Caldwell's autobiographical writings from the 1820s. Henceforth, all references to the memoir are in brackets in the text. Caldwell was born in Ballymoney on 3 May 1769, and died at Salisbury Mills on 7 May 1850; see *Nation*, 6 July 1850 for his obituary, which makes no mention of his memoir.

Observing these developments closely, and experiencing a strong sense of *déjà vu*, were the few surviving members of the first wave of Irish revolutionary nationalist exiles, the men who had created Irish-American nationalism, the United Irishmen in the United States. Most of the leading *émigrés* had long since died – John Daly Burk in 1808, Thomas Addis Emmet in 1827, William James MacNeven in 1841. But men like John Caldwell in New York and John Binns in Philadelphia remained; indeed, Binns was still playing an active role in organizations like the Friends of Ireland and supported Irish American newspapers such as the New York *Nation*. It is no coincidence that Binns and Caldwell both wrote their memoirs in the aftermath of the Young Ireland migration to the United States, and against the background of Richard R. Madden's popular *The United Irishmen: Their Lives and Times*. These men had their own tales to tell, in their own ways – Binns in the form of a book and Caldwell in the form of a family manuscript that he half-hoped might be published one day.[2]

Although Caldwell's memoir has, regrettably, still not been published, it has become an important source for historians of late eighteenth-century Ulster and of the United Irishmen in the United States.[3] But the work has never been considered as a coherent whole and studied in its own right. Around a hundred and twenty thousand words long, it is rich in detail about the cultural milieu of late eighteenth-century County Antrim, and about the familial, religious and social contexts in which Presbyterian radicalism could flourish. The memoir also reveals a great deal, in ways that its author never intended, about hidden tensions within the Ulster-American connection. The political convergence between Ulster Presbyterian radicalism and Jeffersonian democracy was accompanied by a cultural divergence that left Caldwell in a deeply ambivalent position. He identified completely with the American political system, but was culturally alienated in his new home. In this respect, as in others, his experience was shared by many of the Young Ireland *émigrés* who followed in his footsteps.

* * *

The first thing to note about Caldwell's memoir is its title; he described himself as part of a 'North County Irish Family', and not as an 'Ulster Scot'. Caldwell was writing as an Irishman who lived in the north, rather than as an Ulster Scot

2 Richard R. Madden, *The United Irishmen: their lives and times* (Dublin, 1846); *Nation*, 24 June 1848; [New York] *Nation*, 23 October 1849; John Binns, *Recollections of the life of John Binns* (Philadelphia, 1854). 3 See, for example, A.T.Q. Stewart, *A deeper silence: the hidden origins of the United Irishmen* (London, 1993), pp 53–4; A.T.Q. Stewart, *The summer soldiers: the 1798 Rebellion in Antrim and Down* (Belfast, 1995), pp 141–7; Michael Durey, *Transatlantic radicals and the early American Republic* (Lawrence, KS, 1995), passim; David A. Wilson, *United Irishmen, United States: immigrant radicals in the early Republic* (Ithaca, 1998), passim; John Caldwell, Jr., 'Exiled to New York! A United Irishman's memories,' *New York Irish History* 13 (1999), 4–9.

who lived in Ireland; this applies in general to the Presbyterian leaders of the
United Irishmen. Nevertheless, he was inescapably influenced by his ethno-
religious origins. The Caldwell family was part of a tightly knit kin group –
cousins kept marrying cousins – whose ancestors had come from Scotland to
Antrim and Tyrone during the second half of the seventeenth century. Such
intermarriage was common among Ulster Presbyterians and served as a kind of
defence mechanism in an alien and sometimes hostile environment. The first
Ulster Caldwells had been 'deeply impressed with hatred against the Catholic
Church whose persecutions they could not forgive nor forget, but determined to
retaliate with a vengeance now that they possessed the power' (p. 1). Two of
Caldwell's great-uncles remained family heroes for their role in resisting the
siege of Derry in 1688–9 (p. 4). And in 1760, his great-aunt Catherine Ball wrote
that her uncle William was 'for ever dreaming of plots, conspiracies and rebel-
lions, and … thinks he sees a murderer or assassin in every unfortunate Papist
that he meets' (p. 8).

Caldwell could understand such feelings, even though he rejected them
himself. His ancestors in Scotland really had experienced persecution, he
argued, and it was not surprising that anti-Catholic prejudices had been transmitted through the generations (p. 64). But within the Caldwell family during
the second half of the eighteenth century, the views of men like uncle William
appeared increasingly anachronistic. The defeat of Irish Jacobitism, the political
realignment of the remaining Catholic aristocracy, and the increasing social
connections between Catholic and Protestant middle classes all created conditions in which the 'radical' component of the Ulster Presbyterian 'settler radical'
mentality became increasingly influential. If there ever had been a need for legislation to guard against Catholic tyranny, reasoned Caldwell, that time had long
since passed.

In the case of the Caldwells, the shift toward radicalism was facilitated by the
remarkably powerful, well-educated and intelligent women in the family. His
great-aunt Catherine Ball played a particularly important role; a single woman,
she had run the household after John Caldwell's grandfather (Catherine's
brother-in-law) had died. Her own father, John Ball, had been a 'liberal' and
'enlightened' Presbyterian minister from Donegal (p. 5), and Catherine had
imbibed his views. Equally impressive was Caldwell's aunt Sibella. Disfigured
after an illness in her youth, and single all her life, she memorized much of the
Bible, devoured the works of Milton, Pope and Swift, and wrote admiringly of
America (pp 7, 17). Catherine and Sibella were doubtless among the
Presbyterian women of Ballymoney who supported American independence
with their tongues and their needles, as Caldwell put it; they argued in favour of
the revolutionary movement and knitted clothes for its soldiers (p. 4). Within
their own sphere, such women could and did exert immense influence.

There was, in fact, no clear distinction between domestic relations and democratic politics in the Caldwell family. In contrast to the 'Patriarchial [*sic*] Aristocracy' that traditionally characterized relations between fathers and sons in Presbyterian Ulster – and not just Presbyterian Ulster – the Caldwell family emphasized the importance of tender feelings and mutual respect. As Caldwell pointed out, many fathers refused to show affection to their sons and adopted attitudes that 'approached to tyranny'. Relations between fathers and the eldest sons who expected to inherit the land, he continued, were fraught with 'hatred and animosity' (p. 31). During the 1790s, such generational conflicts would often assume political forms; in many cases, the young men who joined the United Irish underground in 1797 and 1798 were rebelling against parental authority as well as British rule.

Even in the relatively close-knit Caldwell family, something of the sort happened. Although the family was well known for its liberal and 'enlightened' values, there were significant generational differences over the question of revolutionary nationalism. John Caldwell senior doubtless sympathized with the objectives of the United Irishmen, but he also believed that a rising would only result in 'slaughter and death', that it would actually postpone the day of freedom, and that peaceful agitation for parliamentary reform would be much more effective. As a result, John Caldwell junior and his brother Richard concealed their revolutionary activities from their father; in retrospect, they would have been better off listening to him (pp 107–8).

The Caldwell family was not only more liberal than most; it was also much richer. As a wealthy linen merchant and substantial landowner, John Caldwell senior was a leading local member of the Presbyterian middle class that had prospered from participation in the Atlantic economy. Among other things, this meant that he could afford to give his children a good education; John junior would attend one of the best-known schools in England. His earliest education, however, took place in Ballymoney and Derry.

As a young boy in Ballymoney, he was taught the rudiments of writing and arithmetic in a small school run by one Mrs Spence and her daughter Miss Cicely. Mrs Spence, recalled Caldwell, believed that fear was a useful stimulus to learning, and scared her slower students with a 'Hobgoblin, a frightful figure on the stairs'. Her daughter preferred physical methods and attempted to instill knowledge through the use of the strap. 'Thus,' commented Caldwell, 'by flagellation of bottom and terror of mind was the science of A.B.C. attempted to be inculcated on the dear little girls and boys of the Town of Ballymoney' (p. 2). Later in life, though, Miss Cicely's students got their revenge by putting cayenne pepper in her snuff box, or placing a grain of gunpowder in her pipe.

After surviving the hobgoblin and the rod, Caldwell was sent to Thomas Templeton's school in Derry; here, the standard form of punishment was being sent to 'a terrific place called the black hole' – good training, he ruefully remarked, for his subsequent imprisonment as a United Irishman (p. 3). Central

to the curriculum was the story of the siege of Derry; 'the cherished history of
that chivalrous act was almost a part of our scholastic exercises', he recalled.
There is no doubt that Caldwell was deeply impressed with the men – including,
of course, his own ancestors – who withstood the siege. The 'zenith of its glory'
came when the Apprentice Boys closed the gates, he wrote, and when the 'brave
little garrison' stood firm in the face of 'treachery, cowardice and timidity within
the walls and an infuriated foe without'. By August 1689, he continued, they
were eating dogs and rats and had been reduced to 'walking shadowy skeletons',
when the British fleet broke the boom and relieved the city (p. 3).

In taking this position, Caldwell revealed the underlying tensions that
remained within the settler-radical position. On the one hand, he wrote with
genuine feeling about the Ulster Catholics who had been 'evicted, slaughtered,
driven to the mountains, or compelled to flee by their ruthless invaders the
Saxons' (p. 1) and noted that the estate of one of his ancestors was 'probably the
spoils of some slaughtered or persecuted aboriginal inhabitant' (p. 5). On the
other, he was proud of 'the gallant deeds of our forefathers' (p. 3) as they resisted
a native Catholic army that had given hope to the dispossessed. Like other
Protestant radicals, Caldwell sustained this apparently contradictory position by
reinterpreting the Glorious Revolution as part of a general struggle for civil and
religious liberty, and by downplaying its anti-Catholic dimensions. In effect, the
radicals were trying to take over the symbolism of the siege from Whigs and
loyalists, and aimed to connect the deeds of their forefathers with the ideological
imperatives of the American and French revolutions.[4]

* * *

Radical Presbyterians in Ulster were mesmerized by the myth of America. The
Caldwells, in common with Presbyterians of all political stripes, were a transatlantic family. During the early eighteenth century, some of them had founded
the town of Londonderry in New Hampshire, while others had become leading
merchants in Philadelphia. Well before the American Revolution, the Caldwells
in Ballymoney looked across the Atlantic with a sense of longing; they were
eager to emigrate in theory, but reluctant to leave in practice. Ireland,
commented John senior, was 'doomed to years, perhaps ages of suffering and
distress' (p. 15). Catholics were persecuted on the grounds that they were
ignorant and violent, argued the Caldwells, and were kept ignorant and violent
by the very act of persecution. Agrarian secret societies such as the Whiteboys
and Hearts of Steel were spreading fear and terror throughout the land, while
'bigotry and arbitrary misrule' (p. 22) were tearing the country apart. 'Could our
brother [John senior] dispose of the family property,' wrote Sibella in 1771, 'we

4 Ian McBride, *The siege of Derry in Ulster Protestant mythology* (Dublin, 1997), pp 32–45.

would all take leave of this unsettled, distracted country' (p. 17). For John senior, writing in 1774, America was a 'happy land' (p. 15) of religious liberty, economic opportunity and political enlightenment, which provided an 'asylum in the wilds' for those who struggled in vain against 'the benighted countries of Europe' (p. 22). There might not have been an actual heaven on earth, but America was as close as it came.

All this was intensified by the American Revolution. When news of the battle of Bunker Hill reached north Antrim in 1775, bonfires lit the midsummer sky to celebrate 'the triumph of America over British despotism' (p. 4). (Meanwhile, further to the south, Irish Catholics celebrated the same battle – which the Americans actually lost – as a victory of American Jacobites over British Whigs.)[5] John Caldwell was six years old; he remembered that his nurse, Ann Orr, took him to the Ballymoney bonfire. 'Look, Johnny dear, look yonder at the west,' she said. 'There is the land of liberty and there will be your country' (p. 4). He also recalled the meetings of the 'little club' his father attended every Wednesday night in Ballymoney:

> On hearing the news from America favourable to their cause, the entire village indeed seemed but as one family united in praying for success for their efforts. This union continued until the famous declaration of the 4th of July 1776 arrived, when Mr Lecky withdrew from the club, and his brethren of the village, who were members of the Established Church thought it incumbent upon them to join in the hue and cry against the rebels, who had proclaimed civil and religious liberty throughout their land. (p. 4)

The split in the Ballymoney club reflected wider divisions within Ulster Protestantism. Most Anglicans drew the line at American independence, as, indeed, did many Presbyterians, while a radical minority continued to embrace the revolutionary cause. As part of this minority, the Caldwells were active participants in the Volunteer movement during the American war, and began in 1783 to argue for Catholic emancipation. In the teeth of considerable opposition, John Caldwell senior, the commander of the Ballymoney Volunteers, secured the election of 'the first Catholic, who bore arms in the Volunteer Army of Ulster', the 'worthy and respectable' Daniel Maxwell. 'From this time forward', wrote John junior, 'bigotry and the little trying sectarian persecutions, which the law authorised and the government fomented or winked at, began to disappear and prepare the way for union of sentiment and feeling' (p. 63).

There was a considerable degree of wishful thinking here; the 'union of

5 Breandán Ó Buachalla, 'From Jacobite to Jacobin,' in Thomas Bartlett, David Dickson, Dáire Keogh and Kevin Whelan (eds), *1798: a bicentenary perspective* (Dublin, 2003), p. 81.

sentiment and feeling' remained more of an aspiration than a reality. But Caldwell's comment about government-sanctioned bigotry and the accumulated impact of 'little trying sectarian persecutions' testifies to his deep alienation from the political and religious system in Ireland. Like most Presbyterians, he resented the power and privilege of the established church. Although Presbyterians were able to vote, subject to property qualifications, and could in theory sit in parliament, the Test Act of 1704 had effectively excluded them from all civil and military offices. They were forbidden to teach in schools, they had to pay tithes to the established church, and their marriages were not legally recognized.[6] 'I might have been considered illegitimate ...', wrote Caldwell, 'if my father and mother had not been married in the parish church, such was the blessed and loving kindness of the Established Church towards Protestant dissenters' (p. 20). Largely as a result of pressure from the Volunteers, the government grudgingly lifted the Sacramental Test for office holding in 1780, and repealed the marriage legislation in 1782. But memories of Anglican discrimination continued to rankle, grievances about tithes persisted, and Caldwell carried on the long family history of opposition to the Protestant Ascendancy, even though he had good personal relations with many Anglicans of comparable social status.

The fundamental problem with Ireland's polity, in Caldwell's view, was that it institutionalized sectarianism; if Presbyterians had experienced discrimination, Irish Catholics had endured oppression. Four-fifths of his countrymen, he wrote, were bound in chains; the 'diabolical policy' of the government had 'provoked and furthered disunion and increased ignorance, superstition and bigotry in a ten fold degree to whatever had been before' (p. 63). All this was buttressed by a 'system of corruption' (p. 63) in which the government bought off its opponents, and the landlords had the franchise sewn up. The economic power of the Ascendancy was perpetuated by the 'unjust institution' of primogeniture, which discriminated against the younger sons (who were consequently 'brought up in reckless idleness and dissipation,' and wound up 'in the Church, the Army, the Navy, or the Pension List'), and which frequently led to the 'utter destitution of the female branches' of the family (p. 53). Corruption, bigotry, persecution, discrimination, oppression and exploitation were the central characteristics of Ascendancy rule, and the social violence of agrarian secret societies was one of the major symptoms; in short, Caldwell believed, the politics of the country were rotten to the core.

But his scathing indictment of Ascendancy rule coexisted with warm, affectionate and humorous accounts of Irish cultural life; Caldwell's memoir crackled with energy when it described the people in and around Ballymoney. There were stories about women like Jenny Valentine, the servant girl who became Lady

6 Ian McBride, 'Presbyterians in the penal era,' *Bullán* 1: 2 (autumn, 1994), 73–86.

Adair after a secret marriage to Sir Robert Adair, an 'eccentric old man of good estate'. Sir Robert's family, believing him to be 'in a state bordering on dotage', had attempted to keep the couple apart; when he died shortly after the honeymoon, they fought the will and pressured Jenny Valentine to relinquish her title, without success. The 'rabble,' Caldwell wrote, 'entered the lists against her'; in contrast, he admired her resourcefulness and tenacity (pp 11–13).

Or again, there was the story of Janet Knox, the 'crazy woman' who once stopped a man from snoring during a Presbyterian service by spitting a plug of tobacco down his open and unsuspecting mouth (pp 17½–18). Caldwell also remembered the hospitality and communalism of Irish life – the nights spent with friends and family, with fiddle music, dancing and storytelling; the festivals when 'we were free from all check and restraint … enjoying all the pleasures of unrestrained merriment and romping'; the trips to Dunluce Castle and the Giant's Causeway on the Antrim Coast, and the 'yearly excursions to the Moravian settlement near Ahoghill and Ballymena' (pp 30–1).

Partly to preserve for posterity a way of life that had disappeared, and partly to demonstrate that Irish culture had deep roots in antiquity, Caldwell supplemented his anecdotes with accounts of 'the manners and customs that prevailed in my early life' (p. 27). He had been deeply moved by the *caoineadh*, or 'Irish Howl', and defended it against the condescension of its English critics. Following in the footsteps of Charles Vallancey, he traced the custom back to the Romans and Greeks, and argued that it had been brought into Ireland by 'a colony of Phoenicians'.[7] 'The Southern neighbours of the Irish,' he commented, 'affect to laugh at and ridicule this custom or ceremony as they do a number of others, but I contend that there are strong historical proofs of their origin, aye and of their civilization too, when the Saxons, Danes, Normans and painted savages were nearly in a state of barbarism' (p. 28). He applied the same argument to Irish wake customs, noting that they permeated all levels of society. It was quite common in wealthier families, he wrote, for the patriarch of the family to exert his control even after death by giving detailed instructions about which class of people were to be entertained in which rooms, who should be out in the barn, and how they should be treated. This was, it is clear, a highly status-conscious society.

Caldwell also recorded the traditional gender divisions in rural Ulster. As elsewhere in Ireland, women were associated with the Otherworld; it was women who keened at funerals and it was women who had the 'second sight'. He recalled that 'the Spae woman of our village' claimed to have predicted the death of the earl of Antrim, since she had heard the Banshee of Dunluce cry a

7 On the view that Irish customs were derived from the Phoenicians, see Joep Leerssen, *Remembrance and imagination: patterns in the historical and literary representation of Ireland in the nineteenth century* (Dublin, 1996), pp 68–77.

fortnight earlier. This greatly enhanced her reputation as a prophetess, he remarked, particularly among those who did not reflect that 'the calamity had taken place previous to the prediction being announced'; predicting the past was always safer than foretelling the future (pp 31–3).

The gender divisions were most marked, however, in traditions about rural work. 'I recollect in early life,' wrote Caldwell, 'how tenacious each sex, particularly the working classes, was of their respective avocations.' It 'would have been thought out of all rule for a man to milk a cow, or a woman to weave', he noted, 'and yet the poor woman, tho' not permitted to throw the shuttle, would be indulged in the most masculine labour of the potatoe garden and the harvest field, whilst the old men and the boys would be indolently knitting stockings and making fishing nets'. 'Happily for society,' he added, 'these prejudices are giving way to better feelings and the industry and talents of both sexes are less restricted' (p. 120); in this respect, nineteenth-century New York appeared to be much more liberal and progressive than eighteenth-century Antrim.

Gender divisions aside, Caldwell generally took a sympathetic approach to Irish rural traditions. Although wakes sometimes led to 'excesses' (p. 28), he argued, they provided a structured way of coping with grief and affirmed community solidarity in the face of death; similarly, he viewed the *caoineadh* as a means of sharing sorrow. Because he believed that such customs were socially beneficial, and because he located them in 'venerable antiquity' (p. 28) rather than dismissing them as 'romish superstitions' (p. 30), he did not share the zeal of moral reformers who were trying to impose respectable rationalism on rural society.

Nevertheless, he believed that these customs belonged to the 'primitive simplicity' (p. 28) of the past, and that enlightened liberalism was the key to the future. His comments about rural customs were themselves a kind of *caoineadh* for a way of life whose time had passed. The establishment of schools for 'the poorer classes of society' (p. 32) was largely responsible for the change, he wrote, but the growth of Methodism in the north of Ireland had also played a significant role. Caldwell remembered John Wesley's visit to Ballymoney in 1785, the initial hostility of the village to his presence, the sheer power of his oratory, and the 'effect which that one night's preaching had on some of the most immoral and intemperate and idle men of the village' (p. 32). 'This indefatigable man under all the opprobrium attached to his name and his doctrines', wrote Caldwell, 'made many thousands of converts in the North of Ireland and also in England' (p. 32). The admiration is obvious; Caldwell himself had felt the power of Wesley's preaching, even though it had not been enough to pull him away from Presbyterianism.[8]

8 Samuel J. Rogal, *John Wesley in Ireland, 1747–1789* (Lewiston, NY, 1993), p. 786.

* * *

Caldwell's Irish Presbyterian identity had been brought into sharper focus during his years at Bromley Academy between 1778 and 1784. He arrived in England with an inferiority complex. 'I had been led to believe and really fancied I should find the English a superior race of beings,' he recalled (p. 34). But when he landed in Liverpool, he found the people 'neither so handsome nor so well bred as those I had left behind in my own country', and remarked 'that they did not speak as good English ... as we did at home' (p. 34). Established by the East India Company, Bromley Academy attracted students from 'all parts of the globe' (p. 37), educated them in writing, mathematics and languages; taught them dancing, fencing and music; and made sure that they all acquired English accents – as John Caldwell did himself (p. 35).

The principal, Richard Bland, supported the American Revolution and gave the students half-day holidays upon the news of each revolutionary victory over British forces. Most of the students were Tories, and included the sons of American loyalists who wanted to insulate their children from republican principles. Nevertheless, the loyalist sons were sufficiently alienated from their English schoolmates to cheer wildly when they learned that the Americans had defeated the British at Saratoga in 1777: 'Hurrah, hurrah, John Bull we have beat you,' they cried (p. 38).

Caldwell shared the sentiments that lay behind the cheering. He found England to be a 'boasting country', characterized by a mixture of arrogance, vulgarity and ignorance; American victories supplied a degree of compensation (p. 35). Contrary to stereotypes about English rationality and Irish superstition, he reckoned that the English were more likely than the Irish to believe in dreams, ghosts and omens. One of the most memorable passages in his memoir described the time that a woman kidnapped him while he was walking in Covent Garden. As she pulled him up to her room, he could see that 'behind a greasy green curtain or screen by accident or design turned aside, was a very tall, pale faced, hideous looking figure of a man, arrayed in a long gown, high cap, long beard, of a cadaverous and emaciated appearance, accompanied by a wand and other insignia of the art of a fortune teller or necromancer' (p. 40). In the end, he managed to escape, but it had been a close call.

His opinion of English life fell further when he experienced the Gordon Riots of 1780; his school was three miles from the epicentre, and he 'could see the flames and witness much of the confusion of the flying and affrighted citizens.' (p. 41). Some of the older schoolboys participated in the riots, 'partaking of the fun and delight of doing up or burning out some unfortunate Roman Catholic whom they did not know and who had never offended them' (p. 41). Eleven years old, he was deeply shocked by the event; later in life, he would connect it to other examples of mob violence that he encountered in Manchester, Liverpool and above all Birmingham. Caldwell visited Birmingham just after the Priestley Riots of July 1791, and expressed his disgust at the 'scandalous outbreak of John Bullism, bigotry, and outrage' of the Church-and-King crowd that destroyed Priestley's house and laboratory. Walking through the still-smoking ruins, he kept a brick from the house 'as a memento of intolerant persecution and British brutality' (p. 78). 'May the Lord in his mercy,' he wrote, 'protect us from the brutality and ignorance of an English mob' (p. 40).

* * *

Caldwell finished his schooling at Bromley Academy with a 'smattering of grammar, bad writing, tolerable arithmetic and mumbling of French' (p. 47). In 1784, he became an apprentice with Samuel Brown of Belfast, a merchant who was involved in the transatlantic trade. After a brief period as a clerk in the newly established Northern Bank in 1787, he became a partner with Brown the following year, and started up his own business in 1793. A New Light Presbyterian, he joined the First Belfast Congregation; its ministers during the 1780s and 1790s, James Crombie and William Bruce, had both been strong supporters of the Volunteers. In Belfast, Caldwell became involved in civic work; he was a director of the Incorporated Poor House and Infirmary and served as secretary and treasurer of the Lamp and Paving Company.

He also joined three inter-related organizations – the Masonic Fraternity, in which he became master of a lodge; the Belfast Green Company, an extension of the Volunteers; and the United Irishmen. 'My object in joining that organization', he wrote of the United Irishmen, 'was to obtain equal rights for all my countrymen of every religious denomination through an independent Irish legislature, whilst I left to others of superior talents or aspiring ambition the honour of aiming to shine in the senate, or the glory of being distinguished on the battlefield of our country' (p. 94).

Although he became a colonel in the United Irishmen, his contributions to the organization were financial rather than military. Rubbing shoulders with radicals such as Wolfe Tone, the millenarian minister Thomas Ledlie Birch and the revolutionary Dublin ironfounder Henry Jackson, he became Belfast's leading fundraiser for the movement. To raise money, he organized lotteries, over the objections of fellow radicals who complained that such activities only encouraged immorality.[9] Having himself won over £300 in a lottery at the age of sixteen, with no apparent damage to his moral principles, Caldwell was not persuaded by such objections (p. 52). The United Irish lottery money was used, he wrote, 'for the partial support of the impoverished patriots, and for

9 Cleland Papers, 7 January 1798, PRONI, D 714/2/14.

law expenses arising from defending the incarcerated' (p. 96). When William Orr was tried for treason in September 1797, Caldwell helped to bring in the high-powered defence team of John Philpot Curran and William Sampson, and also attempted to implement Curran's plan to bribe the jailor and organize a prison break after Orr's conviction (pp 84–6). The plan failed; Orr was executed on 14 October 1797 and became the first Presbyterian United Irish martyr in Ulster.[10]

By this time, the United Irishmen had moved on to a revolutionary footing and expanded their political base through an alliance with the Catholic Defenders. As a middle-class Presbyterian who stood for a non-sectarian republic characterized by political democracy and economic liberalism, Caldwell believed that links with plebeian radicals, whether Protestant or Catholic, were fraught with sectarian danger. Feeling like a *Girondin* about to be overwhelmed by *sans-culottes*, he feared that he and his fellow leaders of the United Irishmen would be swept aside by the 'bad, designing and wicked men' with whom they were working. He perceived a significant parallel between the leading United Irishmen and their followers on the one hand, and the leading Orangemen and their followers on the other. 'I have always pitied', he wrote, 'the better educated of the Orange faction being condemned to associate and hold brotherly intercourse with beings, who were a shame and disgrace to humanized society and the very scum and dregs of it' (p. 94). From this perspective, the men of no property and the men of no popery had more in common than it seemed.

Despite his anxieties, Caldwell continued to support the cause of independence. 'A virtuous and patriotic man', he wrote, 'will not on that account withdraw himself from doing his part for the general weal, or refuse his aid to the salvation of his country tho' he may keep himself aloof from the contagion of the loathsome objects with whom he may for a time be partially associated' (p. 94). It was essential, he believed, to contain and control popular passions and to prevent a premature revolution that would only play into the hands of the British government. Like most United Irishmen, Caldwell convinced himself that the government was attempting to foment a rising, as part of a 'long meditated plot aimed against the independence of the country and to subjugate her more completely to British thraldom [*sic*] and foreign legislation' (p. 99). Although he did not have any evidence for this – not surprisingly, since no such plot existed – his experiences with informers and *agents provocateurs* could easily be fitted into his conspiracy theory. At a United Irish meeting in Ballynahinch, he recalled, Nicholas Mageean had insisted that the radicals 'must spare neither men, women, or children' who were against them; in Belfast, he wrote, John Hughes had urged him to assassinate a tax collector (pp 96, 100). Both Mageean and Hughes turned out to be in the pay of the government; indeed, it was

10 Stewart, *Summer soldiers*, pp 45–51.

Hughes' information that led to Caldwell's arrest in Dublin on 19 May, four days before the outbreak of the Rising.

By blaming the violence of 1798 on the government and its agents, along with the 'depravity and wickedness' that he found 'amongst the people of our party,' Caldwell detached the 'principled' leadership of the United Irishmen from the practical consequences of their ideas and actions. Thomas Paine had made much the same point about revolutionary France: 'It is not because right principles have been violated', he asserted, 'that they are to be abandoned.'[11] In Caldwell's view, the principles of the United Irishmen were self-evidently right and virtuous; the bloodshed of 1798, he believed, resulted from a vicious government and the moral corruption that it had engendered. The vast majority of those who were killed were, of course, on the rebel side; given the balance of forces, it could hardly have been otherwise. But Caldwell never considered the possibility that the leaders of the United Irishmen bore a significant share of responsibility for the violence. However 'virtuous' the leaders may have been, they underestimated the power of the state, the depth and breadth of ethno-religious tensions, and the sheer weight of history that pressed down on contemporary events. Under these circumstances, the attempt forcibly to impose the ideal on the real was more likely to produce civil war than national liberation.

Not surprisingly, Caldwell viewed himself as an innocent victim of British oppression when he was arrested for high treason on 19 May. The arrest itself was conducted along polite eighteenth-century middle-class lines. Major Swan and his assistant searched Caldwell's room for incriminating documents and were then invited to stay for breakfast before taking their prisoner to Dublin Castle. During breakfast, the lady of the house attempted to distract Swan while Caldwell surreptitiously burned a list of United Irish sympathizers who contributed to the lottery. As it turned out, Swan had not been deceived; when the two men left for the Castle, he asked Caldwell to deny having any personal papers when he was arrested, so that Swan would not get in trouble with his superiors (p. 98). Caldwell was interrogated by the privy council and sent to the Birmingham Tower. The following morning, he encountered the Belfast United Irishman William Putnam McCabe, who was one of Lord Edward FitzGerald's closest allies, and who had been brought in for investigation. A master of disguises, McCabe successfully passed himself off as a 'Scotch pedlar', and was duly released. Later in the day, Caldwell glimpsed FitzGerald himself, his 'head bandaged in a bloody handkerchief', after his arrest in the Liberties. He also heard 'in anguish which I cannot describe' the 'heartrending groans' of the men whom FitzGerald had attacked during his arrest; one of them was Major Swan, whom FitzGerald stabbed three times (p. 101). 'In the midst of the horrors I had

11 Thomas Paine, *Age of reason, Part 2*, in Philip S. Foner (ed.), *The complete writings of Thomas Paine* (New York, 1945), i, 516.

witnessed,' he wrote, '… a faintness came over me like … the sickness of death' (p. 102).

He was transferred to Watkins' Tavern on Castle Street, a holding area for United Irish prisoners. Shortly after his arrival, he heard Lord Kingsborough in the next room threaten a fellow prisoner with flogging unless he turned informer; when Kingsborough temporarily left to get a bottle of port, Caldwell whispered encouragement through a hole in the wall (pp 103–4). In general, Caldwell was treated well in prison; the fact that he was respectable and well-connected did him no harm. Joseph Wilson, the American consul in Dublin and a close friend, brought him books; he was provided with a good bed, had his clothes regularly washed, and 'fared sumptuously' on fine food and drink (p. 104). On the other hand, he feared that he had become a hostage to the progress of the Rising. His waiters, who were United Irish sympathizers, reported rumours that the local Orangemen were complaining that the government was treating the rebels too leniently, and were planning to massacre the prisoners if the United Irishmen defeated the British army at Naas. Caldwell was sufficiently worried to sleep with a pair of 'immense carving dinner knives' by his side; in the event, he wrote, the government's opposition to Orange vigilantism, together with the failure of the Rising, meant that the threat passed (p. 105).

In mid July, after eight weeks in Watkins' Tavern, Caldwell was taken to Belfast. As his coach entered the city, he could see 'the terrific sights of the heads of our countrymen, who had been decapitated after being hanged by the sentence of court martial' (p. 106). It was here that he learned about his brother Richard's role in the Rising and the fate that had befallen his family. When the Rising broke out in County Antrim, the seventeen-year-old Richard had been made a United Irish general. At the head of a contingent of Ballymoney men armed with pikes, guns, pitchforks and 'Scythes tied upon sticks,' he marched them to Ballymena, where they joined the United Irishmen who had captured the town. When the tide turned after the loyalist victory at the battle of Antrim on 7 June, Richard crossed the glens to Cushendall and escaped to Scotland, from where he hoped to reach America.

But there was a fifty-guinea price on his head, and his description had been circulated; he was arrested in Scotland, brought back to Ireland, and tried for high treason at a court martial in Coleraine on 13–14 July. He was found guilty and ordered to be 'hanged in the town of Ballymena by the Neck until dead, his head to be severed from his Body & placed upon a spike in the Market House in the town of Ballymoney'; all his property was to be forfeited to the Crown. In a state of desperation, the family did everything possible to save his life. James Parks, his brother-in-law, visited Dublin Castle ten times in one day, secured an audience with Lord Castlereagh and urged John senior to petition the viceroy, Lord Cornwallis. 'Great Moderation must be used,' Parks advised; 'a shew of humility' might produce a pardon. The strategy succeeded; Richard was spared on condition that he leave for the United States and that the rest of the family would follow him. He arrived in Norfolk, Virginia, on 1 September 1798, the first of the family to make it to the 'land of liberty'.[12]

Meanwhile, the family had already been singled out for revenge. Two days after the battle of Antrim, Major William Bacon (who came to be known as 'burning bacon') arrived at their house with a group of soldiers. After eating breakfast with the family, he presented them with an order from Lord Henry Murray, the commander of the Coleraine garrison, that their house and property must be burned down. They were given five minutes to get out, and lost almost everything they had. The local magistrate, Edmund McNaghten, had long viewed the Caldwell family as being 'notoriously disaffected,' but lacked sufficient proof to prosecute them.[13] Now, Richard's actions presented the authorities with the opportunity to demonstrate the price of disaffection. 'Within the allotted few minutes,' wrote Caldwell, 'which time was needed to bring hay and straw from the barn, the humble and comfortable dwelling, the seat of genuine hospitality, whose door was never closed to the distressed nor shut on the afflicted, with the office houses, barns, stock of hay grain etc., were in flames' (p. 108). As Caldwell pointed out, his father had not approved of the United Irishmen's revolutionary strategy; the sins of the son were being visited on the father, 'thus ... reversing the order of the Decalogue' (p. 108). The family was left standing on the lawn in a state of shock; the labour of generations had gone up in smoke. Anger at the injustice of it all stayed with the Caldwells for the rest of their lives and was carried across the Atlantic to America.

Caldwell had hardly absorbed this 'heart breaking news' when he was taken to the makeshift prison in the Donegall Arms and interrogated by John Pollock, the Crown solicitor in Belfast. In contrast to his relatively mild treatment in Dublin, Caldwell was given a much rougher ride in Belfast; there were old scores to settle. Pollock, wrote Caldwell, 'used the most violent and abusive language that a billingsgate blackguard could utter, evidently too much under the influence of the brandy bottle'; when Caldwell refused to become an informer, he added, 'the rage and fury of Pollock became that of a maniac' (pp 110–11). Caldwell was not the only person to describe Pollock in this way; William Steel Dickson left a similar account of his own experiences at the Donegall Arms.[14] Shortly afterwards, Caldwell, Dickson and the other prisoners were moved to the *Postlethwaite* prison ship in Belfast Lough. Caldwell recalled the scene as they

---

12 'Court martial of Richard Caldwell, Coleraine, 13–14 July 1798,' Rebellion Papers, National Archives of Ireland, 620/2/8/8; 620/3/51/5; John Parks to John Caldwell [senior], July 1798, Caldwell papers, PRONI, T 3541/1/1–3, T 3541/5/2; 'To his excellency Charles Marquis Cornwallis Lieutenant General and Governor General of Ireland – The humble petition of John Caldwell [senior],' T 3541/6/2. 13 Stewart, *Summer soldiers*, p. 143. 14 William Steel Dickson, *A narrative of the confinement and exile of William Steel Dickson* (Belfast, 1812), pp 46–50.

marched to the quay: 'Many of the inhabitants, out of respect for our feelings, shut their windows and as I passed the houses of some of my old friends I noticed between the nearly closed shutters the moistened eye and the gentle waving of a white handkerchief' (pp 116–17).

For the next six weeks, they were 'crowded almost to suffocation' (p. 117) in the cramped decks of the *Postlethwaite*, on what they called a 'floating bastille.'[15] There were enough revolutionary Presbyterian ministers on board to have formed a separate republican denomination – the irrepressibly loquacious Thomas Ledlie Birch, preaching millenarianism to his jailers; William Steel Dickson, keeping his fellow prisoners on their knees for long hours in prayer; the licentiate David Bailie Warden, fighting off illness with 'lively, rational, and entertaining conversation'; and the Covenanter William Staveley, 'who annoyed us no little during the tedious hours of darkness by his incessant querulous hard lamentation at his hard fate, as if accusing the Almighty for not having protected him from the evil which had befallen him' (p. 117).[16] Caldwell shared a mattress with the 'worthy and respected' Robert Simms; Castlereagh, in contrast, had described Simms as a traitor of the 'deepest cast'.[17] By August, the word came through that those prisoners who wanted to leave for America would be permitted to do so; Caldwell had already decided to cross the Atlantic. As he returned to Belfast to put his affairs in order, his brother Andrew presented him with a song written in the style of Robert Burns' instantly famous anthem to democracy, *A Man's a Man for 'a that*:

> No hero hang'd, no hamlet burn'd
> No peasant robb'd and a that
> No spiteful spy, no coward turned
> We never dreamt o a that
> The neighbours soon combin'd we saw
> In union, love and a that
> But love was treason by the law
> And sore we pied for a that
> > And a that, and a that
> > And twice as mickle's a that
> > The blessings o America
> > Will make amends for a that. (p. 118)

After the 'dismal night of affliction and almost of despair' in Ireland, America represented 'cheerfulness and hope', a new start in the new republic (p. 117).

---

15 Dickson, *Narrative*, p. 101. 16 David Bailie Warden to —— [*c*. December 1798 – January 1799], David Bailie Warden papers, Maryland Historical Society, MS 871; Thomas Ledlie Birch, *A letter from an Irish emigrant to his friend in the United States* (Philadelphia, 1799), pp 32–4. 17 Castlereagh to —— [1798], McCance Collection, PRONI, D 272/3/23.

***

Actually getting there, however, proved to be a very difficult task. Caldwell set out from Belfast to New York in October, on board the *Pallas*. But the ship ran into a full-scale storm and took refuge in Larne harbour, much to the alarm of the United Irish stowaways who were wanted by the authorities. A week later they set out again, only to hit another ferocious storm that damaged the ship and forced it back to Cork. With the permission of the government, Caldwell returned to County Antrim, where he chartered an American ship, the *Peggy*, Captain John Watson, for New York; it left Belfast on 3 May 1799, Caldwell's thirtieth birthday. Around 144 United Irishmen were on board. They included David Bailie Warden, who became a teacher at Kinderhook Academy (where one of his students was the future president Martin Van Buren) before moving into the diplomatic service and serving as the American consul in Paris. A prolific writer, he was arguably the most intellectually gifted of the United Irish *émigrés* in the United States. Also there was the New Light minister William Sinclair, who became a minister in Baltimore; his religious views were denounced by his fellow passenger the Revd James Simpson, a hard-line Calvinist who 'grumbled so incessantly' during the voyage that he was eventually sent to Coventry (p. 128).

Apart from Simpson's behaviour, the trip began smoothly enough. The weather was fine and the seas were calm; 'we generally amused ourselves on the quarter deck in the afternoons with the fiddle and the dance and spent our mornings in reading, writing and conversation', wrote Caldwell (p. 128). Warden enjoyed it so much that he regretted that the voyage did not last longer than six weeks; this is a far cry from the doom-and-gloom perspective that characterizes much of the historiography of transatlantic voyages.[18] There was, however, one event during the journey that almost ruined all their plans. A few days into the voyage, they were intercepted by a French privateer from Bordeaux. The *Peggy* flew the United States flag; in 1799, France and the United States were in a state of undeclared war, and it was open season on American ships. Caldwell and Watson were taken on board the privateer to meet the captain:

> I descended and was struck with horror on viewing the immense number of guns, pistols, hatchets, pikes, and other instruments of death and destruction with which the cabin was decorated. On looking on Capt. Derrygrand's countenance I beheld the very hideous outline of a bloody pirate. He had only exposed to me, for what reason I know not, one side of his face, which was disfigured by St Anthony's fire and moreover gashed by

18 Warden to —— [*c*. December 1798 – January 1799], David Bailie Warden papers, Maryland Historical Society, MS 871.

severe sword cuts. He then told me that we were a good prize, that the French and American Governments were at war and his peremptory orders were to take and send in, or sink and destroy every vessel under the American flag. We contrived to understand each other in spite of my bad French and his none too good English. He then suddenly turned the other side of his face to me and what was my astonishment in beholding a countenance replete with humanity and kindness. (p. 128)

It is hard to get a more melodramatic image than this – the captain whose face represented for Caldwell the two sides of the French Revolution, the aggressive and the humane. Caldwell told Derrygrand that he was leading a persecuted people to asylum in America; Derrygrand replied that he had orders to bring in all American vessels. Surely, said Caldwell, they would not now be molested by the French, 'in whose struggles we had all felt the most lively interest and who had so lately broken their own shackles and obtained their own freedom' (p. 129). Derrygrand bent but did not break. In desperation, Caldwell tried using a secret Masonic sign; fortunately for him, Derrygrand recognized it, called him a 'trés bon frère,' and finally relented. With some difficulty, he won the agreement of his officers (one of whom was a United Irishman from Portrush), and the *Peggy* was allowed to continue on its journey. Not all the United Irish passengers were pleased; 'one or two young men,' wrote Caldwell, were 'much chagrined at not being sent to France,' and were only silenced when threatened with iron shackles. All the others, however, were delighted, and toasted Derrygrand's health each day for the rest of the trip (p. 129). On 12 June, they arrived safely in New York.

* * *

Here was the land of liberty and here, apparently, was his country. Caldwell wrote with admiration of its constitution, its government, its freedom of religion and its meritocracy. Shortly after he arrived, he stayed at a tavern at Peekskill; the following morning, he learned that the tavern keeper 'had been lately elected a member of the legislature.' This could only happen, he wrote, in 'the democratic republican system of our adopted country, which has so essentially built up the happiness and prosperity of the nation, and raised the man of virtue and talent, be he rich, be he poor, to that elevation of society, which his mental acquirements entitled him to enjoy' (p. 130). Politically, he felt very much at home. But in some other respects, he felt like an outsider in a strange and stressful environment.

'In New York,' he recalled, 'we had but few acquaintances, fewer personal friends and no relatives' (p. 130). To deal with this new reality, he moved through existing Irish-American networks and tried to reproduce in New York the same kind of social milieu he had experienced in Belfast. Continuing his Masonic career (not surprisingly, after the events of his voyage), he became Master of the Erin Lodge and an officer of the Grand Lodge of the State of New York. Here, he rubbed shoulders not only with his fellow countrymen, but also with De Witt Clinton, the Paineite republican who formed close connections with the United Irish *émigrés*, and whose political career was built partly on the radical Irish vote. Along with other exiled Belfast United Irishmen, Caldwell joined (and may have helped to establish) the Hibernian Provident Society, one of the founding organizations of Irish-American nationalism and a key source of support for Clinton in the hotly contested New York elections of 1807. He was equally active in the Friendly Sons of St Patrick, whose members included prominent Irish radicals such as Thomas Emmet and William MacNeven, as well as American sympathizers such as Clinton; in his capacity as vice-president of the society, Caldwell delivered a tribute to Clinton shortly after his death in 1828 (pp 155–6).[19]

Just as he carried over his Masonic and political activities from Belfast to New York, Caldwell also continued in America his earlier Irish career as a merchant. With his brother Richard, and later his brother-in-law John Parks, he moved into the 'wholesale grocery line, linen, flaxseed and commission business,' operating in the Atlantic economy (p. 132). When his father bought land in Salisbury in Orange County, Richard left the firm and helped to develop the grist mill, plaster mill, saw mill and tannery on the estate. Staying in New York, John married Ann Higinbotham on 19 April 1803. Nine months later to the day, his daughter Margaret was born; in 1805, they had a second daughter, Elizabeth. With his new family, his business, his extended kin group, his Masonic connections and his political friends, it seemed that Caldwell was making a successful transition to his new environment.

Yet the process of adjustment turned out to be fraught with difficulty. His business quickly ran into problems; Richard was 'too speculative' (p. 134), John Parks was 'totally unqualified for mercantile pursuits,' and all of them succumbed to the 'mania of ship owning' (p. 132), which proved to be economically disastrous. Meanwhile, in Salisbury, the demands of the estate took a severe toll on his father; worn down by 'untiring industry' and 'excessive fatigue', he died in 1803 (p. 134). 'One disaster succeeded another with most alarming rapidity,' Caldwell wrote. Yellow fever claimed the life of his sister Margaret in 1805. His Aunt Rose and her husband, the United Irishman James Huey, were drowned during a journey to Salisbury. And the increasing stress of John's business affairs damaged his health and left him 'much depressed' (p. 137).

19 See Richard C. Murphy and Lawrence J. Mannion, *The history of the Friendly Sons of St Patrick in the city of New York, 1784 to 1955* (New York, 1962), and Steven E. Siry, *De Witt Clinton and the American political economy: sectionalism, politics, and republican ideology, 1787–1828* (New York, 1989).

To boost his spirits, he took a trip to Europe in the spring of 1809. Combining business and pleasure, he sailed first to Portugal and later to Britain. Despite a near-disaster – he almost drowned when his ship was wrecked in a storm off Holyhead – the trip succeeded in improving his health. The tone of his memoir became much livelier and more energetic. Caldwell provided a vivid description of his run-in with a Liverpool pressgang; led by the famous 'Irish John,' it consisted of 'blacks, whites, and mulattoes' who entertained each other with 'ribaldry and coarse jests' in the 'subterranean apartment' that served as their base of operations (p. 139). 'Irish John' had apparently fought with the rebels in Wexford during 1798 and had been spared on condition that he would join the British army. Had it not been for Caldwell's business connections in Liverpool, he would have been among the many men whom 'Irish John' impressed into the Royal Navy (pp 140–1). From Liverpool, Caldwell travelled to London, where he met some of his old schoolmates, wined and dined with the radical publisher Joseph Johnson, and encountered his 'old acquaintance' John D'Evereaux, who claimed to have been one of Bagenal Harvey's aides at the battle of Vinegar Hill and who was now trying to win British support for an expedition to emancipate South America from Spanish imperialism (p. 141).

Caldwell's journey to Europe was followed in 1810 by a family trip to Canada, where he met the 'brave and gallant' General Isaac Brock (p. 144). Two years later, Brock would be fighting American troops during the War of 1812. When hostilities broke out, Richard Caldwell immediately resumed his brief Irish military career, became a captain in the American army, raised 'a very large company of men' from Orange County, and participated in the march to Canada along the Lake Champlain route. For the United Irishmen in the United States, the war was a means of demonstrating their loyalty to the American Republic and of continuing the fight for Irish liberty. 'Ireland will be rescued from British bondage on the plains of Canada,' asserted one Irish American.[20] In Richard Caldwell's case, there was also the opportunity to avenge 1798 – the torching of his family's home, his court martial and sentence of death, the desperate pleading and prevarication to save his life, and the subsequent exile of the entire family to the United States. But failure in Ireland was followed by disaster in America. Suffering from dysentery, and exposed to a severe storm on Lake Champlain, he died in November 1812, at the age of thirty-five, before he reached the Canadian border (pp 5, 154).

Elsewhere in the United States, virtually all the men in the Caldwell clan were out in arms to defend the Republic against British incursions. In 1813, John took over the Salisbury estate and immediately involved himself in Orange County politics. Recognizing that West Point was vulnerable to attack, he called a county meeting to examine ways of strengthening its defences. Not everyone was

20 *Shamrock*, 26 September 1812.

impressed; 'some individuals of the county,' he wrote, 'insinuated that it was impertinent for a foreigner (for such they termed me) to busy himself in trying to protect his own and their property from the enemy, and that I should be deprived of the credit of even suggesting such a plan of safety' (p. 147). The comment is significant. Even during the War of 1812, when United Irish *émigrés* were demonstrating their American patriotism, asserting their republican principles and placing themselves in the vanguard of the struggle against Britain, someone like Caldwell could still engender resentment as a foreigner who was poking his nose into other people's affairs. Whatever else may have been said about Caldwell, this was clearly not a criticism that could have been levelled against him in Ireland.

For Caldwell, as for most other United Irishmen in the United States, American citizenship was a matter of ideological commitment rather than birth; the attitude of some of his Salisbury neighbours must have rankled. More problematic, though, was the economic situation that he now faced; the purchase of the Salisbury estate left him deep in debt, and his inexperience in the milling business meant that he was 'subject to much imposition from the carelessness or cupidity of hirelings' (p. 145). His 'troubles and vexations' were compounded by personal tragedy; the death of his wife in 1818 left him with feelings of intense loneliness and guilt. Thoughts of his marriage, he wrote, 'were often accompanied by sad and bitter pangs of remorse for many a peevish, cross observation I made and many an act I did to wound the spirit or hurt the feelings of the dear departed.' 'I hope and trust,' he added, 'this candid confession will be a lesson to the reader to avoid giving hurt to any, but particularly to any who are near and dear to them as was the wife of my bosom and mother of my children' (p. 147).

After 1818, the tone of the memoir becomes flat and melancholy. He tried to cut his losses by selling off much of the Salisbury estate in 1824, only to be swindled in the process. The subject was so 'heart rending and hateful' (p. 148) that he could not bear to dwell on it in his writing, except to remark bitterly that 'the labour, the property and the prospects of the family after a struggle of twenty years [was] lost forever' (p. 148). What Major Bacon had done in Ireland by fire had been accomplished by legal chicanery in America – the loss of property, the ruin of hopes, and the removal of Caldwell from the community. The key difference, of course, was that Bacon was acting in the name of the British government, while the American who took over the Salisbury estate was acting entirely for himself.

Returning to New York, Caldwell tried to comfort himself with memories of his years in Ireland and with regular visits to his relatives. But he seems to have lacked a sense of purpose, a sense of direction, and his memoir began to register long periods of boredom. 'The world is a complete masquerade,' he wrote shortly after he left Salisbury, 'and we deceive each other by outward appearances and external show, but in my case at least without intending it. So little has occurred of interest in my operations or situation that altho' I am now writing in January 1825 nothing worth notice will be recorded' (p. 151). The same tone was struck six years later: 'April 1st 1831. I have passed over a year and a half of little interest' (p. 153). 'There are few families in this country,' he commented on another occasion, 'who have come here under flattering auspices, that have during that period experienced more vicissitudes and variations of fortune, more of the ups and downs, more of the ills and cares of life, or the treacherous wiles or smiles of the world than we have done.' 'On the whole,' he continued, 'we have enjoyed as much of its blessings as came to our share, and it is our duty to be thankful for them, and submit with resignation to those reverses, which (no doubt for wise purposes beyond our ken to fathom) we have been tried and afflicted with' (p. 151). The 'blessings of America' were mixed indeed.

* * *

The gap between expectation and actuality, the sense of disappointment that permeates the last pages of Caldwell's memoir, was part of a more general experience among radical Irish exiles in the United States. Although they usually remained committed to the principles of American republicanism, many of the exiles became disillusioned with day-to-day life in the United States. Thus Wolfe Tone in 1795 believed that the government of Pennsylvania was 'the best under heaven,' but also felt that the people of Philadelphia were 'a disgusting race, eaten up with all the vice of commerce, and that vilest of all pride, the pride of the purse'.[21] David Bailie Warden, Caldwell's companion on the *Peggy* in 1799, admired American political institutions but was horrified by the factionalism and careerism that permeated American political practice.[22] Archibald Hamilton Rowan, the United Irish leader who fled to America in 1795, felt the same way. After six months in the United States, he told his wife that he was 'disgusted ... with the rough manners of the people', and with 'the universal rage of money-getting'.[23] Nor was it only the native-born Americans who came under fire; some *émigrés* also complained about the Irish in the United States. 'If you meet a confirmed blackguard,' commented Tone, 'you may be sure he is Irish.'[24] George Cuming, a Belfast United Irishman who stayed with Caldwell

21 Wolfe Tone to Thomas Russell, 25 October 1795, Sirr papers, Trinity College Dublin, 868/2/13–15. 22 Warden to ——, 28 April 1800, David Bailie Warden papers, Maryland Historical Society, MS 871. 23 Archibald Hamilton Rowan to Sarah Rowan, 19 January 1796, in William Hamilton Drummond (ed.), *Autobiography of Archibald Hamilton Rowan* (Dublin, 1840), p. 289. Sarah's reaction to her husband's sentiments is revealing: 'Your picture both of that country [America] and its inhabitants is indeed sufficient to deter any person from going thither. But then you did expect to find perfection there; and I do not think it exists any where...' Sarah Rowan to Archibald Rowan, 1 May 1799, in Drummond (ed.), *Autobiography*, p. 336. 24 Tone to Russell, 25 October 1795, Sirr Papers, Trinity College, Dublin.

when he moved to New York, lamented the 'unhappy divisions' among the Irish Republicans and feared the 'degradation of the Irish character' in the city.[25]

If we move forward from the United Irishmen to the Young Irelanders, from the time that Caldwell left Ireland to the time that he wrote his memoir, a strikingly similar pattern emerges. During his imprisonment in Bermuda in 1849, John Mitchel informed his sister that he would not choose to live in America, on the grounds that the 'ardent and devout worship of the Great God Dollar is too exclusive and intolerant'.[26] Mitchel had not actually set foot in the United States when he made this judgment; but many Young Irelanders who escaped to America in 1848 were equally negative, at least in their private correspondence. Richard O'Gorman admired the 'wondrous energy' and 'self reliance' of the Yankees, but described American politics as 'a filthy pool of shabbiness falsehood and corruption'.[27] Thomas D'Arcy McGee criticized the United States for its 'diseased love of excitement,' its 'education without ethics', its excessive materialism, its lax morality and its loose family ties.[28] And just as Tone and Cuming had written disparagingly of the Irish in America, Thomas Meagher and Michael Doheny made equally scathing comments about their compatriots. 'I have found infinitely more bigotry and intolerance in this country, among our countrymen', wrote Meagher, 'than ever I was sensible of in Ireland.'[29] Doheny went even further: 'If I really thought that an Irish Republic would result in the degeneracy of the people to the extent that they have been generated here,' he wrote, 'I would prefer that Ireland should remain as she is.'[30] These were remarkable sentiments from one of Ireland's most militant mid nineteenth-century republicans.

Perhaps such disillusionment is understandable, even predictable, given the idealism that was invested in the American Republic; the United States had to carry impossibly high hopes on its shoulders. But the common themes are no less revealing for that. Over a fifty-year period, the United States was repeatedly criticized for undermining the true 'Irish character', for its crass, selfish materialism, and for the corrupt factionalism of its politics. Caldwell was much milder in his comments than were many of his fellow exiles, but he shared their concerns, and his sense of unease was unmistakable. Writing to Robert Simms in 1802, he commented that the Irish propensity to live in large towns rather than moving into the interior 'is often attended with ruin to Individuals and

25 George Cuming to Robert Simms, 30 August 1805, and 18 January 1816, 'Emigrant letters to Robert Simms,' PRONI, T 1815.   26 John Mitchel to his sister, 5 March 1849, Hickey Collection, National Library of Ireland, MS 3226.   27 Richard O'Gorman to Smith O'Brien, 1 January 1859, William Smith O'Brien papers, National Library of Ireland, MS 446, f. 3082. 28 See, for example, *American Celt*, 14 April, 12 May 1855.   29 Thomas Meagher to Gavan Duffy, 17 January 1853, Charles Gavan Duffy papers, National Library of Ireland, MS 5757, f. 387.   30 Michael Doheny to Smith O'Brien, 20 August 1858, William Smith O'Brien papers, National Library of Ireland, MS 446, f. 3058.

dishonour to our National Character'.[31] Socially and culturally, the United States sometimes appeared as a snare rather than a blessing; in this sense, things seemed better back home. The communalism that he experienced in Ballymoney and Belfast, the sense of belonging, the hospitality, the colourful characters, the long evenings with fiddle music and dancing, were largely missing from the American section of his memoir. His involvement with the Irish American community in New York went some way to fill the gap, but was not enough to overcome the feelings of loneliness that characterized his later years. Despite being at the centre of a large family, and despite his place in the *émigré* network, he felt isolated in the individualist culture of America.

Caldwell was also ambivalent about American politics. Like other Irish radicals in the United States, he was repelled by the factionalism that characterized American political life, even as he became drawn into it himself. As a strong supporter of De Witt Clinton, he wrote scathingly about the 'many sneers and scoffs and croakings' of the 'political quacks and aspirants' who opposed Clinton's Erie Canal project (p. 155). Elsewhere, he remarked on the 'persecuting spirit' (p. 1) that existed within American politics. On the other hand, he noted that the 'corrupt majority' in the New York House of Assembly that had attacked Clinton was eventually ejected by the electorate, and pointed out that the 'persecuting spirit' in America was 'suffered to expend its virulence in innocuous invective' (p. 1) rather than directly injuring people, as it had done in Ireland.

More generally, Caldwell separated the political theory of American republicanism from much of the practice and from the social and cultural character of American life; in this way, he could continue to view the United States as the land of liberty. He had no choice; to have done otherwise would have been to contradict everything he stood for and to have made much of his life devoid of meaning. For better or worse, America was the only embodiment of democratic republicanism around, and it was the country that had provided an asylum for his family; he had to buy into it. Although he believed that the Irish character was deteriorating in urban America, although he remained something of an outsider in Salisbury and New York, although he was beset by personal tragedy and business problems in the United States, and although he disliked the endemic nastiness of American political debate, Caldwell was proud to bring up his daughters as citizens of the American Republic (p. 145). Culturally, however, he remained Irish – 'North County Irish' – to the marrow of his bones.

31 Caldwell to Robert Simms, 18 October 1802, 'Emigrant letters to Robert Simms,' PRONI, T 1815.

Forging the 'Protestant way of life': class conflict and the origins of unionist hegemony in early nineteenth-century Ulster

KERBY A. MILLER

In 1817 Henry Joy, a prominent Belfast Presbyterian, stated that no 'occurrence of much importance' had transpired in his town since the passage of the Act of Union in 1800. Almost two hundred years later, historian Ian McBride notes that scholars still know little about Ulster Presbyterians' opinions in the early nineteenth century, in part because of official and unofficial repression, and of self-censorship among those who had sympathized with the United Irishmen's 1798 Rebellion or opposed the Act of Union itself.[1] I suggest, however, that Irish emigrant correspondence can dispel some of the darknesses implied by both Joy's and McBride's remarks. Letters sent from America – albeit written from the perspective (and safety) of the New World – provide insights into the motives and attitudes of ordinary Ulster Presbyterian (and other Irish) emigrants. Moreover, missives sent from Ireland to emigrants overseas can illuminate Irish events and developments that most contemporaries preferred to ignore – and, in consequence, that historians have not noticed or have failed to investigate fully. Such is the case with the following letter, written by William Coyne in Belfast on St Patrick's Day, 1816, describing what may have been 'Belfast's first bomb'.[2]

1 [Henry Joy], *Historical collections relative to the town of Belfast: from the earliest period to the union with Great Britain* (Belfast, 1817), p. xiv; Ian McBride, 'Ulster Presbyterians and the passing of the Act of Union,' in Michael Brown, Patrick M. Geoghegan and James Kelly (eds), *The Irish Act of Union, 1800: bicentennial essays* (Dublin, 2003), p. 69; also see McBride, 'Memory and forgetting: Ulster Presbyterians and 1798,' in Thomas Bartlett, David Dickson, Dáire Keogh and Kevin Whelan (eds), *1798: a bicentenary perspective* (Dublin, 2003), pp 478–96. A shorter version of this chapter was published in *Éire-Ireland: An Interdisciplinary Journal of Irish Studies*, 39: 1–2 (spring/summer 2004), 262–80, under the title, 'Belfast's first bomb, 28 February 1816: Class conflict and the origins of Ulster Unionist hegemony.' The author is grateful to Sean Farrell, guest editor of that special double-issue (on Ulster Unionism), and to the regular editors of *Éire-Ireland*, for permission to reprint some of the earlier material in this volume; and to Liam Kennedy, Ted Koditschek, Mark Spencer and David A. Wilson for their helpful comments on the various revisions of the present essay.   2 The author would like to thank Roger Hayden of Ithaca, NY, for providing photocopies and transcripts of Coyne's letter and for granting permission to publish it. The violent incident that Coyne described is omitted from the standard histories of Belfast – J.C. Beckett and R.E. Glasscock (eds), *Belfast: origin and growth of an indus-*

William Coyne was probably a master cooper, and he may have been in his mid-forties when he wrote this, his only surviving letter, to his brother in Duchess County, New York. Very likely William Coyne was a Protestant and perhaps a member of the legally established Church of Ireland. Early nineteenth-century Belfast was a rapidly growing city of migrants, principally from east Ulster's Lagan Valley, and, given the reference in his letter, it is probable that Coyne had moved to Belfast from the predominantly Anglican parish of Magheragall, in the barony of Massareene Upper, in southwest County Antrim.[3]

trial city (London, 1967); George Benn, *A history of the town of Belfast: from 1799 till 1810 ...* (London, 1880); and W.A. Maguire, *Belfast* (Keele, 1993) – but is mentioned briefly in Jonathan Bardon, *A history of Ulster* (Belfast, 1992), p. 259; John W. Boyle, *The Irish labor movement in the nineteenth century* (Washington, DC, 1988), pp 15–16; E.R.R. Green, *The Lagan Valley, 1800–50* (London, 1949), p. 101; and R.B. McDowell, *Public opinion and government policy in Ireland, 1801–1846* (London, 1952), p. 62 – and described in more detail in Andrew Boyd, *The rise of the Irish trade unions* (Dublin, 1985 ed.), pp 30–2.   3 According to the *Belfast Street Directory* (*c.*1813) and *Bradshaw's Belfast Directory* of 1819, William Co[y]ne (or Cain), cooper, lived at 10 Bluebell Entry, off Waring Street. Perhaps he was the same 'Mr William Coyne' who died, aged 75, on 31 August 1846, at his home on the Falls Road. *Belfast News-Letter* (*BNL* hereafter), 4 September 1846; from the death records in the Linen Hall Library, Belfast; which also contains the *BNL* on microfilm. 'Coyne' may be an Anglicization of the Irish surname Ó Cadhain, common in Mayo and elsewhere in Connacht, as well as in south Ulster counties such as Cavan; conversely, it may be a variant of (Mac) Coan (or Cone, commonly Cowan), found in County Armagh and likely derived from the Irish (or Scots Gaelic) *Mac Comhdhain*. The Northern Hiberno-English of Coyne's letter is in mid-Ulster dialect, with few if any Ulster Scots characteristics, as would be expected from his possible origin in south-west Antrim, lying outside the Ulster Scots linguistic domain. In Ulster, however, both language and surname are largely irrelevant to religious identity, and my suggestion that Coyne was likely a Protestant (and affiliated with the Church of Ireland) is based on early census data from Magheragall parish, to which Coyne refers in his letter. In 1766 Magheragall contained 420 households, 365 (86.9 per cent) of which were Protestant, 55 (13.1 per cent) Roman Catholic. Employing the eighteenth-century households-to-persons multiplier devised for Ulster by Dickson, Ó Gráda and Daultrey, in 1766 Magheragall probably contained about 1,840 Protestants and 277 Catholics. By 1831 Magheragall's population included 2,279 Anglicans (67.0 per cent of the total, 74.6 per cent of the parish's Protestants), 646 Presbyterians (20.8 per cent and 23.2 per cent), 63 'other Protestants' (2.0 per cent and 2.3 per cent), and 314 Catholics (10.1 per cent of the total). Thus, by 1831 the Protestant proportion of Magheragall's inhabitants had risen to nearly 90 per cent. However, owing to heavy migration to America, Britain or nearby industrial towns such as Belfast and Lisburn, between 1766 and 1831 the annual growth rates of Magheragall's populations had been extremely low: merely 0.64 among the parish's Protestants, and much less (0.19) among local Catholics. Religious census data for Magheragall in 1766 is in T.808/14,900, in the Public Record Office of Northern Ireland, Belfast; and for 1831 in the First Report of the Commission of Public Instruction, Ireland, *British Parliamentary Papers*, H.C. 1835 xxxiii. Also see D. Dickson, C. Ó Gráda and S. Daultrey, 'Hearth tax, household size, and Irish population change, 1672–1821,' *Proceedings of the Royal Irish Academy*, 82C: 6 (1982), 125–50. For surname origins, see Edward MacLysaght, *The surnames of Ireland*, 6th ed. (Blackrock, County Dublin, 1991). For his analysis of the language of Coyne's letter, I am grateful, as always in linguistic matters, to Professor Emeritus Bruce D. Boling of the University of New Mexico.

In the early 1800s transatlantic mail was expensive and its delivery uncertain. Consequently, Irish immigrant correspondence was filled primarily with information that was vitally important to its authors and recipients but which often seems mundanely personal or familial to contemporary scholars. The principal subjects of William Coyne's letter, however, were very public and quite dramatic, and his missive's exceptional character indicates that he and his neighbours in Belfast considered the developments he described to be extraordinarily significant – and that he assumed his brother in faraway America would consider them equally so. Social and political historians of early nineteenth-century Ulster should also find Coyne's letter of considerable interest.

William and E. Coyne, Belfast, to Henry Coyne, Pleasant Valley, Duchess County, New York, 17 March 1816[4]

Belfast 17th March 1816

Dear Brother

I have rec[d] your Letter of the 24th Dec[r] which give us great Satisfection to hear that you and your Familey were in good health; my aunt also rec,[d] one from you and She and Nancy desires to be remembered to you they are both well and would have wrote but as they had nothing particular to mention they thought the one Letter would do us both, I Showed your Letter to all your acquentainces that is here who was all particularly happy to heare from you, but John Mullan and Michal Roney is both in Scotland; and M[r] M'Pharson,[s] Congregation is disolved his wife Died here and he is in England his Church is Converted into a Muslin ware-house and ocupied by an old acquentaince of yours W[m] Shaw[5] who is an acting Partner in a Concern that is doeing a good dale of business at present however trade is in general but verry flat[6] yet thank God I have had the best of work Since I went to M[r] Bell[7] and the two oldest boys Henry and John is doeing pretty

4 The following transcript reproduces William Coyne's original punctuation and spelling – the latter often indicating his pronunciation, e.g., **dale** (deal), **attact** (attack), **extronary** (extraordinary), **rachedness** (wretchedness), **laveing** (leaving) etc. Occasionally the text is emended by explanatory footnotes or by the insertion of square-bracketed words or letters in the text itself. This minimal editing may cause readers some difficulty, in part because Coyne frequently abbreviated words and/or omitted vowels or entire syllables; thus, **rec[d]** (received); **Dec[r]**, **Feb[y]** (December, February); **Covred, covring** (Covered, covering); **evry** (every); **modrate** (moderate) etc. Also, Coyne often employed commas to replace apostrophes – e.g., **M'Pharson,[s]** (M'Pharson's), **Ruth,s** (Ruth's), **Subscriber,s** (Subscriber's) etc. – or, less commonly, to indicate contractions or abbreviations, as in **rec,[d]** (received) and **per C,[t]** (per cent).   5 W[m] Shaw: according to *Bradshaw's Belfast Directory*, in 1819 William Shaw was a merchant at 24 James's Street, off Waring Street.   6 **but**: only. **trade is in general but very flat**: i.e., in general, trade is only very poor.   7 M[r] **Bell**: *Bradshaw's Belfast Directory* of 1819 lists several merchants, bleachers and cotton manufacturers named Bell – most prominently John Bell & County, cotton

well at the Loom. We have now and then a little Stir as usual between the Weavers and Manifecturiers particularly Thomas How[8] and Frank Johnson[9] Several voilant attacts have been made on the praperty of these 2 individuals but the most dareing of all was on the night of the 28th of Feby on the House of Mr Johnson as his place had been twice Set on fire before he was well prepaird for a third attect haveing the out Side of his windows and door Covred with Sheet Iron and well prepaird in the inside to meet his asealants however notwithstanding they made the attact about 3 Oclock on the morning of the 28th by forseing off the iron Shutters while he[10] and his inmates with Small arms from the uper windows of the House attected the

spinners and manufacturers at John Street, off Donegall and Waring streets; and John Bell, Richard Bell, & County, muslin bleachers, also at John Street – many of whom could have employed Coyne's coopering skills. After the cotton weavers' attack on Francis Johnson's house (see below), John Bell joined the 'Committee of twenty-one Gentlemen,' primarily cotton and muslin manufacturers, appointed to assist Belfast's magistrates and constables to 'seek for and receive information, collect subscriptions [for the rewards offered in return for 'information'], and transact all matters arising out of this disgraceful transaction' (*BNL*, 1 March 1816).   **8 Thomas How**: According to *Bradshaw's Belfast Directory*, in 1819 Thomas How (or Howe) was a muslin manufacturer with business premises in Long Lane, adjacent to his house on Church Street. He was also listed, at 12 Long Lane and 11 Church Street, in *Pigot's Provincial Directory* (London, 1824). According to Mr M'Cartney, one of the attorneys who prosecuted those charged with attacking Francis Johnson's house (see below), the accused weavers had earlier targeted Thomas How, 'whose webs they cut, and [had] attacked those persons who worked [for] him' (*BNL*, 13 August 1816). Thomas How – like John Bell (see n. 7) and Johnson himself – was also a member of the 'Committee of twenty-one' appointed to apprehend Johnson's assailants (*BNL*, 1 March 1816). On 29 June 1838, the *BNL* recorded the death, eight days earlier, of 'Thomas How, Esq., merchant, aged 56 years.'   **9 Frank Johnson**: Francis Johnson, a leading muslin manufacturer at North Street, on Peter's Hill. According to Jonathan Bardon's *History of Ulster*, p. 259, Johnson was a 'hated employer' whose home had been attacked at least once before (as Coyne's letter states), in the summer of 1815, by '[d]esperate weavers' who daubed his front door with tar and set it on fire. According to Boyd, *Rise of the Irish trade unions*, pp 30–1, Johnson twice reduced his weavers' wages – the second time in retaliation for their previous assault. At the trial of those accused of bombing his house on 28 February 1816, one of the prosecuting attorneys charged that, before their final assault on his home, the weavers had also threatened Johnson with anonymous letters, 'made attacks on his person,' and 'even went so far as to warn the Insurance Offices' against insuring his property, 'as they had determined to burn it' (*BNL*, 13 August 1816). On 2 January 1818, the *BNL* printed a lengthy announcement of 'the death of our worthy and lamented townsman, Mr FRANCIS JOHNSON, another victim to the dreadful scourge, Typhus Fever, with which our town is so severely visited.' According to his obituary, Johnson's 'character was held in the most elevated range by his fellow-citizens ... for he was honest, ingenuous, and single-hearted; possessing a cultivated mind, talent, and integrity. In religion and morality, a bright example – in politics, liberal and constitutional – as a merchant, useful and intelligent – and for firmness and unshrinking determination, a man scarcely to be equalled. To his resolute conduct, the country is indebted for the preservation of its most useful manufactures. He was cool, dispassionate, and humane, and amidst difficulties that might have paled a less determined heart, he succeeded in putting down a system of combination which threatened to subvert the very basis of every principle of commercial good order.'   **10 he**: i.e., **Frank Johnson**; see n. 9.

Guards that was covring the working party at the windows when a havy
fireing Commenced on both Sides to[11] the party that was at work forsd the
Shutters and entroudeced either a bomb Shel or Some other extronary
Combustable preperation that Soon exploded and rent the House from top
to bottom not a wall nor inside partation that was not torn to pices yet
despirate as it was and wounderfull to relate not a life was lost on either
Sides,[12] large rewards are offerd for aprehending any one Concernd no less
than £2000 for prosacution and £500 for private information, four quiet
well disposed men have been taken[13] on Suspecion but it is hoped there is
nothing against them that will affect their lives. Jonathan Gardner Stood a
trial at our last Assises for murder and is Still Confind on account of Some
[f]arenciable[14] evidences not comeing forward, the nature of the
Circumstance was thus he haveing kept a public House down Street about
4 Months <ago> he Shut the doar in <debt for> £700 and it was in an
atempt of the Creditors to arest his person that the above accident
haptned,[15] how Soon one trouble Succeeds an other his Son John who was
Clarke in the Bottle House haveing Commited a breach of trust was turnd
out and haveing inlisted a few days after onley got the lenth of England
when he died[16] laveing a wife and 2 Children Ruth,s fortune has been little
better She maried a man of the name of aken and after gowing throw a
Considerable property in a Short time She and her man is in the Antrim
Militia thus the whole Family is reduced to rachedness and distress I have
very little particulars to mention only as I am writeing[17] I have no doubt it
will be a Saticefection to you to hear any thing interesting to the place,
among many valuable institutions that has been established here Since your
departure none deserves more general approbation than the Saveing Bank

11 **to:** until. 12 On the night of the weavers' attack, Johnson's large, three-storey house was
occupied by himself, his wife, six children, two servant women and one male servant, John Lewis,
whom Johnson had recently hired, as a watchman, to guard against nocturnal assaults. Indeed,
Lewis' bravery, in carrying the smouldering 'bomb' from the front parlour into the kitchen at the
rear of the house, may have saved Johnson, his family and servants from death; in the event,
Lewis and Johnson's wife were the only occupants to suffer even minor injuries. 13 **taken:**
arrested. 14 **[f]arenciable**, i.e., 'forensiable': perhaps a hitherto unattested dialect variant of
'forensical' = 'forensic': 'items of evidence suitable for introduction into court proceedings' (see
OED, s.v.). (An alternative reading of the word might be **parmiciable**, i.e. 'permissible.')
Thanks again to Professor Bruce D. Boling for his assistance in this matter (see n. 3). 15 See
the *BNL* of 5 March 1816 for an account of the travails of Gardner, a publican on William Street.
haptned: happened. 16 **Clarke in the Bottle House:** clerk in a glass bottle manufactory or a
bottling plant, perhaps for whiskey. **his Son John ... was turnd out and haveing inlisted a
few days after onley got the lenth of England when he died:** i.e., John Gardner was
dismissed (**turned out**) from his former employment, and a few days afterwards (**after**) he
enlisted in the British army; however, he had travelled only as far as (**the len[g]th of**) England
when he died (presumably on his way to military service overseas). 17 **only as I am writeing:**
i.e., but since I am writing anyway ...

this is instituted for the Saveings of the poor and is Conducted by the foremost of the place a Comettee of 25 is appointed as directors and manager Consisting of the principle Magastrates and Bankers of the town who meets every Friday Evning to receive deposites from evry discription of working people male and female young and old and each Contributer puts in from 10 pence up according as they find it Convenient and as no fines is levied off any member every one makes their payments Convenient to their Silver[18] and when any Subscriber,s payments amounts to 10ˢ they draw interest at the rate of 5 per C,ᵗ this is one of the most valuable institutions ever invented for the benifet of the lower Class of the Community and you may guess the general aprobation it meets with from the Sum alredy Colected in 12 nights onley Since its Commensement amounting to £1256–14–9 I must draw this Letter to an end but I cannot Conclude dear Henry without expressing our Sorrow at your determination in gowing to the Indian teritories if there was any posibelity that you Could get home I think it would be much better than to exile your Self and your Family into Such an uncertain and in all probibility uncomfortable Situation for things are [not] altogether So bad here but working people can live in my openion as Comfortable and Contented as they can do in america[19] for all those that has to earn their Bread by the Sweat of their Brow has to work there as well as here and the rate[20] of our provisions is likely to be very modrate we have not Seen the oat Meal these 2 years more than 15ˢ per C,ʷᵗ,[21] and the rent of Land and Houses is falling in praportion Land in general is down from 25 to 35 per Cent; the rate of victuling at present is Meal from 9ˢ-6ᵈ to 10ˢ per C,ʷᵗ Patatoes from 15ᵈ to 19ᵈ per do[22] Beef from 3¼ᵈ to 6ᵈ per lb fresh Butter from 1ˢ to 1ˢ-3ᵈ per lb Eggs from 3½ to 5ᵈ per doz Sweet Milk 2ᵈ per quart and other things in praportion. Ann Coyne was here last week from Magheragell they are all well there and desires to be remembred to you, Wm Witherops Familey is also well and likewise Sends their Love, Jery Lee,ˢ Sister lives here and desires to let you know that he is dead he was wounded at the Battle of Waterloo and died Shortly after, the name of the man that tom,s wife bore the Child to is John Johnson,[23] I Can add no mor but remains your affectionate Brother and sister Wm & E Coyne.

18 **Convenient to their Silver**: i.e., according to their means (whatever they can afford).
19 **things are [not] altogether So bad here but working people can live in my openion as Comfortable and Contented as they can do in america**: i.e., conditions are bad here, but in my opinion they are not so bad that working people cannot live as comfortably and contentedly (in Belfast) as they can in America. 20 **rate**: cost. 21 **we have not Seen the oat Meal these 2 years more than 15ˢ**: i.e., during the last two years we have not seen oatmeal priced at more than fifteen shillings. **per C,ʷᵗ**: per hundredweight (a unit of measurement equal to 112 lbs). On the prices of oatmeal, potatoes etc., however, see n. 30. 22 **per do**: per ditto (i.e., **per C,ʷᵗ**); see n. 21. 23 **the name of the man that tom,s wife bore the Child to is John Johnson**: this line likely reflects a family scandal. **tom** may be Thomas Coyne, probably William's and Henry's

The urban assault that William Coyne described was made against the house of Francis Johnson, one of east Ulster's most prominent manufacturers and merchants, who employed at least 450 cotton weavers (primarily on the putting-out system) and other workers in and around Belfast. Johnson was also a 'resolute' opponent of 'combinations' – the illegal unions that weavers, printers and other artisans organized to regulate wages and working conditions in the various trades.[24] Indeed, it was Johnson's recent reduction of his employees' wages (or piece-rates) that prompted Belfast's unionized weavers to attack his house. It was not surprising, therefore, that the town's leading citizens mobilized at once to express their 'indignation,' 'horror and detestation' at what they and the *Belfast News-Letter* denounced as 'this foul deed,' this 'unprecedented outrage,' 'this most atrocious offence, the equal of which,' they claimed (conveniently forgetting the legalized butchery that Belfast and east Ulster had witnessed in 1797–9), 'had never before occured in this district of the country.'[25]

On the day following the assault, the town's 'principal inhabitants' met at the stock exchange and appointed a 'Committee of twenty-one Gentlemen,' principally 'in the cotton and muslin trades,' to assist the magistrates and constables in apprehending the 'monsters' 'concerned in this dreadful outrage'. As Coyne's letter attested, the Committee subscribed rewards of £2000 to anyone who would 'discover on, and prosecute [the assailants] to conviction' and of £500 for 'Private Information as may lead to the[ir] discovery and conviction' – plus the promise of 'his Majesty's most gracious Pardon for any Person or Persons implicated … who shall give such information.' Within a week, total subscriptions soared to nearly £8000, and from Dublin the lord lieutenant pledged to pardon anyone willing to 'discover [the culprits'] accomplices.'

At least two thousand printed notices, advertising the rewards, were 'circulated through town and country,' and by mid-May they had proved effective.

brother, who (like William) was listed as a cooper, living at 3 Edward Street (off Patrick Street), in *Bradshaw's Belfast Directory* (1819). Likewise, the **John Johnson** reputed to be the father of **tom,s wife**'s child may have been the same John Johnson, whitesmith, who in 1813 resided at 15 Bluebell Entry, only a few houses removed from William Coyne's abode on the same street (*Belfast Street Directory* [c. 1813]; see n. 3). **24** The description of Johnson is from his obituary in *BNL*, 2 January 1818. The descriptions of the meeting of Belfast's leading citizens, the advertisement for the apprehension of Johnson's assailants, and the weavers' trial, sentencing, execution etc., recounted in the subsequent paragraphs, are in the following issues of the *BNL*: 1 March 1816 (the meeting and advertisement); 5 March, 8 March and 15 March (the advertisement and the lord lieutenant's proclamation); 7 May (the 'hue and cry' for William Gray); 13 August (the trial); 16 August (Judge Day's address to the jury and his sentencing of Johnson's assailants [and of other prisoners]); 3 September (Madden's pardon); 10 September (the executions). On the illegality of Irish 'combinations,' see Patrick Park, 'The Combination Acts in Ireland, 1727–1825,' *Irish Jurist*, 14:2 (1979), 340–59, in addition to Boyle, *Irish labor movement*, pp 7–16, and Boyd, *Rise of the Irish trade unions*, pp 23–6. **25** The floggings and executions that occurred during Belfast's 'Reign of Terror' are detailed in Benn, *History of the town of Belfast*, i, 662, and ii, 20; and in [Joy], *Historical collections relative to the town of Belfast*.

The first fugitive to be apprehended was William Gray, a muslin weaver from Ballymacarret in north Down, although originally from Portadown in north Armagh. Gray turned state's evidence, and by 5 July the authorities had arrested five of his alleged accomplices: John Doe, John Magill, Joseph Madden, James Dickson and James Park. All were cotton weavers from Belfast or north Down and probably members of the Belfast Muslin Weavers' Society. As far as can be determined, all were Protestants.[26]

Their day-long trial took place on 12 August 1816, before the County Antrim assizes at Carrickfergus. By today's standards, the proceedings could fairly be described as a 'show trial,' as the prosecutors and the judge clearly were determined to condemn not only the alleged culprits but also their 'ruinous ... conspiracies' and 'evil system of combinations.' The prosecution's opening statement skillully combined eulogies of Ulster's cotton industry – as patriotic as well as profitable – and of the economic benefits conferred on Ireland by the Act of Union, with dire warnings of the awful consequences for the property rights and public safety of Belfast's citizens if the prisoners were not convicted and punished. As for the latter, the prosecution compared their actions and their 'infernal machine' (the bomb that destroyed Johnson's house) to the savagery of 'the tomahawk and scalping knife' and to the bloody scenes in Paris enacted during the 'Terror' of the French Revolution. 'If this kind of conduct is permitted,' the prosecutor warned, 'this country will soon be not safe to live in.'

After William Gray's testimony, implicating the prisoners in varying degrees, the defence attorney argued that Gray had testified solely for the reward money and to escape punishment – thinking 'it would be better ... to hang others than be hanged [him]self.' The defence also alleged that Gray had a long history of petty thievery in both Ireland and Scotland, and hence his word was doubly untrustworthy, whereas those whom Gray accused were 'honest, ... industrious, hard-working m[e]n,' at least one of whom, as a witness testified, had been asleep in his home on the night of the attack. Yet most critical for the defence was its argument that, under the law, a defendant could not be convicted solely on the testimony of a single informer. Therefore, since Gray's identification of the accused men could not be corroborated, and since all other evidence against them was circumstantial, the jury must acquit.

At this point, however, the prosecuting attorneys made a crucial intervention, later seconded by Judge Day in his address to the jury, forcefully arguing not only that Gray was an exemplary witness but, more important, that criminals in capital cases could indeed be hanged on the word of only one informer. The

26 On the likelihood that the accused were members of the Belfast Muslin Weavers' Society, see Boyd, *Rise of the Irish trade unions*, p. 30. On their probable religious affiliations, see below, n. 63. It is intriguing that although as many as two dozen men reportedly were involved in the attack on Johnson's house, as far as the author can determine only Doe, Magill, Madden, Dickson and Park were ever tried and condemned for the crime.

judge then charged the jury members to do their duty, pausing only to praise 'the fortitude [and] manly firmness' displayed by Francis Johnson and by the other manufacturers whose efforts had secured the prisoners' apprehension.

After two hours' deliberation, the jury declared that Doe, Magill and Madden were guilty of attacking Johnson's house, but that Dickson and Park could be found guilty only of conspiracy to plot the assault. Although the jury recommended mercy, Judge Day sentenced Doe, Magill and Madden to be hanged for their 'malignant and atrocious outrage ... against a Gentleman who was benefiting his country by promoting its manufactures' – and to be hanged in Belfast, rather than in Carrickfergus, 'in order that the[ir] example might have a more powerful and lasting effect in deterring others from engaging in such unlawful associations'. The judge then sentenced Dickson and Park to the 'severest punishment' allowed for their crime – public whippings on the Belfast town scaffold and eighteen months' imprisonment – '[i]n order to teach their associates the impropriety of their conduct and the necessity of obedience to the laws'. Concluding his remarks, Judge Day expressed his trust that the trial's results would bring east Ulster's weavers 'to a sense of their duty, and show them the value of peaceable and industrious habits, and the danger of those unlawful combinations which would vainly usurp the law of the land; they will see,' he declared, 'that however secretly or numerously they associate for their lawless purposes, ... the strong arm of the law will always be found superior to their utmost efforts.'[27]

27 Magill, Doe, Madden, Dickson and Park were not the only prisoners tried and sentenced at the Antrim Assizes on 12 August 1816. Dominick M'Ilhatton and William Eggleston were sentenced to be hanged for breaking into a farmer's house; Michael M'Anally, Patrick M'Kenna and Peter Doran were condemned to transporation for life for robbing bleach-greens (another common crime against Ulster's manufacturing and mercantile interests); and Owen Donnelly was sentenced to transportation for seven years for stealing a hat. Interestingly, most of these 'ordinary criminals' had traditionally 'Catholic' names, although they resided in a county (Antrim) that was overwhelmingly Protestant (and Presbyterian), whereas the 'victims' of their crimes were Protestants, principally manufacturers and merchants – and at least two of them, John Sinclair and Col. Foster Coulson, were members of the 'Committee of twenty-one Gentlemen' who had organized the apprehension of Francis Johnson's assailants. Thus, although this essay argues for the existence at this time of something resembling 'class war' *within* east Ulster's Protestant community – as evidenced in part by the language employed by the judge, the prosecution and the *Belfast News-Letter* in the 'Belfast's first bomb' episode – clearly an alternative pattern already existed whereby 'serious' criminal behaviour, punishable by death or transportation, could 'normally' or 'naturally' be attributed to Catholics. For an example of contemporary popular convictions that Ulster Protestants, especially Presbyterians, rarely committed major or violent crimes, see John Gamble, *Views of society and manners in the North of Ireland, in a series of letters written in the year 1818* (London, 1819), pp 326, 366–7. By mid-century, however, this folk belief had become an integral feature of Unionist ideology, fundamental to the conviction that 'the Protestant "way of life"' was superior to that of Irish Catholics; e.g., see D. George Boyce, 'The making of Unionism,' in Boyce and Alan O'Day (eds), *Defenders of the Union: a survey of British and Irish Unionism since 1801* (London, 2001), p. 23;

For unknown reasons the lord lieutenant commuted Joseph Madden's death sentence to transportation for life, but on 6 September 1816 John Magill and John Doe were hanged, on Belfast's High Street, in an 'awful spectacle' designed to 'display the power and the terror of the law in the most impressive manner.' Whether to overawe the 'immense multitude of spectators' or to prevent expressions of sympathy (or rescue attempts) by the crowds, a 'strong military guard' escorted the prisoners from Carrickfergus jail to Belfast, where they joined yet another 'strong detachment of military, both horse and foot', from the city's army barracks. At least four clergymen were present at the hangings, before which the condemned men prayed and made speeches (designed for publication) of confession and repentance. Both prisoners played the contrite and pious roles expected in such rituals, albeit in quite different ways. John Doe, a member of an evangelical sect, attributed his transgressions solely to personal, moral failings: to his 'cohabitation' with 'a woman of bad character', by whose influence he was 'cut off from the Church' and led 'step [by] step' to 'the awful deserved chastenings of the Lord'. By contrast, John Magill addressed the socio-political issues involved and expressed sorrow that he had 'acted under the influence of mistaken views.' 'I now see the evil of all such combinations and outrages,' he concluded; 'I see I have offended God, dishonoured religion, and injured society, for which I am sincerely sorry.' After Magill's presentation, the prisoners were 'launched into eternity', meeting their deaths with 'manly fortitude' and 'calm resignation', each leaving 'a wife and child to lament their untimely fate.'[28]

Thus was smashed what the *Belfast News-Letter* later called 'a system of combination which threatened to subvert the very basis of every principle of commercial good order.'[29] Yet in truth, commerce and industry in early nineteenth-century Belfast and in Ulster, generally, were scarcely in 'good order'. Indeed, the assault on Johnson's house and business premises can be understood only in the contexts of the profound economic dislocations and often severe distress that afflicted northern Irish society in the decades following the Act of Union.

Between 1782 and 1800 Belfast's population had increased from about 13,000 to 22,000, and by 1831 it rose to more than 53,000, as men and women from rural Ulster migrated to the city or its hinterland to work as handloom weavers or as spinners in cotton factories and, increasingly after 1830, in linen mills. In 1800, according to the Revd John Dubourdieu, the cotton industry employed about 13,500 people in Belfast alone, plus another 27,000 within ten miles of the city.

Catherine Hirst, *Religion, politics and violence in nineteenth-century Belfast: The Pound and Sandy Row* (Dublin, 2002), pp 27–8, 32, 36.   28 A week after their comrades' executions, Park and Dickson endured their public floggings. Park received 314 lashes, Dickson 269; both fainted during their ordeals, after which they were returned to Carrickfergus jail to serve their eighteen-month sentences; see Boyd, *Rise of the Irish trade unions*, p. 32.   29 *BNL*, 2 January 1818.

However, economic growth was unsteady and its rewards were distributed very unevenly. The American Non-Importation and Embargo acts of 1806 and 1807, respectively, followed in 1812 by the outbreak of the Anglo-American War, cut off Belfast's cotton supplies and caused bankruptcies and unemployment. In 1815 the return of peace precipitated a depression in the textile industry, the effects of which on the labouring poor, in town and country alike, were exacer-bated by poor harvests, rising food and fuel prices, outbreaks of typhus, and the return to the labour market of thousands of demobilized soldiers and sailors. In the following year (when Belfast's weavers attacked Johnson's home) the city's poor were ravaged by starvation and fever, falling wages and rising unemployment, responding with food riots and a wave of 'normal' crimes against property. In the mid-1820s the economic situation again deteriorated sharply, as severe industrial depression throughout the United Kingdom coincided with parliament's withdrawal of tariff protection for Irish cotton goods. By the early 1830s Ulster's cotton industry had been eclipsed by linen manufacturing, but although the latter expanded rapidly, most of its new factories and economic advantages were concentrated in the province's eastern corner. Beyond the vicinity of Belfast and a few other east Ulster towns, cottage wages and industries collapsed. Rural spinners could not compete with cheap, factory-spun thread, and country weavers could rarely survive far from eastern supplies of yarn and the industry's principal markets. Social conditions among the North's rural poor markedly deteriorated.[30]

Moreover, according to many contemporaries, living standards among weavers in Belfast and other towns also declined sharply. In 1802 a visitor to Belfast reported that its cotton weavers earned at least 18s. per week, but their wages had begun to decline before 1815, and by the mid-1820s, when one-third of the citys weavers were unemployed, wages had fallen to merely 7s. per week. In 1827 William Ritchie, when petitioning the British government on behalf of

---

30 On Belfast's population, see Benn, *History of the town of Belfast*, i, 300, and ii, 82. For contem-porary accounts of the Ulster cotton and linen industries, see: Revd John Dubourdieu, *Statistical survey of the County of Antrim* ... (Dublin, 1812), pp 389–411 (1800 employment data on p. 404), and *Statistical survey of the County of Down* ... (Dublin, 1802), pp 235–36; Gamble, *Views of society and manners in the North of Ireland*, pp 415–16; Henry D. Inglis, *Ireland in 1834: a journey throughout Ireland, during the spring, summer, and autumn of 1834* (London, 1835), ii, 224–63 passim; and Edward Wakefield, *An account of Ireland, statistical and political* (London,1812), I, pp 680–708. See also the secondary sources cited in n. 31 below. On the Belfast food riots of 1816, see Boyd, *Rise of the Irish trade unions*, p. 31. The cost-of-living indexes compiled by Professor Liam Kennedy of Queen's University, Belfast, indicate steeply rising prices for oatmeal, potatoes and other necessities in 1816–17; thereafter prices generally declined but rose sharply again in 1824–7, 1831–2, and 1837–42; my thanks to Professor Kennedy for sharing this data. In the early nineteenth century, many of the thousands of Irish petitions sent to the British Colonial Office, begging for assisted emigration, were written by or on behalf of demobilized soldiers and sailors, now landless and unemployed, who had served in the British forces during the French Revolutionary and/or Napoleonic wars (see below, n. 31).

two hundred Belfast-area weavers desperate to emigrate, described a house-to-house survey which revealed that 'three fourths of the operative weavers' had weekly wages of only 2*s*. to 4*s*., while the remainder earned merely 4*s*. to 5*s*. 'We have no prospect in future of ever paying our rents,' Ritchie lamented; hence, '[we] are completely in the power of our Landlords, who can at pleasure take from us our little all. It is with the greatest difficulty [even] the best workmen can procure subsistence for their families, and we could produce instances of those who have lately died here in a state of starvation.'

Considerable testimony suggests that conditions for east Ulster's weavers improved little, if any, during the following decade – despite the rapid shift from cotton to linen manufacturing and the latter's much-vaunted 'prosperity.' In the early 1830s the *Belfast News-Letter* reported that the weavers in the Belfast suburb of Ballymacarret, across the Long Bridge over the River Lagan, were obliged to eat 'oatmeal unfit for cattle' and were 'reduced to skeletons from overwork and lack of sleep.' In 1838 local weaver James Boyd claimed that he and his peers laboured daily from fourteen to eighteen hours for as little as 3*s*. 6*d*. per week, while others testified that Belfast's working-class neighbourhoods were 'a mass of filth and misery.' In 1840 Cæsar Otway contended that the 'physical condition of [Ulster's] weavers' was 'worse ... than that of any [other] class of Irishmen.' Throughout the pre-Famine decades, British officials were besieged by similar reports – not only from Belfast but also from Ballymena, Moy, Newry, Rathfriland and other towns in east and mid-Ulster, as well as from places such as Dunnamanagh and Ballyshannon in south and west Ulster – penned by weavers who complained that low wages and uncertain employment rendered it nearly 'impossible [for them] to make a living'.[31]

31. Bardon, *History of Ulster*, pp 259–60; Beckett and Glasscock, *Belfast*, pp 82–7; Boyd, *Rise of the Irish trade unions*, pp 24–5; Boyle, *Irish labor movement*, p. 28; F. Geary, 'The rise and fall of the Belfast cotton industry: some problems,' *Irish Economic and Social History* 8 (1981), 30–49; Green, *Lagan Valley*, pp 100–2; Maguire, *Belfast*, p. 31; and, more broadly, Líam Kennedy and Philip Ollerenshaw (eds), *An economic history of Ulster, 1820–1939* (Manchester, 1985), chs 1–2; and Eoin O'Malley, 'The decline of Irish industry in the nineteenth century,' *Economic and Social Review* 13:1 (Oct. 1981), 30–2. W.P. Ryan, *The Irish labour movement* (Dublin, 1919), pp 78–111, contains much testimony by and about weavers in Belfast and elsewhere in Ulster during the 1830s; much of this qualifies Henry Inglis' highly favourable impressions in 1834, but even he acknowledged that, over the previous fifteen years, the condition of rural weavers and spinners had deteriorated; see Inglis, *Ireland in 1834*, ii, 220. The best general work on the North's linen weavers is W. H. Crawford, *The handloom weavers and the Ulster linen industry* (Belfast, 1994). An excellent local study of socio-economic changes in Belfast's western hinterland is Marilyn Cohen, *Linen, family and community in Tullylish, County Down, 1690–1914* (Dublin, 1997), which includes Cæsar Otway's observation on p. 75; Cohen notes (pp 83–4) the weavers' testimony that their conditions were worse when they were employed by manufacturers – i.e., on the putting-out system and/or in weaving shops, as were Francis Johnson's assailants – than when they worked independently. A unique primary source of testimony about socio-economic conditions in Ulster (and elsewhere in Ireland) is the 384 series of Colonial Office (C.O.) Papers, vols 1–75,

One would expect that such severe distress might engender conflicts between Ulster's Protestant weavers and their employers – as well as among Protestant landlords, tenants, subtenants and labourers, generally – and, indeed, examples of such strife had been common at least since the Oakboy and Steelboy uprisings of the 1760s and early 1770s. In the 1780s poor northern Protestants' affiliations with the violent activities of the Peep o' Day Boys and, in the 1790s, of the United Irishmen and the Loyal Orange Order also had stemmed, at least in part, from economic anxieties. In the same decades, struggles between Belfast's cotton weavers and their employers appear to have been particularly intense, provoking condemnation from Presbyterian businessmen and editors of all political persuasions. After the Act of Union, the unsettling processes and inequitable results of industrialization (including the de-industrialization of most of Ulster's countryside) generated among the North's poor – especially among proletarianized weavers in and around Belfast – new waves of anger, organization, protest and reprisal against perceived exploitation. As early as 1802–4 the *Belfast News-Letter* expressed mounting concern about renewed trade unionism among the town's workers – 'How would trade go on or the town improve,' asked the paper's editor, 'if such actions were permitted?' – and applauded the trials and punishments of workers who combined and went on strike for higher pay. Yet in 1811 Lisburn's cotton weavers formed another union and destroyed the webs and looms of those who would not work for what its members deemed 'fair wages'. In March 1815 a 'mob of apprentice lads' rioted in Belfast against rising food costs, and in April a march on the city by Lisburn's weavers, protesting wage reductions, ended in tumult and bloodshed when police tried to arrest their leaders.[32]

Thus, in 1816 the north Down weavers' attack on Francis Johnson's house was only one of the most dramatic examples of contemporary class conflict.

in the Public Record Office, Kew, England, which contains thousands of letters written by (or on behalf of) weavers, farmers and others who, between 1817 and the mid-1840s, petitioned the British government for information about assisted passages to and/or land grants in British North America (primarily in Upper Canada – now Ontario). Quoted in this and the preceding paragraph are the petitions of weavers William Ritchie et al., Belfast, 13 April 1827 (C.O. 384/14), and of John Tovil, Kinnary, near Moy, County Tyrone, 16 April 1842 (C.O. 384/69). Similar weavers' petitions include: John Shaw, Belfast, 17 January 1817 (C.O. 384/1); James Smily et al., Bracky, County Armagh, n.d. [recd 19 August 1823] (C.O. 384/9); John Burton, Cookstown, County Tyrone, 13 April 1827, and David Kennedy, Clough, County Down, 21 June 1827 (C.O. 384/16); J. Beatty, Rathfriland, County Down, 28 March 1831 (C.O. 384/24); Hugh McComb, Newry, County Down, 6 January 1831, and Daniel Lunney, Dunnamanagh, County Tyrone, 18 March 1831 (C.O. 384/25); Robert Ritchey, Galgorm, Ballymena, County Antrim, 13 May 1833 (C.O. 384/31); and John Moore, Belfast, 6 August 1842 (C.O. 384/69).   32 Benn, *History of the town of Belfast*, ii, 22, 36, 47; Boyd, *Rise of the Irish trade unions*, pp 23–32; Boyle, *Irish labor movement*, pp 15–16; Green, *Lagan Valley*, p. 101; McDowell, *Public opinion and government policy*, p. 62; and Hirst, *Religion, politics and violence in nineteenth-century Belfast*, pp 26–7.

Indeed, the execution of Johnson's assailants seems to have had no immediate effects. Throughout 1816 the *News-Letter* continued to bewail the 'outrages' – rivaling in frequency and severity those in proverbially 'disturbed' Catholic Munster – committed largely by Presbyterian weavers and other poor Protestants on the persons, livestock, homes and businesses of east Ulster's landlords, agents, bailiffs, strong farmers and manufacturers.

On 5 August 1816, for instance, the *News-Letter* lamented the numerous 'outrages' that recently had 'disgraced' the neighbourhood of Ballynahinch, County Down, in the parish of Magheradroll (roughly three-fourths of whose inhabitants were Protestants – of whom the same proportion were Presbyterians).[33] During the winter and spring 'property to a very considerable amount, consisting of dwelling-houses and offices, a bleach-mill, a flaxmill, a corn-mill, and kilns, [had] been destroyed by fire', in addition to 'cattle shot and mutilated – notices posted up, threatening death and destruction to individuals if they took certain farms, or went beyond a certain rent for their lands – houses attacked and fired into'. As late as July, 'notices were posted, … calling for a reduction of rents, and breathing vengeance against several individuals'. The same issue of the *News-Letter* also reported the County Antrim grand jury's 'great concern … at finding [before it] a list of so many unprecedented and atrocious crimes, … written in characters of blood', that had been committed in that overwhelmingly Protestant and allegedly law-abiding county. In response, Judge Day 'emphatically' asked the grand jury's members whether the local gentry were prepared to allow Antrim to 'become the Tipperary of the North?'[34]

Judge Day's analogy was suggestive, for the minds of élite Irish Protestants and British officials could easily associate Ulster's class conflicts with much wider and more profound threats to law and order. The upper- and middle-class British and Irish Protestant rhetoric of class was virtually identical to that of anti-Catholicism, as both 'papists' and the poor were stigmatized as lazy, immoral and dangerous. Revealingly, the term 'combinations' signified not only the largely or exclusively Protestant trade unions in Belfast and Dublin, but also the equally illegal Whiteboys and the other Catholic secret agrarian societies that terrorized Tipperary and other counties in southern Ireland. Members of both

33 In 1831 nearly 72 per cent of the inhabitants of Magheradroll (or Magheradrool) parish were Protestants; of the latter, almost 73 per cent were Presbyterians. See above, n. 3, for the source of 1831 religious census data.   34 *BNL*, 5 August 1816 (the Antrim grand jury met on 3 August); additional reports of crimes and 'outrages' appear in later issues, for instance in that of 6 September 1816. James G. Patterson has noted the continuance in east Ulster of rural violence, perpetrated by disaffected Presbyterians, in the years after the 1798 Rebellion; however, his study ends with Robert Emmet's and Thomas Russell's abortive rising in 1803, whereas the evidence presented here indicates that certain kinds of unrest either persisted well into the first two decades of the nineteenth century or at least resurged after the Napoleonic Wars. See James G. Patterson, 'Continued Presbyterian resistance in the aftermath of the Rebellion of 1798 in Antrim and Down,' *Eighteenth Century Life* 22:3 (November 1998), 45–61.

organizations challenged capitalist relations – for instance, the Thrashers of County Mayo tried to regulate weavers' wages as well as rents – hence, George Cornewall Lewis' characterization of the Whiteboys as 'a vast trades union for the protection of the Irish peasantry'. And in varying degrees both were suspected, by Dublin Castle and affluent Irish Protestants alike, of harbouring subversive political ideas and intentions. It was feared, for instance, that Belfast's weavers had been radicalized by the ideals of the French Revolution, spread by the writings of Thomas Paine and the activities of the United Irishmen, and the city's historian John Gray even speculates that old ideological links between radical politics and the weavers' combinations might have informed their violent activities in 1816 – or at least inspired the government's savage repression. In that light, moreover, alarmed officials could regard such assaults on property not only as implicit threats to the Union – still insecure after only fifteen years – but also as part of a broader, 'Jacobinical' pattern of escalating labour unrest and demands for sweeping political reform that, in the immediate post-war years, quite explicitly threatened the social and political order in Great Britain itself. Thus, the treatment of the Belfast weavers accused of destroying their employer's house must be viewed in light of the government's 'deliberate policy of enforcing examplary punishments' to quell lower-class 'outrages' and political dissent on both sides of the Irish Sea.[35]

In Britain, workers' unrest and political protests would continue to mount through the 1840s. In Belfast, however, the cotton weavers' combination collapsed in the 1820s, and wages fell so low that Scottish manufacturers began sending cotton yarn to be woven there, rather than in Glasgow or Paisley, both to reduce labour costs and to break the Scottish weavers' unions. To be sure,

35 On the rhetoric of class in early and mid-nineteenth-century Ireland and Britain, see Margaret Preston, 'Discourse and hegemony: race and class in the language of charity in nineteenth-century Dublin,' in Tadhg Foley and Seán Ryder (eds), *Ideology and Ireland in the nineteenth century* (Dublin, 1998), pp 101–2. On secret agrarian societies, generally, and their similarities to workers' combinations, see: George Cornewall Lewis, *Local disturbances in Ireland* (London, 1836; 1977 reprint); Kerby A. Miller, *Emigrants and exiles: Ireland and Irish emigration to North America* (New York, 1985), pp 61–7; and George O'Brien, *The economic history of Ireland from the Union to the Famine* (London, 1921; 1972 reprint), p. 398. On the suspected radicalism of Belfast's weavers, see John Gray, *The Sans Culottes of Belfast: the United Irishmen and the men of no property* (Belfast, 1998), pp 29–38; and, generally, Jim Smyth, *The men of no property: Irish radicals and popular politics in the late eighteenth century* (Dublin, 1992). On contemporary labour and political unrest in Britain, and the official panic and repression produced thereby, the classic work is E.P. Thompson, *The making of the English working class* (New York, 1963); while the official responses in London and Dublin are detailed in Brian Jenkins, *Era of Emancipation: British government of Ireland, 1812–1830* (Kingston and Montreal, 1988), e.g., pp 123–5; and in Stanley H. Palmer, *Police and protest in England and Ireland, 1780–1850* (Cambridge, 1988). Jenkins notes (p. 68) that, in the language of Robert Peel and his Tory associates in Dublin Castle, 'illegal combinations' also included the upper- and middle-class Catholic associations that campaigned for Emancipation.

occasional strikes by cabinetmakers, printers and others still occurred in the next decade.[36] But by the 1830s evidence of serious or violent social conflict among Protestants in Belfast and elsewhere in Ulster seems to have virtually disappeared – along with any lingering suspicions of the Protestant lower classes' fidelity to the Union and the crown. The mass actions that had marked the Oak- and Steelboy agitations in the east Ulster countryside never recurred, for example, and in 1837 Jonathan Binns, a member of parliament's recent poor law inquiry commission, described class relationships among rural Protestants in east Ulster as entirely quiescent, despite the extreme competition for land and leases. In Belfast, James Campbell, a local manufacturer, testified in 1838 that weavers' combinations had been extinct for more than a decade; ever since 1825, Campbell reported, 'labour [was] perfectly free' – that is, non-unionized – in the city's textile industries, and he rejoiced that, even when faced with wage cuts, his workers behaviour was 'very respectful and proper'. In the same period a Belfast weaver, also testifying before a parliamentary committee, pleaded that the government maintain low Irish wages in order to afford protection and encouragement to capital. Likewise, although in Belfast and elsewhere in Ulster the franchise (especially after 1829) was extremely restricted and political power monopolized by a wealthy few, the 1830s witnessed in Protestant Ulster no workers' movement for equal rights that was remotely comparable to the Irish-led Chartist agitation in Britain itself.[37]

To be sure, there were complaints that workers' *attitudes* still remained less than fully satisfactory. As late as 1833, for instance, the co-owner of Belfast's enormous York Street Mill lamented that many of his workers, often recent migrants from the Ulster countryside, were 'as yet scarcely accustomed' to the demands of the new 'factory system'. However, it was precisely during this period that visitors to Belfast and to east Ulster, generally, became lavish in their praise for the 'industriousness' and 'steadiness' exhibited by the city's and the region's inhabitants. Significantly, observers, native as well as foreign, almost invariably associated this 'spirit of commercial enterprise' with Protestantism, the benign effects of the Act of Union and equally salutary 'British' influences. Thus, in 1834 Henry Inglis reported that, because of its 'Scottish' character, the

36 Gray, *Sans Culottes of Belfast*, pp 37–8; Boyd, *Rise of the Irish trades unions*, pp 29, 40–3; McDowell, *Public opinion and government policy*, pp 62–3.   37 Jonathan Binns, *The miseries and beauties of Ireland* (London, 1837), i, 54 and passim; Boyle, *Irish labor movement*, pp 26–7; E. Strauss, *Irish nationalism and British democracy* (London, 1951; 1975 reprint), p. 76. On politics in early nineteenth-century Ulster, see Peter Jupp, 'County Down Elections, 1783–1831,' *Irish Historical Studies* 28:70 (Sept. 1972), 177–206; Brian Walker, 'Landowners and parliamentary elections in County Down, 1801–1921,' in Lindsay Proudfoot (ed.), *Down: history & society: interdisciplinary essays on the history of an Irish county* (Dublin, 1997), pp 297–307; and especially Frank Wright, *Two lands on one soil: Ulster politics before Home Rule* (New York, 1996), chs 2–3; and on the Irish role in British Chartism, see Dorothy Thompson, *Outsiders: class, gender and nation* (London, 1993), ch. 4.

North had 'nothing in common with the rest of Ireland', and in 1843 the Halls concluded that Belfast was full of 'English' virtues – 'so much bustle, such an aspect of business, a total absence of all suspicion of [that] idleness' – 'improvidence' and 'insubordination', as other observers decried – that allegedly characterized the Catholic populace of southern Ireland.[38]

Such testimony suggests that it was these pre-famine decades that witnessed the emergence and elaboration of what Unionists often called 'the Protestant "way of life"': a complex of pious, loyal and resolutely *bourgeois* norms that became the touchstone of modern Ulster Protestant identity and of Ulster Unionist political culture. In this now-familiar formula, Protestant religion, British ethnicity, loyalty to the crown, obedience to the laws, respect for property, sturdy self-reliance and steady, sober, industrious behaviour were allegedly inextricable. Protestantism, Unionism and respectability, in short, were supposedly synonymous. Thus, by 1854 a Protestant missionary in Belfast naturally equated 'respectable' behaviour with Protestantism and found it difficult to believe that the people he encountered in Sandy Row, who did not behave 'respectably', could possibly be Protestants.[39]

Yet how and why had this remarkable transformation supposedly occurred? How had Ulster's turbulent Protestant underclass allegedly been transformed into exemplars of industry and deference? Put another way, how had Protestant Ulster's upper and middle classes, so beleaguered in the early 1800s, succeeded in forging a sense of pan-Protestant identity and community, characterized by Unionist verities and capitalist values, that ideally transcended social and denominational divisions? To what degree was the alleged transformation reflective of an altered reality? Was the 'Protestant "way of life"' merely a *bourgeois* aspiration, itself rooted in Protestant Ulster's class relationships, that obscured as much as it revealed? Why and how did it become a communal badge, integral to Ulster Protestants' cultural and political identity?

Unionist spokesmen often argued that the industry, sobriety and loyalty which they attributed to Ulster Protestants were virtually primordial – inherent in their religion and British heritage. In the late eighteenth century, however, observers had been hard-pressed to discover anything resembling a 'Protestant ethic' at work among the great majority of the North's tenants, craftsmen and labourers. In 1776–9, for example, the English visitor Arthur Young, an enthu-

38 Cormac Ó Gráda, *Ireland: a new economic history, 1780–1939* (Oxford, 1994), p. 329; Inglis, *Ireland in 1834*, ii, 217–18, 249–51; Maguire, *Belfast*, p. 33. As early as 1825 the conservative *Belfast News-Letter* claimed that the city's mechanics were much more interested in scientists and inventors such as Newton, Boyle and Arkwright than in martyred United Irishmen like Emmet, Russell and Tone; McDowell, *Public opinion and government policy in Ireland*, pp 58–9. 39 The phrase became ubiquitous in Unionist rhetoric; see Charles Townshend, *Ireland: the twentieth century* (London, 1998), p. 58. A useful summary of Unionism ideology is in Boyce, 'The making of Unionism,' p. 23. Hirst, *Religion, politics and violence in nineteenth-century Belfast*, p. 36.

siast for capitalist development, complained that the Protestant small farmers and weavers in and around the east Ulster towns of Antrim, Hillsborough, Lurgan, Newry and Warrenpoint were 'in general apt to be licentious and disorderly'. Despite the consequent 'misery and inconvenience', they subdivided their smallholdings, repeatedly and 'universally', to enable their sons to marry young. Moreover, they refused to 'work more than half what they might do, owing to the cheapness of provisions making them idle, as they think of nothing more than the present necessity'. '[W]hen meal is cheap, they will not work,' but instead they 'spend much of their time in whiskey houses' or hunting hares; 'a pack of hounds is never heard', Young lamented, 'but all the weavers leave their looms, and away they go after them by hundreds.' In the early decades of the nineteenth century, both foreign and native observers continued to make similar remarks. In 1810 John Gamble, a Presbyterian from Strabane, County Tyrone, bemoaned the notorious uncleanliness of his co-religionists' bodies, homes, clothes and eating and cooking utensils, and two years later the English visitor, Edward Wakefield, noted that northern Presbyterians were as fond of holidays and whiskey, and as averse to the law, as their Catholic neighbours. As noted above, even in the 1830s some middle-class observers commented that Belfast's weavers often still entertained 'erroneous opinions of the relations of employers and labourers, of masters and servants.'[40]

Also, during the late 1700s landlords and officials had complained incessantly about the rampant 'insubordination' and 'disloyalty' among east Ulster's Protestants – especially among its Presbyterians – and with good reason, for in the 1790s the United Irishmen were more thoroughly organized in north Down, the Route and in other overwhelmingly Protestant and Presbyterian parts of east Ulster than anywhere else in Ireland. And, again, well into the early 1800s observers such as Wakefield and Gamble (the latter now in 1818) remarked on Ulster Presbyterians' continued alienation from – even hostility to – their landlords, the Church of Ireland and the laws. Indeed, in 1812 Wakefield alleged that northern Dissenters remained 'Republicans in principle ... [and] in their hearts decided enemies to the established government.' Thus, the historian Ian McBride concludes that, for some time after the Act of Union, Ulster 'Presbyterian political attitudes remained almost instinctively anti-government in character.'[41]

40 Arthur W. Hutton (ed.), *Arthur Young's tour in Ireland (1776–1779)* (London, 1892), i, 120, 127, 130–4, 150–1; John Gamble, *Sketches of history, politics, and manners, in Dublin, and the North of Ireland, in 1810* (London, 1826 ed.), pp 262–3; Wakefield, *An account of Ireland*, ii, 739–40; Hirst, *Religion, politics and violence* , p. 28.   41 On the United Irishmen in east Ulster, see Nancy J. Curtin, 'Rebels and radicals: The United Irishmen in County Down,' in Proudfoot (ed.), *Down: history & society*, pp 267–96; Curtin, *The United Irishmen: popular politics in Ulster and Dublin, 1791–1798* (Oxford, 1994); and A.T.Q. Stewart, *The summer soldiers: the 1798 Rebellion in Antrim and Down* (Belfast, 1995). Wakefield, *An account of Ireland*, ii, 546–7 (I am grateful to Prof. David W. Miller, of Carnegie Mellon University, for this reference); Gamble, *Views of society and*

Of course, for the Revd Henry Cooke and many others, by the 1830s and after it was Belfast's and east Ulster's celebrated economic growth that largely explained their Protestant inhabitants' growing contentment with both the Union and élite rule, and their all-class unity in the face of Catholic nationalist agitation. But as we have seen, the North's prosperity was by no means widespread, even among Protestants. Another explanation for Protestant workers' apparent docility was put forth by Alexander Moncrieffe, a Belfast manufacturer, who in 1838 testified before a parliamentary commission that 'Catholic and Orange rivalries made trade unionism impossible and ensured a supply of cheap labour.'[42] Yet Moncrieffe's explanation was too simple and superficial. It reflected an assumption that Protestant-Catholic animosities were, if not primordial and inevitable, at least always sufficient *in themselves* to mitigate intra-communal class conflict and to ensure that poor Protestants would defer to the leadership and embrace the capitalist values of their wealthier coreligionists.

The processes by which Ulster's Protestant élites achieved socio-cultural and political hegemony over the Protestant poor were in fact much more complex than either Cooke's or Moncrieffe's explanation implied. Rather, it is arguable that the construction of the Ulster Unionist community, united in defence of the Protestant way of life, had many of its most important origins neither in shared Protestant prosperity nor in Protestant–Catholic strife (local or national), but instead in the upper- and middle-class resolutions of the class struggle revealed by the violent incident described in William Coyne's 1816 letter.

For example, in the early 1800s it was by no means certain that Ulster's predominantly Anglican upper class and its largely Presbyterian middle classes (themselves bitterly divided over contemporary political and religious issues, including the United Irishmen's legacy) could join to present a united front to their own subtenants and labourers.[43] Yet in the aftermath of the weavers' assault on Francis Johnson's home, Belfast's and east Ulster's gentry, magistrates, merchants and manufacturers – Anglicans and Presbyterians, Whigs and Tories – united as 'Gentlemen' and mobilized their considerable resources against the workers' threat to property and order. This was not an isolated instance of such convergence. Given the prevalence of lower-class unrest and violence in the early 1800s, the mobilization of élite opinion, if not overt power, concerning class

manners in the North of Ireland, pp 87, 191, 197–8, 211–12, 367–9; and McBride, 'Ulster Presbyterians and the passing of the Act of Union,' 75.   42 Boyle, *Irish labor movement*, pp 28–9; Moncrieffe's statement is also summarized in Boyd, *Rise of the Irish trade unions*, p. 25, and in Ryan, *Irish labour movement*, p. 84.   43 Significantly, the *Belfast News-Letter*'s campaign against east Ulster's lower-class Protestant combinations occurred simultaneously with a movement (orchestrated by the Cabinet and Dublin Castle, but spearheaded by local Presbyterian conservatives) to purge the city's Academical Institute of faculty and students who allegedly harboured 'disloyal' and 'heretical' opinions; e.g., see the issue of 7 May 1816. On this controversy, see Peter Brooke, *Ulster Presbyterians: the historical perspective, 1610–1970* (Dublin, 1987), pp 137–45; and Finlay Holmes, *Henry Cooke* (Belfast, 1981), pp 14–15.

issues must have become semi-permanent and self-perpetuating, creating common interests and sympathies that could transcend other differences.[44]

Equally important is that after 1800 a re-formed Ulster Protestant élite could no longer rely solely or even primarily on *its own* legal and military resources to confront lower-class insubordination. Whereas in 1792 Belfast's gentry and businessmen had relied on the city's own Volunteers to suppress workers' combinations – and even to evict a defiant tenant who lived twenty miles from town! – after the Union both statutory power and its ultimate enforcement were now centred in London and Dublin Castle. To be sure, Ulster Protestant landlords and magistrates often chafed at British reforms that, by professional-izing the Irish legal and policing systems, reduced their autonomy and increased their dependence on British authority. In the crisis of the early 1800s, however, when it appeared that 'commercial good order' teetered on the brink of collapse, their own spokesmen cried out for strong, effective action that could emanate only from Westminster and Dublin. Thus, in late 1816 the *Belfast News-Letter*'s exasperated editor announced that, since 'declarations, resolutions, and subscriptions have been tried and found unavailing[, new] energy must be infused, [new] measures must be matured and acted upon to reclaim the misguided multitude'. If landlords and manufacturers could not convince their tenants and workers by traditional means of 'the illegality of their proceedings, ... stronger [methods] will have to be resorted to'; for otherwise, he warned, 'the turbulent [will only] become more audacious'.[45]

In short, Ulster's Protestant upper and middle classes were obliged not only to unite but also to rely heavily on the coercive mechanisms of the post-Union British state to regain authority over their refractory inferiors. In the process, they inevitably developed a community of interest both among each other and with the Union that was now their first and last reliance in their efforts to tame the nocturnal armies of 'idle vagabonds' who assailed them.[46] After all, the

---

44 *BNL*, 1 March 1816. Mary McNeill's *The life and times of Mary Ann McCracken, 1770–1866: a Belfast panorama* (Dublin, 1960), is particularly revealing of such convergence. Although Henry Joy McCracken, the executed leader of the United Irish rebels in Antrim, lamented that 'the rich always betray the poor,' after the Rebellion his own brothers, prosperous cotton manufacturers, were quick to join his former political foes in condemning Belfast workers' illegal combinations; see pp 241–4. 45 Gray, *Sans Culottes of Belfast*, pp 15–17, 21–2. *BNL*, 5 August 1816. In 1816 the *News-Letter* also lobbied intensively for the creation of a more effective police force in Belfast; e.g., the issue of 6 September; in the same year the British parliament responded with a Police Act that inceased the authority of the city's police commissioners. On the period's police and magisterial reforms, and élite Irish opposition to them, see Jenkins, *Era of Emancipation*, and Palmer, *Police and protest in England and Ireland*; also useful are the early sections of Brian Griffin, *The Bulkies: police and crime in Belfast, 1800–1865* (Dublin, 1997); Virginia Crossman, *Local government in nineteenth-century Ireland* (Belfast, 1994); and Crossman, *Politics, law and order in nineteenth-century Ireland* (New York, 1996). 46 *BNL*, 6 September 1816.

Union not only protected Irish Protestants, generally, by submerging Ireland's Catholics in a British Protestant majority. At least equally important, it protected propertied Irish Protestants against Protestant men of no property by merging the interests of the smaller, weaker and more vulnerable Irish élite with those of Britain's ruling classes – then perhaps the most dynamic and powerful in the world.

In 1817 the old Belfast Presbyterian liberal, Henry Joy, expressed the conviction of most propertied Protestants that the Union was their best and only security. In return, for example, the historian Peter Jupp has noted the 'slavish support' which Irish members of parliament gave the British government in 1800–20, and the works of historian Brian Jenkins illustrate numerous instances of élite Irish dependence, ranging from patronage to economic policies. Among the latter, and of special relevance to the issues discussed in this chapter, are Irish Chief Secretary Robert Peel's successful efforts, in 1812, to persuade the cabinet to veto the Board of Trade's proposal to remove the tariff on foreign linen goods, as well as his support for the corn laws, enacted (1815) in part at Irish landlords' behest. Equally notable is visitor Henry Inglis' vague but tantalizing reference in 1834 to 'the peculiar favour and protection which the north of Ireland has enjoyed from the [British] state'. Of course, British support for the Irish landlord and commercial élites was designed primarily to serve imperial interests, and both Peel and his successor in Dublin Castle, Henry Goulbourn, believed that the Union could best be maintained by keeping Ireland's Protestants and Catholics divided – 'I hope they will always be disunited,' Peel wrote, and the 'great art is to keep them so ...' – a strategy that ensured both Protestant dependence on British power and what scholar Frank Wright calls 'reactionary dominance throughout the nation,' including 'the metropolis itself'. In the eyes of propertied Protestants, the internal and external, the social and political, projects were inseparable, since a 'valuable employee' was regarded *per se* as 'a more loyal subject to the British Empire'.[47]

Thus, unlike Ireland's propertied Catholics, who felt alienated and betrayed when denied their promised Emancipation for three decades after 1800, their Protestant peers soon enjoyed every reason to be loyal to a British government that long proved able, in Ireland and Britain alike, to protect essential upper-class privileges, to placate middle-class (Protestant) demands and to suppress or neutralize lower-class challenges. For seventy years after the Act of Union,

47 McBride, 'Memory and forgetting: Ulster Presbyterians and 1798,' 485–6; P. J. Jupp, 'Irish M.P.s at Westminster in the early nineteenth century,' in *Historical Studies VII* (London, 1969), p. 73; Jenkins, *Era of Emancipation*, and 'The chief secretary,' in Boyce and O'Day (eds), *Defenders of the Union*, pp 49, 55; Inglis, *Ireland in 1834*, ii, 218; on Castle officialdom and patronage, also see Edward Brynn, *Crown and Castle: British rule in Ireland, 1800–1830* (Dublin, 1978), e.g., pp 80, 119; Wright, *Two lands on one soil*, p. 53; Preston, 'Discourse and hegemony,' 108.

Westminster denied Ulster farmers' every plea for the legalization of tenant-right, passing instead a series of laws that facilitated evictions, forbade tenants' subdivision of their farms and in other ways augmented landlords' authority over the occupants of their estates. Ulster's manufacturers were no doubt equally gratified, as in 1803, for example, when parliament legislated for Ireland a special anti-combination act, the terms of which were 'decidedly harsher' than the draconian measures that applied only to British workers.[48] In addition, the Union's alliance of Irish and British property buttressed Ulster's Protestant élite in its self-interested interpretation and enforcement of such laws. For example, in late 1816, only a few months after Doe and Magill were hanged in Belfast for bombing Johnson's home, John McCann, a manufacturer in Lisburn, was acquitted of murdering his own employee, Gordon Maxwell, the leader of the muslin weavers' union, on Belfast's Malone Road, despite Maxwell's dying declaration that McCann was his killer. And of course it was ultimately by British authority that thousands of Irish men and women were transported to the Australian penal colonies – nearly 6,000 between 1825 and 1835 alone – often for challenging the 'principle[s] of commercial good order'.[49]

Many mechanisms of élite persuasion, however, depended neither on overt force nor on British legislative or administrative authority, although those constituted both the ultimate resort and the essential context. Indeed, if ordinary Ulster Protestants were to internalize the lessons which their superiors wished to inculcate, the latter needed to initiate a variety of measures offering rewards as well as punishments. It was significant, to be sure, that 1816 witnessed not only the weavers' assault on Johnson's premises but also the establishment in Belfast of a House of Correction – a new prison with a strict work regimen designed to instill 'morals and industry' among its 75 to 100 inmates.[50] At least

48 J. Dunsmore Clarkson, *Labour and nationalism in Ireland* (New York, 1925), pp 55–6; and Park, 'Combination Acts in Ireland,' 356.   49 Barton, *History of Ulster*, p. 259; Boyle, *Irish labor movement*, pp 15–16, 37; Green, *Lagan Valley*, p. 101; and *BNL*, 2 January 1818. Much cheaper and more effective than transportation, of course, would be the 'voluntary' mass emigration of the 'disaffected' or of those likely to become either disaffected or a burden on upper- and middle-class charity. Indeed, it is arguable that the British government's relaxation in the late 1820s of its prior restrictions on Irish (and British) emigration was determined not only by the growing popularity of 'free labour' theories and Malthusian apprehensions but also by the recognition, particularly during that decade's severe industrial depression, that mass lower-class emigration could relieve severe social and political pressures on the upper and middle classes in Ireland and Britain alike. Of course, the 'problem' with which British officials wrestled in the 1820s was that, without massive financial assistance from government or landlords, most of the Irish deemed particularly 'superfluous' or 'dangerous' could not afford to emigrate. See Gerard Moran, *Sending out Ireland's poor: assisted emigration to North America in the nineteenth century* (Dublin, 2004), chs 1–2.   50 *Bradshaw's Belfast Directory ... 1819* (Belfast, 1819), xx. Significantly, also, Belfast's House of Industry, to relieve and discipline the poor, was founded in 1809, partly in response to the effects of severe recession in the city's cotton industry; see Dubourdieu, *Statistical survey of the County of Antrim*, pp 410, 544–5. Yet, as Margaret Preston notes, applying

equally important, however, was the sort of initiative that William Coyne described in his eulogy of the new Belfast Savings Bank, 'instituted for the Savings of the poor and ... conducted by ... the principle Magastrates and Bankers of the town'. Such charitable and morally instructive efforts by Ulster's upper and middle classes were most obvious in cities such as Belfast but were not confined there, as during the early 1800s benevolent loan societies, almost invariably sponsored by local landlords and Protestant clergymen, sprang up in towns and villages throughout the island. Visiting Ireland in 1834, Henry Inglis noted approvingly how such loan societies engendered both dependence and good moral effects among the grateful debtors: 'Habits of punctuality are encouraged, 'he observed, 'and so is sobriety' – 'since this virtue is essential to obtaining a loan'.[51]

At least equally pervasive and effective were the pan-Protestant revivals of the Second Reformation and the host of charitable and educational institutions that were established or transformed and invigorated under their inspiration. The financial, political and ideological linkages between Irish revivalism and upper- and middle-class Irish (and British) Protestant loyalism and conservatism are well known, as all sought to purge Protestant (as well as Catholic) Irish society of the Jacobin 'French diseases' of political radicalism, religious infidelity and lower-class insubordination. In this respect, the new Hibernian Sunday Schools that flourished in east and mid-Ulster were but one example of the new forces that contributed to what historians David Hempton and Myrtle Hill have described as 'the inculcation of religious respectability which was so prominent a feature of nineteenth-century Ulster life'. To be sure, the historian Mary McNeill contends that Mary Ann McCracken, sister of the United Irish leader, was typical of Belfast's Presbyterian middle classes in channelling the political reformist zeal of the late 1700s into charitable and benevolent activities, targeting the city's poor, in the early and mid-1800s. Yet although McNeill argues for continuity between the old and new reform impulses, it seems clear that the overwhelming majority of McCracken's efforts were conducted under new evangelical auspices and control, and that, whereas the late-eighteenth-century activities had *challenged* a hierarchical order that was loyal/aristocratic, the 'busy benevolence' of the post-Union era *confirmed* a new one that was loyal/ bourgeois.[52]

Also of major importance were the quasi-charitable and material benefits of

---

historian Gareth Stedman Jones' insights to the sponsors of nineteenth-century Irish charity and missionary work, 'The policeman and the workhouse were not sufficient. The respectable and the well-to-do had to win the "hearts and minds" of the masses' as well; Preston, 'Discourse and hegemony,' 107. **51** Inglis, *Ireland in 1834*, I, pp 37–8. **52** David Hempton and Myrtle Hill, *Evangelical Protestantism in Ulster society, 1740–1890* (London, 1992), pp 59–60; see also Cohen, *Linen, family and community in Tullylish*, p. 15. McNeill, *Life and times of Mary Ann McCracken*, pp 257–87; McDowell, *Public opinion and government policy in Ireland*, p. 30.

lower-class Protestant membership in the Orange Order and in Ulster's disproportionately large Yeomanry corps. Despite its 'plebeian' rank-and-file
membership, reportedly drawn (as in County Armagh) from 'the lowest orders',
the historian K. Theodore Hoppen concludes that Ulster's Anglican gentry and
magistrates were in the forefront of the Orange Order, and that 'the heart of the
movement' was supplied by 'the substantial farmers who predominated as local
leaders' in the countryside, supplemented in the towns by men in managerial (for
example, foreman) or clerical posts.53 Thus, the Orange Lodges were uniquely
able to execute what surely were some of their most vital functions: to ensure
ordinary Orangemen received preferential legal treatment, of course, but also –
and of at least equal importance – to insulate them against the dangers of
eviction, unemployment and emigration.54 The Yeomanry was also a hierarchical
property-based force, and hence a means by which landlords exercised control
over their tenants. Moreover, during the economically distressed early 1800s the
pay as well as the preferential treatment that ordinary Yeomen earned for their
service was perhaps at least as important as – indeed, was inseparable from – the
political and psychological status conferred by this evidence of their
commitment to the Union and to their élite officers' definitions of law and
order.55

53 K. Theodore Hoppen, *Elections, politics and society in Ireland, 1832–1885* (Oxford, 1984), pp
320–1. Scholars who emphasize the sometimes contentious relationships between élite and
plebeian Orangeism may question this essay's implicit argument as to the importance of the
Orange Order's role in enforcing upper- and middle-class hegemony. I believe, however, that the
distinctions and tensions some historians discern between the two phenomena have been greatly
overdrawn.   54 On Orangeism and emigration, see n. 75.   55 Martin W. Dowling, *Tenant right
and agrarian society in Ulster, 1600–1870* (Dublin, 1999), p. 99, paraphrasing Frank Wright's
argument concerning Orangeism in his *Two lands on one soil*. On the Yeomanry, see Allan
Blackstock, *An ascendancy army: the Irish Yeomanry, 1796–1834* (Dublin, 1998); e.g., pp 222–4;
quotation on p. 271. Blackstock notes that '[o]nly in Ulster were there sufficient numbers of
yeomen to make an impact on internal disorder, *yet there they were needed least*' (p. 251; my
emphasis). However, if we conceptualize Ulster society not merely according to a simplistic 'Two
Traditions' (Protestant *vs.* Catholic) model, but also in terms of intra-Protestant class and
denominational divisions, then the heavy concentration of Yeomen in Ulster (especially in
overwhelmingly Presbyterian east Ulster) seems a logical response to the kinds of social-control
problems dramatized by the Belfast weavers' 1816 assault on Francis Johnson's house, as well as
providing a Castle-funded and an Anglican gentry-led means by which the region's Presbyterians
could be managed by – if not integrated within – a pan-Protestant Tory-Orange bloc. The
Orange Order and the Yeomanry had other symbiotic relationships that greatly benefited their
overlapping memberships. For instance, Yeomen enjoyed easy legal and financial access to
firearms, which in turn gave Orangemen an enormous advantage over their Catholic competitors;
note the generally huge discrepancies between Protestant and Catholic casualty rates resulting
from early nineteenth-century Orange-Green clashes, as chronicled in Sean Farrell's *Rituals and
riots: Sectarian violence and political culture in Ulster, 1784–1886* (Lexington, KY, 2000). At the
risk of cynicism, moreover, it may be conjectured that one of the Orange Order's important, if
unacknowledged, functions was to provoke what would be denominated as 'Catholic aggression'

Like the Petty Sessions Courts (established in 1827), such bodies reinforced hierarchy and deference on local levels and connected those local relationships with supra-local or metropolitan rules, institutions and power structures. In Ulster especially, perhaps, they not only strengthened traditional, cross-class social bonds but also instilled, encouraged and rewarded new proto-*bourgeois* habits and outlooks compatible with the needs of commercialization and industrialization.[56] Equally important, in the process they sifted Ulster's and Ireland's inhabitants into two broad, dichotomous groups – the 'loyal' *versus* the 'disloyal', the 'respectable' *versus* the 'disreputable', the 'worthy' *versus* the 'unworthy' of patronage and respect.

Of course, those who formulated and benefited from this Manichean scheme ultimately determined that the most vital and enduring distinction between the two opposing groups, as 'characterized' in 'moral' terms, would almost invariably be made on an allegedly 'natural', sectarian – Protestant *versus* Catholic – basis. To be sure, in 1816 Belfast's Protestant magistrates and élites were willing, perhaps even eager, to enrol the city's parish priest and future Catholic archbishop, William Crolly, as a member of the Committee of Gentlemen that arranged the capture of Francis Johnson's assailants. And no doubt both Crolly and many affluent Protestant liberals would have been happy, on that and similar occasions, to enlist other 'respectable' Catholics among the 'friends of order'.[57] A combination of external and internal circumstances, however, aborted any chance for the emergence of the sort of interdenominational, class-based alliance of men of property that the Protestant liberal, Henry Grattan, had promoted in the late 1700s, or that the southern Catholic bishop, James Doyle of Kildare and Leighlin, continued to advocate – as a union of the

against the 'Protestant community' or 'rebellious conspiracy' against the Union, either of which demanded the Yeomanry's mobilization and hence extra service pay for its members. Naturally, evidence to corroborate such conjectures is extremely difficult to uncover, but Dublin Castle officials often expressed suspicions that many of the Irish gentry's and magistrates' pleas for military intervention, to suppress alleged Catholic insurrections in their districts, were motivated by either paranoia or material self-interest. 'Before we became acquainted with the true state of affairs,' complained one British soldier in 1814, 'they [Irish local officials] made us complete hacks, calling us out to assist in every drunken squabble which took place, often through their own insolent behaviour'; cited in Crossman, *Politics, law and order in nineteenth-century Ireland*, p. 41. **56** *Bradshaw's Belfast Directory ... 1819*, xix. For a unique study of these processes, focusing on Thomastown, County Kilkenny, see Marilyn Silverman, *An Irish working class: explorations in political economy and hegemony, 1800–1950* (Toronto, 2001), esp. pp 119–41. **57** On Crolly, see Ambrose Macaulay, *William Crolly: archbishop of Armagh, 1835–49* (Dublin, 1994). As far as can be determined, Fr Crolly was the only Catholic member of the 'Committee of twenty-one Gentlemen,' appointed on 29 February 1816 to raise money and otherwise arrange for the capture of Johnson's assailants (*BNL*, 1 March 1816). However, Crolly's name disappears thereafter from the *BNL*'s record of the case, presumably because those arrested and convicted turned out to be Protestants; for example, Crolly was *not* among the clergymen who attended Doe's and Magill's executions on 6 September (see *BNL*, 10 September 1816).

good and the virtuous – as late as the 1820s.[58] Instead, for three crucial decades after 1800 the Tories largely controlled the British government and Dublin Castle. The Tories' alliance with Irish ultra-Protestantism and the Orange Order, and their refusal to grant Catholic Emancipation, ensured the adversarial growth of Catholic alienation and Nationalism which, in turn, effectively guaranteed that Irish Unionism would develop as an almost exclusively (and militantly) Protestant phenomenon. Yet the internal factor may have been even more crucial. Given the rampant class-conflict of the early 1800s, and in the context of the long depression following the Napoleonic Wars, the Protestant élite's successful imposition of capitalist relationships and mores on Ulster's Protestant poor virtually necessitated the creation and continual reinforcement of a sectarian 'moral economy' that paradoxically combined 'free labour' ideology with the selective reality, or at least the seductive rhetoric, of Protestant privilege and patronage.[59]

Discrimination of various kinds was present, of course, in the operations of charitable and other institutions, as well as in many less formal social relationships: most obviously in instances of Protestant preferment or in blatant manifestations of anti-Catholic prejudice, as implemented or expressed by ultra-Protestant landlords, magistrates and employers, and/or by ordinary Orangemen and Yeomen (the latter often synonymous). Thus, Catholic spokesmen complained bitterly that in the Protestant-controlled town corporations in Ulster and elsewhere, '[e]very species of Catholic industry and mechanical skill is checked, taxed, and rendered precarious' by 'uncertain and unequal ... justice' and by 'fraud and favoritism daily and openly practiced to their prejudice'.[60]

58 Grattan's career is described in many sources, e.g., James Kelly, *Henry Grattan* (Dundalk, 1993), but particularly relevant to the arguments in this chapter is Maurice O'Connell's 'Class conflict in a pre-industrial society: Dublin in 1780,' *Dalhousie Review* 9:1 (fall 1963), 43–55. On Bishop James Doyle, see Miller, *Emigrants and exiles*, pp 82–3, 89, and passim; as well as Doyle's own *Letters on the state of Ireland; addressed by J.K.L. to a friend in England* (Dublin, 1825), esp. pp 14 and 169–75. As W. P. Ryan notes, 'Bishop Doyle, and priests of his diocese, were in favour of the organizing of "respectable" citizen patrols, accompanied by some police and military,' to counter the Whiteboys in south Leinster. 'Among other activities, it was suggested that they should call at night at the houses of suspected persons to see if they were at home. Dr Doyle desired that the counter-associations should be armed in order to "terrify evil-doers," who should also be dismissed from their employment'; Ryan, *Irish labour movement*, p. 27. 59 On the ideological and practical tensions in Unionism between sectarian privilege and free-market capitalism, see Kerby A. Miller, 'The lost world of Andrew Johnson: sectarianism, social conflict, and cultural change in Southern Ireland during the pre-Famine era,' in James S. Donnelly, Jr., and Miller (eds), *Irish popular culture, 1650–1850* (Dublin, 1998), pp 222–41. 60 Miller, *Emigrants and exiles*, p. 89; this particular complaint was made in 1812 by Daniel O'Connell. Sympathetic Protestants concurred; for criticisms of Tory-Orange perversion of the legal and judicial systems in Ulster, for instance, see Thomas Reid, *Travels in Ireland, in the year 1822, exhibiting brief sketches of the moral, physical, and political state of the country* (London, 1823), pp 193–4. For one historian's assessment of Orange bias in Ulster's 'notoriously partisan judicial

At least initially, however, both élite and plebeian Protestants made important distinctions between the 'loyal-respectable-worthy' and the 'disloyal-disreputable-unworthy' within the Protestant population itself. For much longer than Unionist mythology would later allow, critical discriminations were made among Protestants on denominational grounds: between proverbially 'loyal' Anglicans and reputedly 'disaffected' Presbyterians.[61] As a result, during the 1798 Rebellion, liberal (but loyal) Protestant Dissenters in Donegal and elsewhere were fearful that the Orangemen, then overwhelmingly Anglican, were 'Sworn to Distroy all Prisbitearans as well as Rommans': an apprehension that helps explain Presbyterians' subsequent, if underrepresented, membership in both the Orange Order and the Yeomanry. Suspicions about Presbyterian fidelity to the Union long lingered, however, and officials in Dublin Castle feared that many Presbyterians' enrollment in Ulster's Yeomanry Corps was merely expedient or even insincere. For their part, as Edward Wakefield, John Gamble and others testified, ordinary Presbyterians remained socially and politically alienated: resenting the rents they paid to Anglican landlords, despising tithes and regarding the Church of Ireland clergy with 'sovereign contempt'.[62] To be sure, it is more difficult to discern whether animosities were common between Anglicans and Presbyterians who shared the *same* social status.[63] In the circum-

system,' see Farrell, *Rituals and riots*, pp 44–5. **61** Historians as varied in perspective as Ian McBride and Kevin Whelan concur that Ulster Presbyterian alienation, and Presbyterian-Anglican divisions, lasted long after the Act of Union; see McBride, 'Ulster Presbyterians and the passing of the Act of Union,' 75; and Whelan, *The Tree of Liberty: radicalism, Catholicism and the construction of Irish identity, 1760–1830* (Cork, 1996), p. 155. **62** James Steele, Raphoe, County Donegal, 15 May 1797, cited in Miller, *Emigrants and exiles*, p. 230. Blackstock, *Ascendancy army*, p. 129. Also see McBride, 'Ulster Presbyterians and the passing of the Act of Union,' 80, where he argues that, although the Yeomanry offered 'propertied Protestants' a 'route to rehabilitation' after 1798, Presbyterians remained greatly under-represented and, as one Anglican magistrate feared, may have joined Yeomanry corps (and the Orange Order) primarily to 'screen themselves' from loyalist suspicions and reprisals. Wakefield, *An account of Ireland*, ii, 548. At least into the 1830s, Ulster's leading Whig-Presbyterian newspaper, the Belfast *Northern Whig*, continued to denounce tithes on the Presbyterians' behalf; see Flann Campbell, *The Dissenting voice: Protestant democracy in Ulster from plantation to partition* (Belfast, 1991), pp 145–53. There is evidence, however, that suggests a lessening of Presbyterian animosity toward tithes between the early 1800s, when Presbyterians in Aghaloe parish, County Antrim, murdered a tithe-proctor (ca. 1822), and the 1830s and 1840s, when some observers claimed that tithes no longer agitated east Ulster's Dissenters because the region's landlords allegedly had assumed responsibility for paying them. If the latter is true, one might speculate whether such landlord paternalism was a significant cause or consequence of the creation of pan-Protestant Unionism. See Thomas Reid, *Travels in Ireland, in the year 1822*, p. 221; Inglis, *Ireland in 1834*, ii, 206–7; and Binns, *Miseries and beauties of Ireland*, i, 77. **63** Nevertheless, it may be revealing that, judging from their respective domiciles, William Gray, the weaver-conspirator turned informer in 1816, was probably an Anglican, whereas those who suffered from his betrayal were most likely Presbyterians. The *Belfast News-Letter*'s detailed account of the trial testimony makes clear that William Gray, although then a resident of Ballymacarret (in Knockbreda parish, north County

stances, however, perhaps it was no wonder that, at least by the 1820s, most loyal Protestants (and increasing numbers of Presbyterians) felt obliged to all show themselves in the annual Twelfth of July parades, for, as one Orangeman demanded, 'how [else] could we tell whether they are of the right or wrong sort?' As Thomas Reid, a visiting Scottish reformer, concluded, 'it is not the poor Catholics alone whose allegiance is suspected; poor Protestants are also thrown into the back ground; none but Orangemen are the "right" sort'.[64]

Furthermore, overlapping and reinforcing pressures were imposed hierarchically, across class lines, as well as on a denominational basis. Protestants of property and influence, Anglicans and Presbyterians alike, also stigmatized as 'unworthy' those Protestants of lesser wealth and status, regardless of their church affiliations, who did not conform to the emerging *bourgeois* Unionist order. During the social crises of the early 1800s, for example, Irish municipal authorities often instructed parish relief committees not to grant charity even to Protestant applicants who lacked certificates of 'good character' from their landlords, clergymen or employers – testifying, for example, to the petitioners' non-membership in working-class combinations.[65] In the same period, east

Down), was originally from the neighbourhood of Portadown, County Armagh, where his father and sister still resided. Portadown is in Drumcree and Seagoe parishes, the total populations of which were *c.*54–57 per cent Protestant in 1766 and 70 per cent Protestant in 1831, and whose Protestant populations in 1831 were each slightly more than 88 per cent Anglican. (In 1766 Anglicans comprised roughly 77 per cent of Seagoe's Protestants; no comparable 1766 data exists for Drumcree.) By contrast, the condemned weavers were all described as residents of Belfast or adjacent areas in north Down, and Doe and Magill were buried in Knockbreckan, a townland located in the north Down parishes of Drumbo and Knockbreda. No 1766 census figures survive for either parish, but in 1831 Drumbo's and Knockbreda's total populations were 97 per cent and 94 per cent Protestant, respectively, and their Protestant populations were 83 per cent (Drumbo) and 78 per cent (Knockbreda) Presbyterian. For the sources of this religious census data, see above, n. 3. It may also be significant that one of the other prisoners, James Park, who was sentenced only to flogging and imprisonment, had almost certainly been a member of the Yeomanry before his arrest. See *BNL*, 16 August 1816, in which Judge Day, while sentencing Park and Dickson, remarked that the former 'had evinced his guilt by resisting a magistrate, with a musket which had been committed to him ... for the protection of [the law].' Unfortunately, the connections that Joseph Madden enjoyed, to persuade the lord lieutenant to commute his death sentence to transportation for life, can only be conjectured, since the *News-Letter* was unusually reticent on the matter. Intriguingly, extensive research by Dr Jennifer Harrison, of the University of Queensland, was unable to discover any evidence that Madden was ever actually transported (communication to author, 22 Oct. 2004); my thanks to Dr Harrison for her efforts in this regard.   64 Reid, *Travels in Ireland, in the year 1822*, pp 189, 368. Similarly, in 1810 John Gamble noted that the Orangemen in Newtown-Stewart, County Tyrone, despised the Protestant (mostly Presbyterian) populace of nearby Strabane – as 'worse than Catholics,' as 'renegadoes who had deserted the good old cause' – because they had showed, in Gamble's view, 'good sense' and charity to their Catholic neighbours by refusing to allow the Order to march through the town on 12 July; in revenge, the Orangemen invaded Strabane in force and terrorized its inhabitants; Gamble, *Sketches of history, politics, and manners*, pp 269–70.   65 Boyle, *Irish labor movement*, pp 18–19.

Ulster's few remaining rhyming weavers – formerly the heralds of socio-political discontent and religious liberalism – learned, often from bitter experience, that élite patronage and publication prospects were generally closed to those who resisted the tides of convention. Likewise, and especially after 1831, the North's Protestant schoolmasters increasingly fell under the sway of conservative clergymen. Meanwhile, the Presbyterian clergy's own ranks were successively purged of disloyalty and heresy by Tory allies, such as the Revds Robert Black and Henry Cooke, who increasingly dominated the Ulster Synod and other religious bodies and who distributed government bounties and their own resources according to political and doctrinal criteria, to ensure what one critic called a 'pious and loyal servility'.[66]

Over time such formative influences, and other forms of conditioning less obvious but continuous, were instrumental in shaping the *mentalité* of ordinary Protestants in the economically unstable and socially stratified world of pre-famine Ulster. Surely it was critical, for example, that such influences were brought to bear initially and most insistently during the three decades immediately following the Act of Union – decades marked by escalating competition and heightened insecurity wrought by a lethal combination of explosive population growth, severe economic hardships and profound dislocations, and capitalist 'modernisations' in agriculture and manufacturing alike: all operating in a society that yet remained rigidly hierarchical and characterized, even among Protestants, by a strikingly unequal distribution of power and resources. As Robert Peel noted with satisfaction during the economic crisis of 1816–17 (when the Belfast weavers launched their ill-fated attack on Johnson's house), severe distress eventually 'promoted peace and good order', because, he wrote, 'The lower classes became in many parts completely dependent upon the bounty of their wealthier neighbours, and soon found the policy of fortifying their claims to compassion by peaceable behaviour.'[67]

On the provincial level, certainly, after 1798 Ulster's ordinary Protestants had no lawful *political* alternatives to docility and loyalty. In parliamentary elections (on the rare occasions when contests among competing candidates actually occurred), the North's Protestant voters (most of whom were disfranchised in

---

66 On the rhyming weavers, generally, see John Hewitt, *Rhyming weavers and other country poets of Antrim and Down* (Belfast, 1974). Frank Wright argues that it was the debate over implementation of the Irish National Education Act (1831) that forged the alliance between Presbyterian orthodoxy (with its demand for the 'open bible') and an 'Anglican landlord conservatism [that] was employing its political and institutional resources to link opposition to national "Godless" education to a generalized opposition to the Whig government and all its works'; see Wright, *Two lands on one soil*, p. 67. On the political and doctrinal struggles in Ulster Presbyterianism, generally, see Brooke, *Ulster Presbyterianism*, pp 129–74; and, on the selective distribution of the *regium donum* to create a conservative clergy, also see McBride, 'Ulster Presbyterians and the passing of the Act of Union,' 75 (quotation in text); and Holmes, *Henry Cooke*, pp 14–15.
67 Jenkins, *Era of Emancipation*, p. 132.

1829) simply concurred in their landlords' choices, either from deference or coercion, and parliamentary seats in Antrim, Down and nearly all other constituencies were the virtual monopoly of a handful of Ulster's wealthiest magnates. To be sure, some of east Ulster's most powerful families, such as the Downshires, were Whigs; and Belfast itself was a centre of Whig Party strength. However, although traditionally the 'Presbyterian party', the Whigs were scarcely more sympathetic to lower-class Protestants' economic grievances than their 'Church and King' adversaries among the Conservatives. At least Tory landlords, especially those affiliated with the Orange Order, offered ordinary Protestants the prospect – or the comforting illusion – of upper-class pater-nalism. By contrast, Ulster's Whigs – especially the Presbyterian *haute bourgeoisie* (including most of Belfast's leading merchants, bankers and manufac-turers) – espoused a free-market capitalism which, however potent a rhetorical weapon against 'Tory aristocracy', translated into attitudes and legislation at least as prejudicial to working-class combinations and to Ulster's poor, generally, as anything Tory landlords could devise. Moreover, the Whigs' chronic political weakness in the North – in part a result of their inability or unwillingness to address poor Protestants' economic concerns – made the party heavily dependent on support from British Whigs and (in return for championing Emancipation) on Irish Catholic voters and the Catholic hierarchy: the former naturally reinforced the Whigs' own commitment to the Union and to Britain's ruling classes, whereas the latter only made them more vulnerable to the pan-Protestant appeals of the Tory–Orange alliance.[68]

68 On Ulster politics in the early nineteenth century, see: Hoppen, *Elections, politics and society in Ireland*, pp 265–6; Peter Jupp, *British and Irish elections*, 1784–1831 (Newton Abbot, 1973), pp 153–60; 'County Down Elections, 1783–1831,' 177–206; and 'Irish M.P.s at Westminster in the early nineteenth century,' 65–80; Brian M. Walker, 'Landowners and parliamentary elections in County Down, 1801–1921,' 297–307; and *Ulster politics: the formative years, 1868–86* (Belfast 1989), chs 1–3 and pp 47–9; and Wright, *Two lands on one soil*, chs 2–3. Whig Party loyalties offered few rewards even to Ulster's middle-class Presbyterians; the Conservatives dominated electoral politics in nearly all constituencies, as by 1850 the Tories were 'enthroned as the "natural" party of Protestantism' (Hoppen, p. 266); moreover, the Whig Party itself rarely rewarded Presbyterians with seats in Parliament (according to Hoppen, p. 265, in 1832–57 only four of twenty-five Ulster Whig MPs were Presbyterians, with Anglicans [and one Quaker] comprising the remainder). Nor did Party power at Westminster translate into local influence and patronage power for Ulster's Whig Presbyterians; as late as 1884 nearly three- fourths of Ulster's justices of the peace were members of the Church of Ireland (Walker, *Ulster politics*, p. 23). In addition, although Irish and especially Ulster Whigs were strongly opposed to tithes, save for a few mavericks like W. Sharman Crawford they were lukewarm or at best ineffective in protecting tenant-right. And on issues directly affecting the welfare of Ulster's Protestant poor, they generally espoused classic 'liberal' positions in support of property rights, 'free labour,' and 'scientific' charity. For example, in 1816 and in 1825–6, Irish Whig MPs led demands for the Tenants' Recovery Act (facilitating evictions) and the Subletting Act, respectively, and their support for Catholic Emancipation was accompanied by a willingness, at the least, to disfranchise Ireland's 40s. freehold voters (who included thousands of Ulster Protestants); see McDowell,

The lack of regional or national alternatives meant that local circumstances would be instrumental in determining the future of Protestant Ulster's social ethos and political culture. And on local levels, what were no doubt most crucial and pervasive were a multitude of everyday signals, hierarchically imposed but laterally reinforced, that conformity to 'respectable' and 'loyal' norms of behaviour and opinion – the two at least rhetorically indivisible – were essential prerequisites for favourable leases, steady employment, decent wages, extended credit, rapid promotion and charity during hard times – as well as for the subtler comforts of social and religious fellowship, for a sense of 'community,' that lessened the sting of poverty in psychological if not material ways. The most important signals, especially at first, were made by those who had the greatest resources and power to bestow or withhold rewards, but eventually they were reinforced by sub-élites, social intermediaries, and, in the end, by all those who, consciously or unconsciously, acknowledged their legitimacy and thus adhered – however sincerely, pragmatically or superficially – to the norms demanded by 'the Protestant "way of life"'. Thus, the early and mid-nineteenth-century transformation of the Harshaws, Presbyterian farmers in west Down, from open sympathizers with Catholic Emancipation and Repeal into staunch Unionists and Orangemen, was instructive and perhaps typical, as its younger members were enmeshed in webs of credit and other obligations to members of the Orange Order, while the older ones were publicly attacked by local clergymen for refusing either to join the Order or to acknowledge the Unionist dictum that Protestantism, loyalty and respectability were synonymous and interdependent.[69]

Indeed, some pressures for conformity may have been even more intimate and intense. As the historical sociologist Marilyn Cohen has noted, whereas the evangelical Protestantism of the New Reformation offered Ulster's upper classes 'a creed which reaffirmed old values and supplied a rigorous defense of social and political conservatism', it also sanctified *bourgeois* family relationships and

Public opinion and government policy in Ireland, pp 74, 99. Likewise, Belfast's middle class Whigs were particularly energetic (on both economic and moral grounds) in their support for the government's campaign to eradicate illegal whiskey distillation, a vital income source for poor rural Protestants (as well as Catholics) in de-industrializing west and south Ulster; see Wright, *Two lands on one soil*, p. 75. For Belfast's beleaguered workers, Francis Dalzell Finley, editor of the *Northern Whig*, must have appeared a quintessential middle-class Liberal, as he negated the popular effect of his criticisms of landlordism with strident opposition to unions, even after they became legal in 1825; in 1836 he broke the city's printers' union by importing scab printers from Dublin and Scotland, and, when that failed, by training pauper children from local charity institutions to replace his workers; see Boyd, *Rise of the Irish trade unions*, pp 42–3; Gray, *Sans Culottes of Belfast*, pp 37–8; McDowell as above, pp 58–91; and Brian Inglis, *The freedom of the press in Ireland, 1784–1841* (London, 1954), p. 16. **69** For the Harshaws' story, I am grateful to Marjorie Robie, of Ipswich, MA, who generously shared the results of her important research which, when published, will expand significantly historians' understanding of the local dynamics of east Ulster Protestant society in the early and mid-1800s.

enshrined the special roles of wives and mothers in propagating and guarding the norms of 'respectability' (industry, cleanliness, piety, sobriety, chastity) that were allegedly associated with Protestantism, threatened by Catholicism (and by the 'improvident' lower classes, generally), and hence protected by the Union with Protestant Britain. In this context, it may be accurate to speak of the domestication and even the feminization of Unionism, complementing the latter's 'outdoor' and overtly masculine expressions in the Orange Order. Indeed, from the 1870s on, Orangeism itself would become more respectable, domesticated, and to a degree, even feminized through the adoption of the Orangemen's now 'traditional' 'marching uniform' (suits and bowler hats) as well as of 'ladies' auxiliaries'. Arguably, however, it was in the early nineteenth century, with the rise of the *bourgeoisie* in tandem with evangelicalism, that Unionism and its associations became embedded in the heart of Ulster Protestant family culture.[70]

Finally, the success of these hegemonic pressures was both revealed and ensured by two other critical factors that historians of Ulster society and political culture have largely ignored: namely, the massive size and the selective character of early and mid-nineteenth-century Ulster Protestant emigration. Between the end of the American Revolution and the beginning of the Great Famine, at least one quarter-million and probably much closer to one half-million Protestants left an Ulster which, near its demographic peak in 1831, contained less than 1.1 million Protestants.[71] Moreover, both denominational and social-class factors heavily determined *which* Protestants would emigrate and which would not. Modern analyses of census data confirm contemporary reports that Ulster's Protestant emigrants were disproportionately, indeed overwhelmingly, Presbyterians as well as predominantly cottage artisans (principally weavers) and small to middling tenant farmers or their children.[72]

70 Cohen, *Linen, family and community in Tullylish*, p. 15. To my knowledge, no scholars have examined the development of Ulster Unionism through these perspectives. My arguments are extrapolated from my research into the Johnston family correspondence from Ballymahon, County Longford (see Miller, 'The lost world of Andrew Johnston,' cited in n. 59) and by analogy with scholarship on industrialization, evangelical religion, middle-class domesticity and gender in early and mid-nineteenth-century America; e.g., Paul Johnson, *A shopkeeper's millennium: society and revivals in Rochester, New York, 1815–1837* (New York, 1978); Colleen McDannell, *The Christian home in Victorian America, 1840–1900* (Bloomington, IN, 1986); and Mary P. Ryan, *Cradle of the middle class: the family in Oneida County, New York, 1790–1865* (New York, 1981). For information about the Orangemen's marching attire and women's auxiliaries, I am grateful to Professor Donald MacRaild of Victoria University, Wellington, New Zealand.   71 According to computations of the parish data in the First Report of the Commission of Public Instruction, Ireland (see n. 3), in 1831 Ulster contained approximately 1,077,500 Protestants (and 1,197,100 Catholics). (Strictly speaking, the nine-county North would not become 'the Protestant Province of Ulster,' as Unionists liked to call it, until 1871.) On contemporary Ulster emigration, see Miller, *Emigrants and exiles*, chapters 5–6; Ó Gráda, *Ireland: a new economic history*, p. 76; and William Forbes Adams, *Ireland and Irish emigration to the New World from 1815 to the Great Famine* (New Haven, 1932).   72 See above, n. 49. For

To be sure, eighteenth-century links with America no doubt encouraged much northern Protestant emigration in the early 1800s. So allegedly did competition with Catholics for land and employment – perhaps especially in Protestant-minority areas in south and west Ulster – in part because many landlords merely paid lip-service to the 'moral' claims of 'Protestant community' and leased farms on their estates to the highest bidders, as Protestant tenants often complained.[73] Yet more important causes are strongly suggested by the

evidence as to the 'character' of pre-famine emigration from Ulster and elsewhere in Ireland, taken from contemporary observers' reports and ships' passenger lists, see Miller, *Emigrants and exiles*, chapter 6. The author plans to publish a full, census-based analysis of the denominational and social composition of early and mid-nineteenth century Ulster emigration, but some preliminary conclusions can be found in: Kerby A. Miller et al., *Irish immigrants in the land of Canaan: letters and memoirs from Colonial and Revolutionary America, 1675–1815* (New York, 2003), Appendix 2: 'Irish migration and demography' (with Líam Kennedy); in Kerby A. Miller and Bruce D. Boling, with Líam Kennedy, 'The Famine's scars: William Murphy's Ulster and American odyssey,' *Éire-Ireland* 36:1–2 (spring/summer 2001), 98–123, reprinted in Kevin Kenny (ed), *New directions in Irish-American history* (Madison, 2003), pp 36–60; and in May Kao Xiong, 'Shadows in the land of *Eoghain*: the Great Irish Famine in County Tyrone, 1845–50' (MA thesis, University of Missouri-Columbia, 2003), which examines census data for 1821–41 as well as for 1841–51. It may be notable as well that, at least in the post-famine period, Ulster Protestant emigration (especially from east Ulster), relative to the Catholic exodus from the three southern provinces, also appears to have been disproportionately male; see Miller, *Emigrants and exiles*, p. 371. 73 In the nineteenth century, the allegation that 'unfair' Catholic competition was a – or even *the* – primary cause of Irish Protestant emigration became an integral aspect of Unionist ideology and rhetoric. (E.g., see Boyce, 'The making of Unionism,' p. 23.) However, in the 1700s it had rarely featured in Ulster Presbyterian discourses on emigration, and in the 1800s it rarely appeared as a cause of complaint in Ulster Presbyterian emigrants' correspondence. In both, by contrast, attributions of emigration to 'landlord tyranny,' tithes and taxes, and (after 1800) to British misgovernment were much more common. Although instances of Catholic competition displacing Ulster Presbyterians (and other Protestants) undoubtedly occurred, and although the latters' fears of such competition became widespread (as attested by relatively impartial observers such as John Gamble and Jonathan Binns), the demographic evidence indicates that widespread Catholic displacement of Presbyterians in the North did *not* take place (see text below). It is arguable, therefore, that Ulster (and Irish) Unionists, and many ordinary Protestants, embraced the 'Catholic competition = Protestant emigration' thesis for several closely related ideological and practical reasons. Ulster Presbyterian emigrants' traditional self-portrayal – as oppressed 'victims' of landlord oppression, Anglican clerical avarice and British misgovernment – was incompatible with Unionism's demand for pan-Protestant solidarity and loyalty; indeed, it was dangerously similar to Irish Catholic Nationalists' argument that emigration was forced 'exile.' By contrast, blaming Protestant emigration on Catholic competition reinforced Protestants' traditional 'settler ideology,' portraying the latter as once more under 'siege' by the 'natives.' That contention also reinforced notions of Protestants' inherent 'respectability' and 'superiority,' because, in contrast to their Catholic competitors, who allegedly were content to live in filth and misery in order to pay rack-rents, Protestant tenants deserved and proudly demanded 'decency and comfort' (Boyce, 'The making of Unionism'). In addition, the explanation enabled Protestant tenants to employ Unionist appeals for Protestant solidarity against their landlords; although their spokesmen's frequent complaints suggest that such pleas may at best have enjoyed only partial success, ordinary Protestants (having abandoned the

overall differences between the high rates of Ulster Presbyterian emigration and the low rates of Ulster Anglican emigration that can be inferred from the significant disparities between their respective annual growth rates in 1766–1831 and in 1831–61. Furthermore, it is significant that those disparities were greatest in the mid-Ulster region, in the so-called Linen Triangle, centred on north and central Armagh but also including west Down and east Tyrone. Of course, in the late 1700s and early 1800s this religiously mixed district experienced Ulster's highest population growth, the most intense competition over land and employment, and the most profound socio-economic dislocations. But at least equally important, perhaps, is the fact that mid-Ulster was also the epicentre of Anglican loyalism and, after 1795, of Anglican loyalism as institutionalized and mobilized in the Orange Order. Indeed, in many parts of mid-Ulster the denominational balance between Anglicans and Presbyterians changed so radically in the early and mid-1800s that it is difficult to avoid the conclusion that formal or informal, overt or subtle, forms of discrimination practised by Anglican landlords, employers and magistrates, as well as by ordinary Orangemen, may have been critical in stimulating such disproportionately high rates of Presbyterian (as well as Catholic) out-migration.[74]   .

Steelboys' option) had no lawful option but their insistent, Orange-dressed reiteration (see Miller, 'The lost world of Andrew Johnston'; also Wright, *Two lands on one soil*, p. 28). Indeed, it may be that the 'Catholic competition' argument's most important function, especially in Ulster, and its most crucial contribution to pan-Protestant Unionism, was in deflecting attention from the *intra*-Protestant social-class and denominational conflicts that the actual patterns of Northern emigration both reflected and revealed (see text below). Surprisingly, no scholar has investigated the social or political consequences in Ulster of the disfranchisement of *Protestant* 40s. freeholders, despite widespread claims that large numbers of former *Catholic* voters were evicted after 1829. For evidence (or allegations) of Ulster landlords replacing Protestant tenants with Catholics, however, see Whelan, *Tree of liberty*, p. 51 (shortly after Waterloo, in Armagh and Cavan); Gamble, *Views of society and manners in the North of Ireland*, pp 421–2 (1818, west Ulster); and Binns, *Miseries and beauties of Ireland*, i, 78–9 (late 1830s, in Down); but see also Binns, i, 315, for evidence of Ulster landlords (especially evangelical leaders and/or Orange district masters) evicting Catholics to replace them with 'loyal' Protestants – a complaint made frequently by Catholic Nationalists and priests in the pre-famine decades, and probably with at least equally good cause.   74 For examples – as from Moira parish, in west Down, where in 1766–1831 the Presbyterian proportion of the population fell from 34 per cent to merely 19 per cent, while the Anglican share soared from 34 per cent to 54 per cent – see Miller et al., *Irish immigrants in the land of Canaan*, Appendix 2, esp. pp 663–8. See also Miller, 'Ulster Presbyterians and the "two traditions" in Ireland and America,' in Terry Brotherstone, Anna Clark, and Kevin Whelan (eds), *These fissured isles: varieties of British and Irish identities* (Glasgow, forthcoming). Signficantly, Anglican-Presbyterian differentials in rates of population decline and emigration rates continued into and beyond the Famine era, again suggesting that patronage from a landlord class and a magistracy that was overwhelmingly Anglican, plus membership in the Orange Order, may have sheltered poor Anglicans in large part from the economic pressures that encouraged emigration – and in 1845–50 caused severe suffering – among less-favoured Protestants. See Miller et al., 'The Famine's scars,' esp. pp 98–103 and 110–11. Also noteworthy

Of course, whether Ulster Presbyterian (and other) emigrants left Ireland primarily from ambition, frustration, intimidation or desperation is problematic. Historians' judgments as to the relative importance of 'push' and 'pull' factors – of economic, cultural, religious or political causes and motivations – are often based as much on their ideological predilections as on the emigrants' actual circumstances. Yet whatever the reasons, the fact is that in early and mid nineteenth-century Ulster, generally, and in mid-Ulster particularly, Presbyterians were most liable to emigrate, whereas Anglicans were most likely to stay.[75]

is Marilyn Cohen's conclusion that the poor Protestant weavers in west County Down who best survived the Famine crisis were those who had become fully proletarianized and hence totally dependent on their employers, whereas the yet independent or even semi-independent farmer-weavers with 5–10 acres fared far worse; although Cohen scarcely mentions the Orange Order or denominational distinctions in her study, her data suggest the inextricable nature of socio-economic, ethnic, religious and political factors in determining who persisted, emigrated or perished; Cohen, *Linen, family and community in Tullylish*, pp 134–55. Intriguingly, also, it was not until the 1880s that Ulster Presbyterian and Anglican population decline and emigration rates converged, becoming virtually identical through 1926; moreover, it was in 1881–1926 that Presbyterian numbers declined at rates significantly lower than those of Ulster's Catholics, whereas before 1881 the North's Presbyterians and Catholics had shared very similar demographic experiences. Of course, historians contend that it was in the mid-1880s when Ulster's Presbyterians finally joined the Orange Order *en masse*, thereby not only demonstrating pan-Protestant solidarity in opposition to Home Rule but perhaps also acquiring whatever relative immunity from emigration Orangeism had traditionally conferred on the province's Anglicans. Of course, it may also be the case that, by the 1880s, decades of heavy emigration had so 'simplified' Ulster Presbyterian society that, despite the rural crisis of the 1880s, there remained few lower-class Presbyterians on whom pressures to emigrate could operate. Denominational rates of population decline, 1881–1926, computed from the data in W.E. Vaughan and A.J. Fitzpatrick (eds), *Irish historical statistics: population, 1821–1971* (Dublin, 1978), pp 57–73. **75** In the mid-1830s, the Revd Mortimer O'Sullivan, Anglican rector of Killyman parish (straddling Counties Armagh and Tyrone, in the heart of the Linen Triangle), testified before a parliamentary commission that five-sixths of Killyman's Protestants were members of the Orange Order because Orangeism 'gave Protestants courage to stay rather than emigrate,' despite their alleged fears of being 'exterminated' by their Catholic neighbours, who numbered roughly half the parish's inhabitants. Religious demographic data, however, illuminates O'Sullivan's claims. It is intriguing that the proportion of Killyman's Protestants whom O'Sullivan claimed to be Orangemen was almost identical to the proportion that was composed of members of the Church of Ireland. Yet O'Sullivan's allegation that, prior to the advent of the Orange Order, Protestants had fled Killyman because of competition from, or fear of, Catholics is highly questionable, since between 1766 and 1831 the parish's Protestant population had increased by about 276 per cent whereas the number of Catholic inhabitants had risen only 126 per cent. Finally, between 1831 and 1861 it appears that in Killyman (as in the rest of Ulster) only Anglicans (not 'Protestants' generally) gained through Orangeism sufficient 'courage' (or economic advantage?) not to emigrate, for although the local Church of Ireland population declined merely 12 per cent (compared with Catholic losses of nearly 34 per cent), the number of the parish's Presbyterian inhabitants fell almost 26 per cent. (The figures for 1831–61 in County Armagh, generally, were Anglicans -8 per cent, Catholics -16 per cent, and Presbyterians

Certainly, in the circumstances any Ulster Protestants – Anglicans or Presbyterians (and perhaps especially the latter) – who hoped to *avoid* emigration altogether (or to emigrate on the most advantageous terms – with landlord or government assistance, perhaps even with free land grants or jobs waiting in a British colony) knew that their chances of success would be immeasurably enhanced if they proclaimed themselves to be 'Protestants from time immemorial,' 'Loyal and submissive to their government', as well as 'industrious[ly and] peaceably ... inclined'. It would be even better if they could 'prove' their claims, for example by reference to Catholic 'persecutions' they had suffered for their loyal service, as in the Yeomanry, and by producing written 'characters' from what one petitioner called 'the highest toned protestants in Ireland': landlords, clergymen, employers and/or Orange lodgemasters. Sadly, of course, the images conjured up by grovelling petitions such as that of James Gibson, who 'cast [him]self at the feet of [his lordship's] protection', scarcely comported with the 'sturdy, independent' self-image of Ulster Protestant and Unionist mythology.[76]

-31 per cent.) For O'Sullivan's testimony, see Wright, *Two lands on one soil*, p. 97. Percentages computed from population data for Killyman parish in 1766 (T.808/15,266, Public Record Office of Northern Ireland, Belfast); in 1831 (First Report of the Commission of Public Instruction, Ireland; see n. 3); and in 1861 (Irish Census, 1861, *British Parliamentary Papers*, H.C. 1863, liv [Vol. 3, Ulster]). For demographic patterns in the entire province, particularly in mid-Ulster, see the sources cited in ns. 72 and 74. **76** Of course, the great majority of the petitions written and sent between the 1810s and 1840s by Irish Protestants (and Catholics) to the Colonial Office in London, begging for free passages to, and/or land grants in, British North America (and later, Australia), expressed loyal sentiments in varying degrees. My arguments, however, are: first, that Ulster (and other Irish) Anglicans were greatly advantaged in that usually they could rely on traditional, recent and contemporary 'proofs' of their loyalty, as in 1798 or simply by virtue of Church of Ireland membership; second, that to gain comparable leverage Ulster Presbyterians, traditionally and – often with good reason – recently under suspicion from landlords and magistrates, needed to (at least) match their Anglican neighbours in demonstrations of fidelity to the established order; and, third, that Catholics, proverbially suspect and unable to join either the Orange Order or (usually) the Yeomanry corps, would inevitably become the 'other': the foils against whom both Anglicans and Dissenters could contrast their own 'love and veneration for, and obedience to, his majesty's Government,' as well as their claims to superior industry, sobriety and respectability. The petitions quoted in this paragraph of the text (and above) are: James Campbell, Portadown, County Armagh, 5 April 1819 (C.O. 384/4); William Burroughs, Magherafelt, County Derry, 22 March 1822 (C.O. 384/8); James Smily et al., Bracky, County Armagh, n.d. [recd. 19 August 1823] (C.O. 384/9); James Gibson, Omagh, County Tyrone, 12 April 1828 (C.O. 384/19); Patrick Clark, Dunleer, County Louth, 5 November 1829 (C.O. 384/21); and Robert Ritchey, Galgorm, County Antrim, 13 May 1833 (C.O. 384/31). Other petitioners testifying to their Protestantism and/or their loyal service (in the Yeomanry or the police, as informers etc.), offering certifications of 'character' from clergymen, Orange Lodges etc., and/or alleging victimization by 'disloyal' Catholics, include: James McConnel, Enniskillen, County Fermanagh (C.O. 384/10); Revd Alexander McEwen (on behalf of his Presbyterian congregation), Kirkcubbin, County Down, n.d. [1826] (C.O. 384/14); David Kennedy, Clough, County Down, 21 June 1827 (C.O. 384/16); James Rogers, Bailieboro, County Cavan, 6 October

By contrast, from the early 1800s to mid-century the letters written by Ulster Presbyterians who emigrated to the United States often exuded alienation and even 'manly' defiance, as they perceived or at least portrayed themselves as economic and even political refugees from an inequitable and repressive society. Many such migrants, for example, were like David Robinson, a farmer's son from County Derry, who from his Kentucky refuge declared he 'could never brook the idea of cringing to a despotic tyrant', or like John McBride, a weaver from County Antrim, who declared he had left Ulster so he would not 'have to stand like a beggar at a manufacturer's door.'[77] Others included the predominantly Presbyterian small farmers and craftsmen whom John Gamble observed, shortly after the Napoleonic Wars, who explained their decisions to emigrate in language that mixed bitter criticism of landlordism and of post-Union Ulster's social and political inequities with republican dreams of the political freedom and socio-economic independence they hoped to enjoy in America. 'Borne down by poverty and oppression,' Gamble wrote of his Presbyterian countrymen, 'they carry their industry, talents and energy, to a distant and happier land, and never think of the one they have quitted but with loathing, and of its government, with a feeling, for which hatred is but a feeble word.'[78] And, finally, still others were the weavers and labourers who migrated to northern England's industrial towns where, in the early 1800s, they became notorious for the radicalism of their trade unionism and political activities, and where – in another revealing example of Irish and British élite convergence – they often fell victim to spies and informers whom the British government recruited among yet other Ulster migrants who were members of the Orange Order.[79]

In conclusion, of course, what might be termed the 'taming' of Ulster's Protestant lower classes would be a prolonged, uneasy and even transatlantic development. It would involve the transformations of 'wild Irish' in America and in the United Kingdom into respectable 'Scotch-Irish' and 'loyal Britons', as well as the creation of staunch Unionists in northern Ireland itself.[80] Even the

1830 (C.O. 384/23); and John MacRay, Butler's Bridge, County Cavan, 23 May 1844 (C.O. 384/75). See above, n. 31, for the full citation to the Colonial Office petitions. It should be noted that Orange Lodge transfer certificates, signifying membership in good standing, were invaluable aids for many Irish Protestant emigrants, especially those intending to settle and find employment in British North America; see Cecil J. Houston and William J. Smyth, *The sash Canada wore: a historical geography of the Orange Order in Canada* (Toronto, 1980). **77** David Robinson, Lexington, KY, 4 May 1817, full text in Miller et al., *Irish immigrants in the land of Canaan*, pp 681–3; John McBride, Watertown, NY, 9 January 1820, cited in Miller, *Emigrants and exiles*, pp. 202–3. **78** Gamble, *Views of society and manners in the North of Ireland*, p. 191; also see pp. 197–8, 202, 367–8, 421. **79** Kevin Haddick-Flynn, *Orangeism: the making of a tradition* (Dublin, 1999), pp 202–8. See also Boyd, *Rise of the Irish trade unions*, pp. 37–40; Strauss, *Irish nationalism and British democracy*, pp 125–6; and Thompson, *Outsiders: class, gender and nation*, chs 4–5. **80** With regard to the development of 'Scotch-Irish' identity and community in late eighteenth- and early nineteenth-century America, this argument is elaborated

latter process would remain bedevilled by intra-communal conflicts – over tenant-right and industrial relations, for example – as Ulster's Protestant upper, middle and lower classes sought to define Unionism's practical implications – and distribute its material rewards or burdens – in different ways. In the end, of course, as at the beginning, their residents' loyal defence of 'the Protestant "way of life"' would have quite different outcomes in Belfast's upper-, middle-, and working-class Protestant neighbourhoods. Yet from at least the middle of the nineteenth century, such issues would be contested almost invariably within the Unionist family: within a hegemonic framework of shared political, social and cultural assumptions that had been forged, disseminated and, at times, quite harshly imposed by Ulster's Protestant élites in the early 1800s. Thus, Belfast's first bomb in 1816 was by no means the most destructive that would be exploded during the next two centuries. To historians, however, it may signal the importance of a hitherto-unappreciated intra-communal social conflict, the resolution of which was of momentous importance for the future of Ulster and Irish society.

in Miller et al., *Irish immigrants in the land of Canaan*, especially in chapters 49–68. On the creation of 'loyal Britons,' see Linda Colley, *Britons: forging the nation, 1707–1837* (New Haven, 1992).

Contributors

DAVID W. MILLER is Professor of History at Carnegie Mellon University. His publications include *Church, state and nation in Ireland, 1898–1921*, *Queen's rebels: Ulster loyalism in historical perspective* and a number of essays on eighteenth and nineteenth century Irish history. He is writing a book under the working title 'Ulster Presbyterians and Irish Catholics in the Famine era, 1829–1869'.

KEVIN JAMES is Assistant Professor of History at the University of Guelph and a faculty member in the University's Scottish Studies Programme. His research focuses on rural labour, textile manufacture and garment production in Ireland and Scotland. His work has appeared in *Saothar*, *Scottish Economic and Social History*, *Textile History*, and the *Canadian Journal of Irish Studies*, and he is the author of a forthcoming study of hand-loom weaving in the nineteenth-century Irish linen industry.

MARK G. SPENCER is Assistant Professor of History at Brock University. He is the author of *David Hume and eighteenth-century America* (2005), the co-editor of *Utilitarians and their critics in America, 1789–1914* (4 vols, 2005), and the editor of *Hume's reception in early America* (2 vols, 2002). He has also published essays in academic journals such as the *William and Mary Quarterly*, *Eighteenth-Century Studies*, and *Hume Studies*, and in numerous scholarly reference books.

PETER GILMORE is a doctoral candidate in social history at Carnegie Mellon University, Pittsburgh, Pennsylvania, where his work is directed by David W. Miller. His research centers on Ulster Presbyterian emigration to western Pennsylvania in the period between the American Revolution and the Irish famine. He has previously written on Ulster Scots music and language.

KATHARINE L. BROWN has been an Adjunct Professor of History and Art at Mary Baldwin College since 1982. She has worked as Director of Research and Collections at the Museum of American Frontier Culture, and was Executive Director of the Woodrow Wilson Birthplace Foundation. She is the author or co-author of the histories of four Presbyterian and two Episcopal churches in Virginia, of several essays and articles about the Scotch-Irish, and of a history of cattle in Virginia from 1607 to 2000. She has presented numerous papers on aspects of the Scotch-Irish experience and on the United Irish immigrants to America.

KERBY A. MILLER is Professor of History at the University of Missouri-Columbia and former Senior Research Fellow at the Institute of Irish Studies at Queen's University, Belfast. His works include the prize-winning studies, *Emigrants and exiles: Ireland and the Irish exodus to North America* (1985), and *Irish immigrants in the land of Canaan* (principal author, 2003); as well as the co-edited *Irish popular culture, 1650–1850* (1998).

DAVID A. WILSON is Professor of History and Celtic Studies at the University of Toronto. His books include *Paine and Cobbett: the transatlantic connection* (1988), and *United Irishmen, United States: immigrant radicals in the early Republic* (1998).

Index